MISSIONS TO THE

# MOON

THE STORY OF MAN'S GREATEST ADVENTURE
BROUGHT TO LIFE WITH AUGMENTED REALITY

FOREWORD BY **GENE KRANZ**
FORMER NASA FLIGHT DIRECTOR

ROD PYLE

ANDRE
DEUTSCH

**Right** Charlie Duke works at Plum Crater with the Lunar Rover in the background.

THIS IS AN ANDRE DEUTSCH BOOK

This updated edition first published in 2018 by André Deutsch
First published in the UK by André Deutsch in 2009
A division of the Carlton Publishing Group
20 Mortimer Street, London W1T 3JW, UK



ISBN 978-1-787-39177-2

Printed in Dubai

# CONTENTS

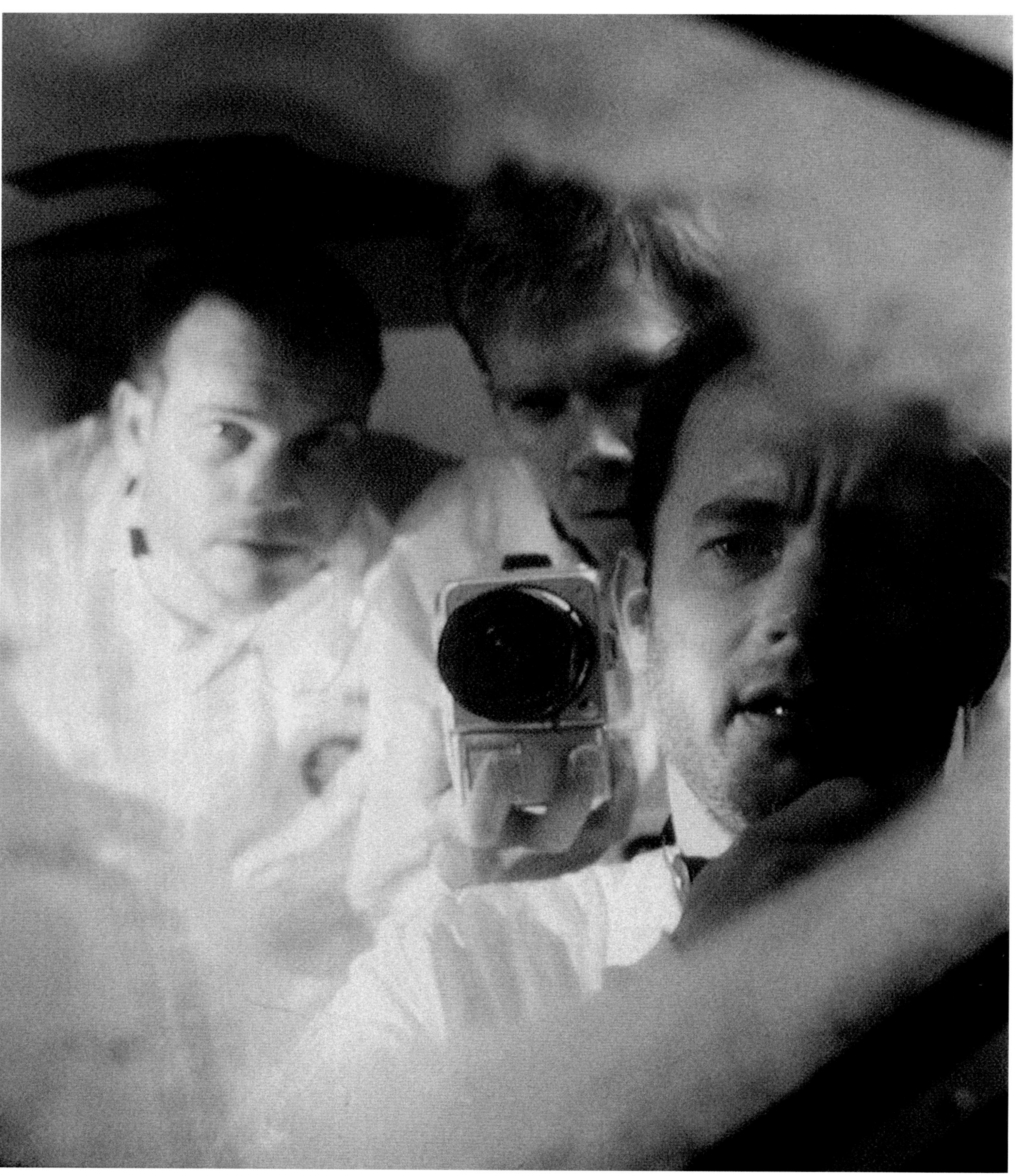

# FOREWORD

## THE IMPACT OF THE *APOLLO 13* MOVIE ON THE PEOPLE OF THE WORLD BROUGHT HOME THE CHALLENGES AND THE RISKS OF AMERICA'S LUNAR JOURNEYS.

Young teams in Mission Control using primitive technology with a credo that "failure is not an option" met every mission challenge with split-second decisions. The story of Mission Control is one of leadership, trust, shared values and teamwork that defied the odds, and in our first decade of spaceflight, they brought every crewman home safely. The safe return of the Apollo 13 crew after an oxygen tank explosion was one of our "finest hours".

But there is much more to the incredible story of Apollo and mankind's exploration of the moon, and that story is well chronicled within the pages of this book.

My spaceflight career began with the Mercury programme in 1960, working under the first Flight Director, Dr Chris Kraft. Soon I was serving in that position myself during the Gemini and Apollo programmes. Much of the credit for our success in space should go to the dedicated team of young engineers and technicians who worked with me in Mission Control.

The people who worked on the Mercury, Gemini and Apollo programmes bonded as a family like no other. Each programme demanded our very best, and only by working together were we able to realize our goal of reaching the moon.

The struggle to reach the moon is documented in innumerable books, television specials and museum exhibits, but there is nothing quite like reading original sources from the era to bring the programme to life. The reproductions in this book allow you to do just that. Here you'll find the early documents of Dr Wernher von Braun, memos of the critical decisions surrounding the lunar effort, excerpts of my own Flight Director's Log from Apollo 13, and more. Looking through these historically significant mementos will take you on an insider's tour through humanity's first journey into space.

Our work in space is unfinished and my hope is that a new generation of explorers will once again find the leadership, the spirit and the courage to boldly go forward and complete what we started.

This book is a meaningful step in that direction.

**Gene Kranz**
*Former NASA Flight Director, 1962–1974*

**Opposite** In this still from the film, the Apollo 13 crew surveys the cold emptiness from the Lunar Module Aquarius, their lifeboat in space. From left: Bill Paxton as Fred Haise, Kevin Bacon as Jack Swigert and Tom Hanks as Jim Lovell.

# INTRODUCTION

## FROM 1968 THROUGH TO 1972, THE UNITED STATES HURLED NINE TINY SPACECRAFT TOWARDS THE MOON.

Six made successful landings and each built on the successes of its predecessor. It was an amazing time and has come to be regarded as the Golden Age of space exploration.

But many other efforts by other nations have also been extended towards our nearest neighbour. Notably, the Soviet Union spent vast amounts of rubles and energy on attempting to beat the US to the moon, and they almost made it (as is detailed inside this book). Japan, India, China and others have sent, or are planning to send, unmanned probes to the moon, and one of these nations – China – is planning an aggressive assault on the moon with crewed flights. There may be Chinese taikonauts roving the moon at about the same time that NASA returns there after a 50-year hiatus.

However, we are getting ahead of ourselves. This book is primarily about the history of the exploration of the moon. There are vast tracts of fascinating material left by these pioneering missions, the most accessible of which are those of NASA in the United States and, slightly less so, those of the former Soviet Union. In these archives, amazing stories of a struggle of heroic proportions can be found, much of it unseen by casual observers. Some artefacts are what you might expect: internal memos, flight summaries and planning studies take up a mile of shelf space. But hidden in these archives are also gems of space history...

Some examples of both the usual and the extraordinary are inside this book. A mission report for Apollo 11, still compelling reading today, resides near a faded memo hidden away for years, regarding an attempt to change the name of "Project Mercury" to "Project Astronaut". Also included are a newspaper describing the USSR's triumphs, the Apollo 11 descent map and the original, handwritten Flight Director's log of the Apollo 13 crisis, in the steady handwriting of Gene Kranz and others.

Sifting through this has been a pleasure and a thrill. Short of actually going into space, haunting these archives is perhaps the best way of all to taste the thrill of space exploration. It is a bit like gaining access to that last scene from *Raiders of the Lost Ark* – you just never know what you'll find in the warehouse.

If you get a chance to visit the US National Air and Space Museum, the Kansas Cosmosphere, the Kennedy Space Center, the Johnson Space Center or any of the many international museums dedicated to spaceflight, treat yourself. There is nothing quite like seeing the technology to make it all more real and give mankind's greatest explorations deeper meaning.

Hopefully this book, with its many very special inclusions, will also increase your understanding and fuel your passion for the exploration of the cosmos. Because, as Dave Scott, the commander of Apollo 15 famously said, "Man must explore".

**Rod Pyle**
*Author*

**Opposite** The Stars and Stripes are erected on the moon. This time, though, the explorers were able to drive the flagpole deeper into the surface and it didn't fall over at liftoff as the Apollo 11 flag did. Pete Conrad, during a more serious moment, is unfurling the flag, which is held aloft via a wire running through the top as there is no air to make it "wave" on the moon.

# HOW TO USE THIS BOOK

## MISSIONS TO THE MOON

### WITH AUGMENTED REALITY

**1.Download**

the free Missions to the Moon app from www.apple.com/itunes or www.android.com/apps and open it on your smart device.

**2.Scan the pages with these interactive icons**

**AR** Video

AR-fueled images activate videos from NASA's archives, allowing you to experience history first-hand.

**AR** Audio

AR-fueled images activate audio clips that tell the story through the voices of those involved.

**AR** Document

These icons trigger important documents relating to lunar exploration. Rifle through these on your smartphone or tablet.

**AR** Model

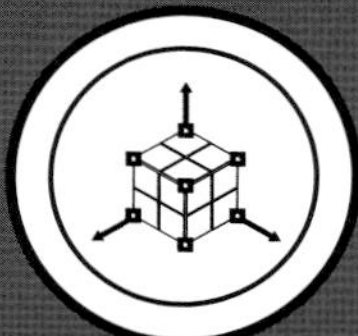

These icons trigger 360° renderings of iconic spacecraft. Explore them by rotating your device.

Powered by **Digital Magic**®

# MAN AND THE MOON

NEVER WAS THERE A TIME WHEN HUMANS DID NOT LOOK SKYWARD TO THE MOON AND WONDER, IF ONLY FOR A MOMENT, ABOUT HER NATURE. IN MANY CULTURES SHE HAD AN IMPORTANCE FAR BEYOND BEING AN OBJECT OF MERE CURIOSITY.

After all, relative to the planet it orbits, the moon is the largest known satellite in our solar system. As such, and with an orbit less than half a million miles in diameter, it dominates our skies in any phase save new moon. Its visage has driven poets, astrologers, calendar-makers, priests and warlords alike. It inhabits our thoughts, illuminates our nights and loiters in our dreams. The moon is the night-time lamp of the human psyche.

A vast body of mythology, folklore and legend has arisen around the moon. Early accounts date back to ancient Sumer, where the moon was known as Nanna or Nammar, who ruled over measurements and calendars. For the Egyptians the moon was referred to as the god Thoth, "the mind and tongue of Ra", and sometimes Osiris, the god of life, death and fertility.

The Greeks called the moon Selene, the goddess of night. She was the sister of Helios, god of the sun, and Eos, goddess of the dawn. Thus Selene was the central part of the night cycle. Later, Selene was identified with Artemis, a goddess of nature. In Roman times, the moon was linked to the goddess Luna, and later Diana.

Other cultures had varied interpretations of the moon. The ancient Chinese, for example, imagined a rabbit on the moon, a companion to the goddess Chang'e, for whom the rabbit forever prepares the elixir of immortality. However, it was not until the early seventeenth century, when the famed astronomer Johannes Kepler wrote a treatise called *The Dream*, in which a young man voyages to the moon, that the idea of travelling to the moon seemed even vaguely practical.

In 1865, Frenchman Jules Verne took a considerable step forward when he published *From the Earth to the Moon* (*De la Terre à la Lune*). In this story a trio of self-made businessmen launch themselves to the moon in a giant cannon shell called Columbiad, only to meet with an uncertain fate.

A Russian schoolteacher, Konstantin Tsiolkovsky, wrote some of the first serious enquiries into real lunar travel. His 1883 publication *Free Space* explored the use of chemically fuelled rockets for space travel. He further discussed the need for a portable atmosphere, multiple stages and advanced cryogenic fuels. This and other works inspired a generation of space pioneers in Russia and the West.

On the heels of such masters, H G Wells penned *The First Men in the Moon*, originally published in 1901. Lacking the scientific rigour of Verne, but with considerably more imagination, Wells writes of an

**Left** The Roman goddess of the moon, Luna, as descended from the Greek Selene, one of the oldest of the Greek deities. The crescent moon rides atop her head.

## THE BAT-MEN OF LUNA

In 1835, the *New York Sun* published an article entitled:
***GREAT ASTRONOMICAL DISCOVERIES LATELY MADE BY SIR JOHN HERSCHEL, L.L.D. F.R.S. & c. At the Cape of Good Hope***

The piece detailed how John Herschel, a prominent astronomer of the day, had discovered life on the moon. The creatures Herschel was credited as discovering included lunar buffalo, living beachballs, blue unicorns, intelligent bipedal beavers and, perhaps most alluring of all, bat-men. The article was a hoax, penned by Cambridge graduate Richard Adams Locke, and was thought to be responsible for a great boost in circulation. The paper never officially admitted to the fabrication.

**RIGHT** Winged bat-men (and women!) and other fanciful creatures populate the moon in the 1835 hoax printed in the *New York Sun*. Herschel, famed astronomer, was not consulted prior to the publication and was not amused.

> **That orbed maiden with white fire laden Whom mortals call the Moon**
> (Percy Bysshe Shelley, "The Cloud")

iron sphere covered in anti-gravity paint that transports an eccentric inventor and his ne'er-do-well partner to the moon. Once there, they are confronted by lumbering lunar cows, dangerous plants and an advanced race of humanoid insects called Selenites. Only the partner returns – the inventor stays behind and educates the Selenites about the evil nature of man.

Both *From the Earth to the Moon* and *The First Men in the Moon* paint vivid pictures of Victorian-era space travel to Earth's nearest neighbour. It is an alluring vision, supported by a fine scientific thread via the writings of Tsiolkovsky. However, it would be the 1930s before a young, charismatic German aristocrat would take these ideas, combine them with others, and begin to create the foundation for rocket that would ultimately propel men to the moon.

## LA LUNE DE FRANCE

**Above** A still from Georges Méliès film *Le Voyage dans la Lune.*

**Below** A young Jules Verne. Widely considered to be the father of modern science fiction, Verne wrote with an unbridled passion for science and technology.

In 1902, when the movie business was in its infancy, a Frenchman named Georges Méliès created a cinematic masterpiece entitled simply *A Trip to the Moon* (*Le Voyage dans la Lune*). It was created within a set constructed using a system of flats and pulleys, similar to those used in operetta, and featured exploding moon beings and many other effects which were impressive for the day. Drawing its inspiration from both Verne and Wells, the opening scenes utilize the cannon-shell spaceship from the Verne novel.

**Opposite left** Jubiliation! It's departure day in Jules Verne's *From the Earth to the Moon* (*De la Terre à la Lune*), 1865.

**Opposite right** Up and away: Verne's Columbiad moonship is fired from the huge 274-metre (900-feet) cannon into space.

**Above left** Published in 1865, Jules Verne's *From the Earth to the Moon* broke new ground when it asserted the possibility of travelling to the other planets via a spacecraft, albeit from the muzzle of a cannon.

# VENGEANCE TAKES FLIGHT

IN MARCH 1912, JUST AS WAR WAS THREATENING EUROPE, WERNHER MAGNUS MAXIMILIAN FREIHERR VON BRAUN WAS BORN IN WIRSITZ, THEN PART OF THE GERMAN EMPIRE, TO A CIVIL-SERVANT FATHER AND A MOTHER DESCENDED FROM THE MEDIEVAL GERMAN NOBILITY.

As a young man, von Braun observed the moon and planets through his small telescope. By 1932 he was an engineer as well as an avid reader of the works of Hermann Oberth, considered to be the father of German rocketry. Such works include *By Rocket into Planetary Space* (*Die Rakete zu den Planetenräumen*). Von Braun's background was in science, but he also possessed an active imagination, a combination that would serve him well in later life.

Heavily influenced by Oberth and other visionaries, von Braun found an outlet for his passion for rockets in Adolf Hitler's Nazi war machine. Von Braun's aristocratic lineage, and his doctoral thesis (*Construction, Theoretical and Experimental Solutions to the Problem of the Liquid Propellant Rocket*), led to his swift integration into Germany's growing war preparations.

By 1937, von Braun was an official Nazi and was working on rocket-powered weapons at Peenemünde, Germany. Whether he joined the Nazi party by choice or coercion has never been established by either the US or German Governments, but von Braun himself had something to say about the matter:

**VON BRAUN:** I was officially demanded to join the National Socialist Party. At this time [1937] I was already Technical Director of the Army Rocket Center at Peenemünde... My refusal to join the party would have meant that I would have had to abandon the work of my life. Therefore, I decided to join. My membership in the party did not involve any political activity... in Spring 1940, one SS-Standartenführer (SS Colonel) Müller... looked me up in my office at Peenemünde and told me that Reichsführer-SS Heinrich Himmler had sent him with the order to urge me to join the SS. I called immediately on my military superior... Major-General W Dornberger. He informed me that...
if I wanted to continue our mutual work, I had no alternative but to join...

Michael Neufeld, Von Braun: Dreamer of Space, Engineer of War, 2007

**Below** Von Braun in 1930, during his early days as a rocket enthusiast (second from right). He quickly dismissed the old fireworks-derived solid-fuelled devices for more complex, but powerful and controllable, liquid-fuelled versions.

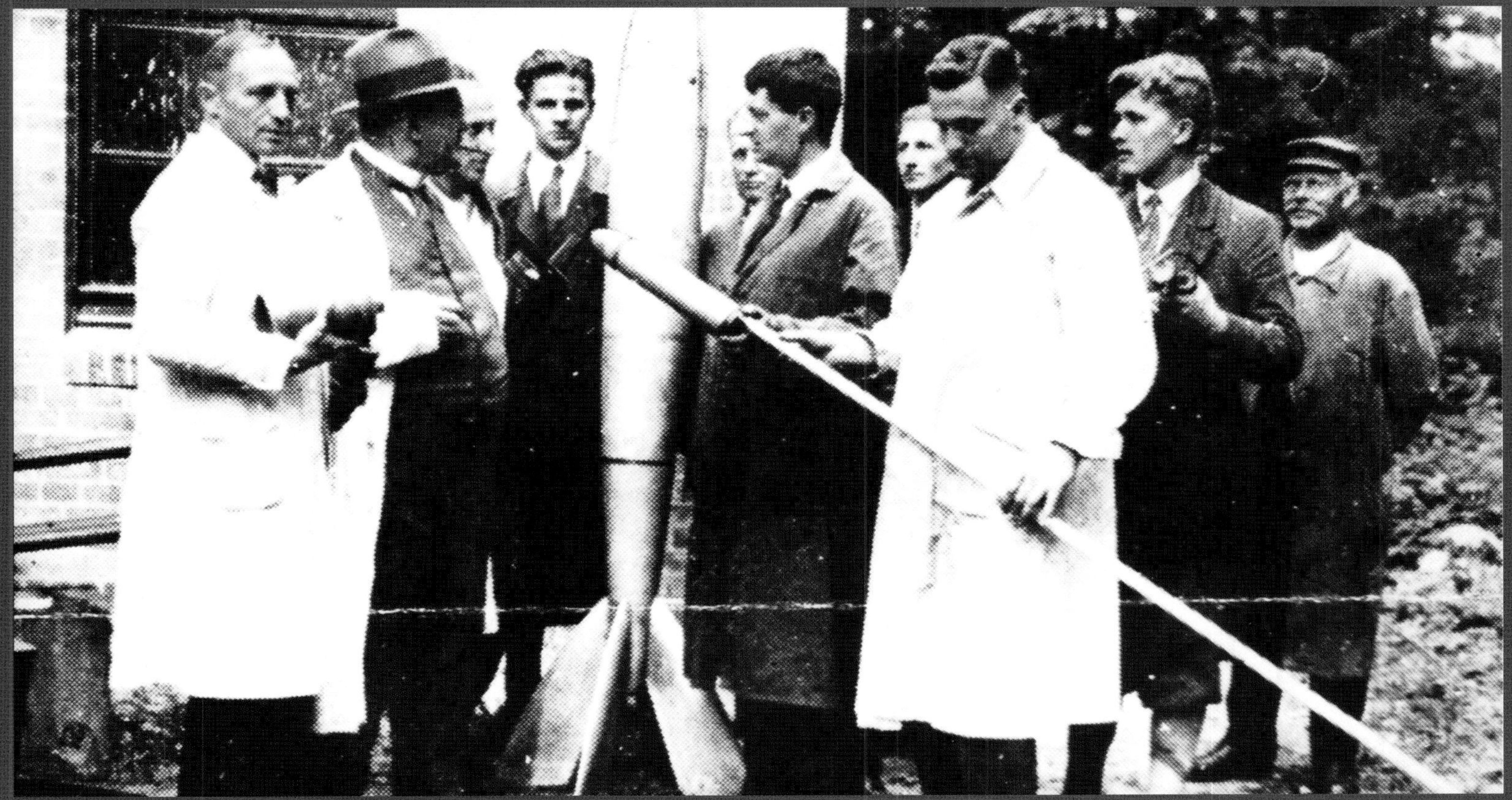

## TARGET: MANHATTAN

Hitler dreamed of striking at the heart of America with his wonder weapons. In the early 1930s, Eugen Sänger, a German student, designed a rocket-glider (or "skip-bomber") that he thought could accomplish the task. It was eventually called Silverbird, and would be launched off a 3.2-kilometre- (2-mile-) long rail track. Then, using its own rockets to ascend to 144.8 kilometres (90 miles), it would begin to descend and "skip" along the denser atmosphere below to reach its target, delivering 1,816 kilograms (4,000 pounds) of bombs. It was theoretically interesting but impractical, and never got beyond wind-tunnel testing.

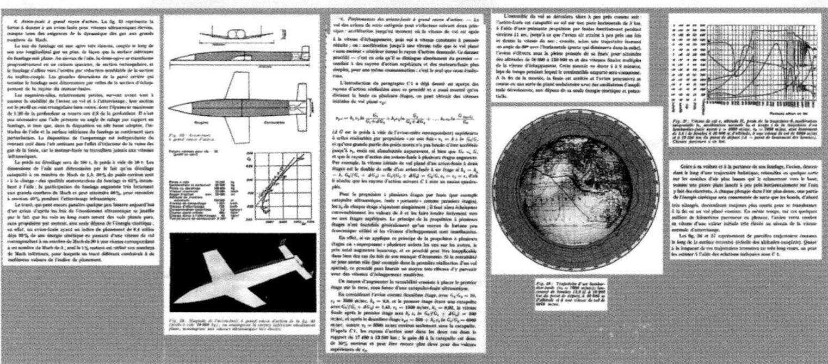

**Above** An article printed in France in 1948. Impressive on paper, the Silverbird skip-bomber would never have been able to withstand atmospheric heating at the speeds it was intended to travel.

At the advanced research centre in Peenemünde, von Braun created, tested and launched the so-called "vengeance weapons" against Allied targets. The Vengeance 1, or V1, was a rocket plane, powered by a pulsejet, a valveless self-sustaining engine requiring only fuel input to operate during flight. This "buzz bomb" or "doodlebug", as the British called it, was soon reduced to a mere nuisance by the RAF, but had set the stage for the amazing weapon that was to follow.

His next (and most famous) accomplishment was the V2 rocket. Related to the V1 by little more than a prefix, the V2 was the world's first ballistic missile. First launched on 7 September 1944, the missile carried a large enough bomb load to wreak local havoc, and was a true terror weapon as it fell at supersonic speeds from the skies onto its targets.

The rocket, which carried a payload of almost 997 kilograms (2,200 pounds) of explosives, was 13.8 metres (46 feet) high and almost 1.8 metres (6 feet) at its widest. It was fuelled by alcohol and liquid oxygen, generating 72,480 kilograms (160,000 pounds) of thrust, and had an operational range of about 320 kilometres (200 miles). Guiding the craft was an elaborate (for the day) gyroscopic control system, which was accurate to within a few miles at impact. While not impressive by today's standards, it was quite advanced in the era of manually aimed aeroplane-dropped bombs.

Upon hearing the news of the first successful raid on London, von Braun is alleged to have said: "The rocket worked perfectly except for landing on the wrong planet…"(NASA historical website, http://sse.jpl.nasa.gov/). He claims to have fallen into a deep depression having been told of the attack. Over the course of the war he would have almost 3,200 more chances to experience his regrets.

Soon after the initiation of V2 flights, the Allies bombed Peenemünde so mercilessly that von Braun's entire operation was moved into the Harz Mountains in Northern Germany. There, in a vast complex tunnelled dozens of miles deep into the rocks, tens of thousands of Jewish, Polish and other prisoners of the Reich worked, often to death, building Hitler's rockets of war.

The legacy of the V2 includes the Redstone rocket, which launched the first Americans into space, and the progenitors of the Saturn V and the early Saturn rockets. However, a darker legacy remains from the war – while the V2 killed almost 7,300 people in attacks, a full 20,000 of Germany's enslaved labourers died during its construction. It was a shameful heritage for a brilliant machine, but technology rarely advances in a moral vacuum.

As the defeat of Germany loomed, von Braun and his comrades realized that they were marked men – the Russians and Americans wanted their rocket expertise, and Hitler wanted them dead, in order to deny their knowledge to the enemy. In a cloak-and-dagger exercise worthy of the theatre, von Braun arranged for himself and 120 members of his team to surrender to the Americans, and on that day, however indirectly, Project Apollo was born.

**Opposite below** A German V2 rocket is prepared for testing in Germany, 1944. The white-and-black paint scheme was for observation purposes, and would be replaced by camouflage for use in combat.

**Left** V2 rocket departs Peenemünde, Germany, under the supervision of Wernher von Braun. Fuelled by liquid oxygen and alcohol, the rockets had a range of about 320 kilometres (200 miles) and a large explosive warhead.

**Above** A view of a precursor to von Braun's V2 rocket, being pulled out of a storage shed. Note the camouflauge wrapping over the tailfins.

## VENGEANCE 1

A predecessor to the V2, the V1 winged bomb was a new approach to terror from the skies. An early cruise missile, it was launched from an angled ramp in Germany towards targets in Belgium and England. A self-sustaining pulsejet engine, in which combustion occurs in pulses, powered the vehicle. But the "doodlebug" was noisy and slow, and the British developed tactics which allowed them to shoot down or disable many V1s before they reached their targets. The V2 programme took precedence thereafter.

**Left** A V-1 under power. The engine would quit well before it reached its target, and it would glide to its ultimate destination, exploding on impact.

## INVESTIGATION MEMO

Some in the US Government had misgivings about von Braun's background. Rumours swirled about possible Nazi party affiliations and SS membership. This November 1948 memo details some of the results of the ongoing investigation.

From 532 page file on VON Braun

Federal Bureau of Investigation
United States Department of Justice

202 U. S. Court House
El Paso, Texas
November 30, 1948

CONFIDENTIAL

CLASSIFIED BY: 9145/
DECLASSIFY ON:

AIR MAIL SPECIAL DELIVERY

ALL INFORMATION
HEREIN IS UNCLASSIFIED
EXCEPT WHERE SHOWN
OTHERWISE

DIRECTOR, FBI

RE: ~~WERNHER MAGNUS MAXIMILIAN FREIHERR~~
VON BRAUN
SPECIAL INQUIRY - DEPARTMENT OF
JUSTICE, GERMAN SCIENTISTS UNDER
THE PROTECTIVE CUSTODY AND CONTROL
OF THE JOINT INTELLIGENCE OBJECTIVES
AGENCY

Dear Sir:

Reference is made to Albany letter dated November 24, 1948, copies of which were furnished to the Bureau.

b7c b7d

It is noted that [redacted] made statements to the effect that, in his opinion, VON BRAUN was an avowed Nazi Party Member and that his opinion was based on VON BRAUN's actions and talk and the personal impression he gained from conversation with VON BRAUN. He also stated that he had learned from British Intelligence that VON BRAUN held a commission in the SS and was personally decorated by HITLER for his work on the V-2.

b1

It is set forth in the report of Special Agent [redacted] [redacted] dated September 25, 1948 at El Paso, that VON BRAUN's commission in the SS was known to American Army officers who requested VON BRAUN to come to the United States [redacted] [redacted] there was no information available at Fort Bliss, from the military associates of VON BRAUN indicating any apparent Nazi sympathies.

The Albany Division is being requested to reinterview [redacted] [redacted] and submit a report containing more specific information.

COPIES DESTROYED
15 MAY 20 1960

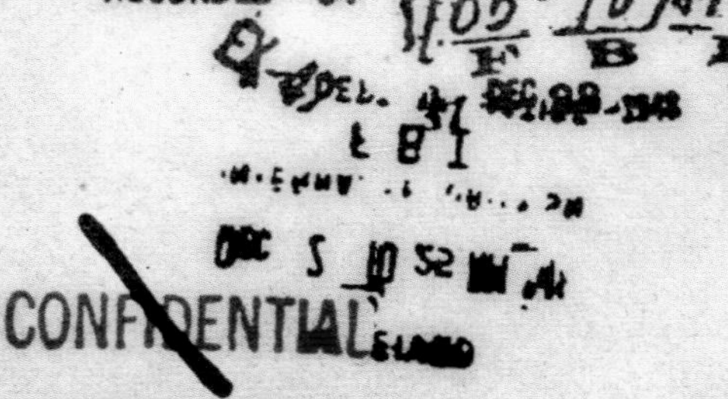

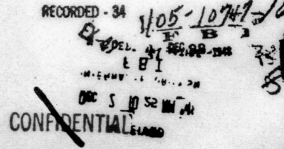

CONFIDENTIAL

# SPACE STATION SKETCH

After considering various configurations, including a large orbiting wheel, von Braun sketched a design for a simpler space station in 1964. Utilizing existing Saturn rocket hardware, the small orbital workshop never got off the drawing board. A similar design would later be realized as Project Skylab in the early 1970s.

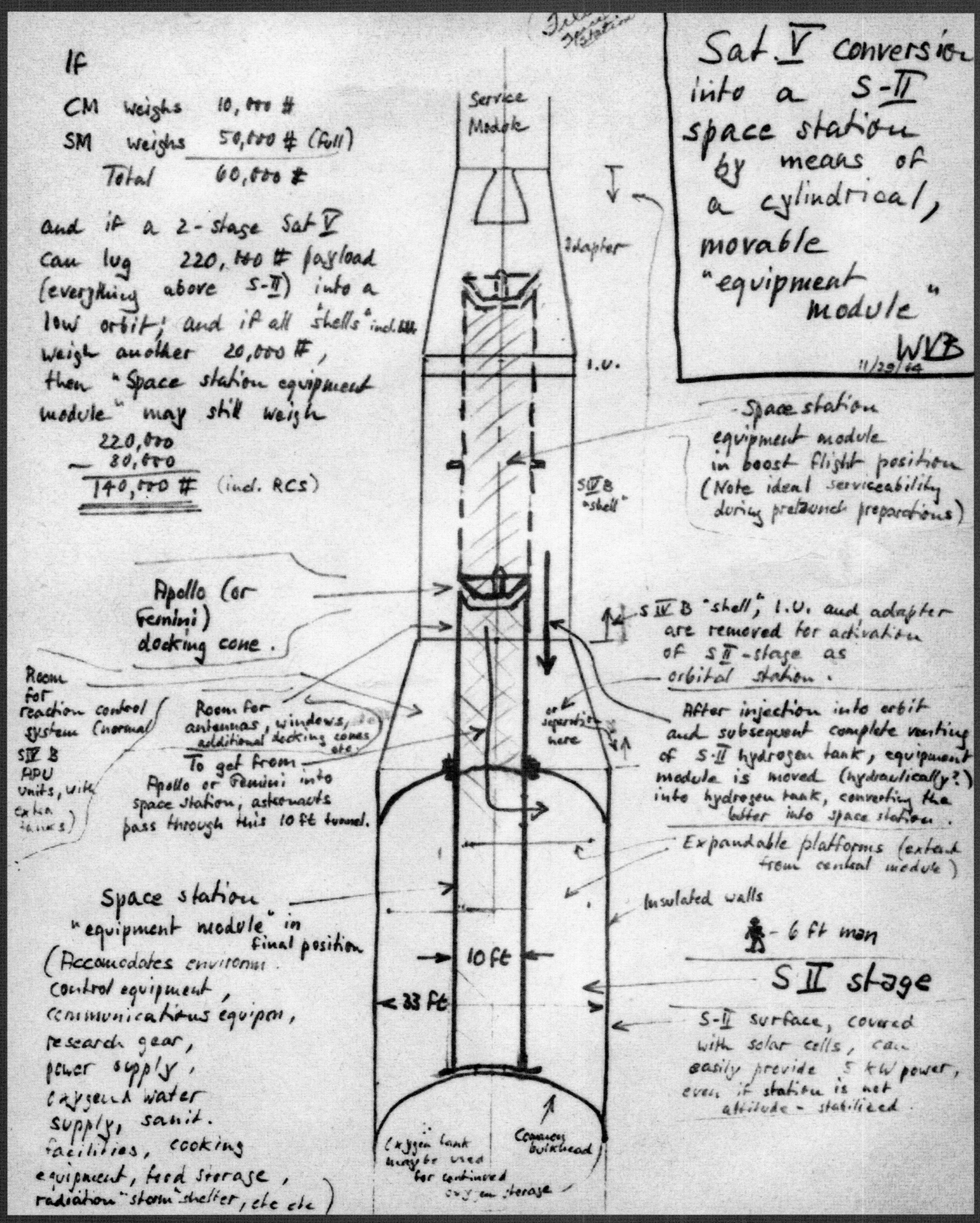

# CHAPTER THREE

# SLEEPING UNDER A RED MOON

IN 1957 BRITISH PRIME MINISTER ANTHONY EDEN RESIGNED, US TROOPS FORCED RACIAL DESEGREGATION IN LITTLE ROCK, ARKANSAS AND THE US AND USSR BOTH SUCCESSFULLY TESTED INTERCONTINENTAL BALLISTIC MISSILES (ICBMS).

Of all the tidal shifts in the world in that year, however, Sputnik 1 was the most far-reaching.

In one brilliant move, the Russians catapulted themselves into technological prominence, leaving the US and its oft-delayed Vanguard satellite programme in the backwater. The American public was outraged, and the free world looked at the US in doubt. Lyndon B Johnson, then a senator, railed: "Control of space means control of the world!" (Alan Wasser, "LBJ's Space Race: what we didn't know then", *The Space Review*, 2005).

US efforts soldiered on. The Navy's Vanguard programme struggled to launch a melon-sized satellite in a forlorn claim to space.

## LAIKA

Sputnik 2 was launched on 3 November 1957. Inside was Laika, a three-year-old, five-kilogram (11-pound) stray dog found on the streets of Moscow. Sergei Korolev, the Soviet Chief Designer, had grown fond of the animal and was deeply disturbed by her early demise. She died after just a few hours in space instead of the anticipated ten days, as the thermal control system had failed. She would have been euthanized by a gentle poison had she survived. Sputnik 2 eventually re-entered five months later, and both spacecraft and deceased passenger were incinerated.

**Above** The thermal control system failed shortly after launch, and the dog Laika lived for only about 6 hours. Her early death was concealed for decades.

**Above** Vanguard's ignominious ride. On 6 December 1957, it flew to the height of a few inches and exploded in full view of the assembled press. "Kaputnik!" raged the headlines. Vanguard finally flew on 17 March 1958, three months after von Braun's Explorer 1.

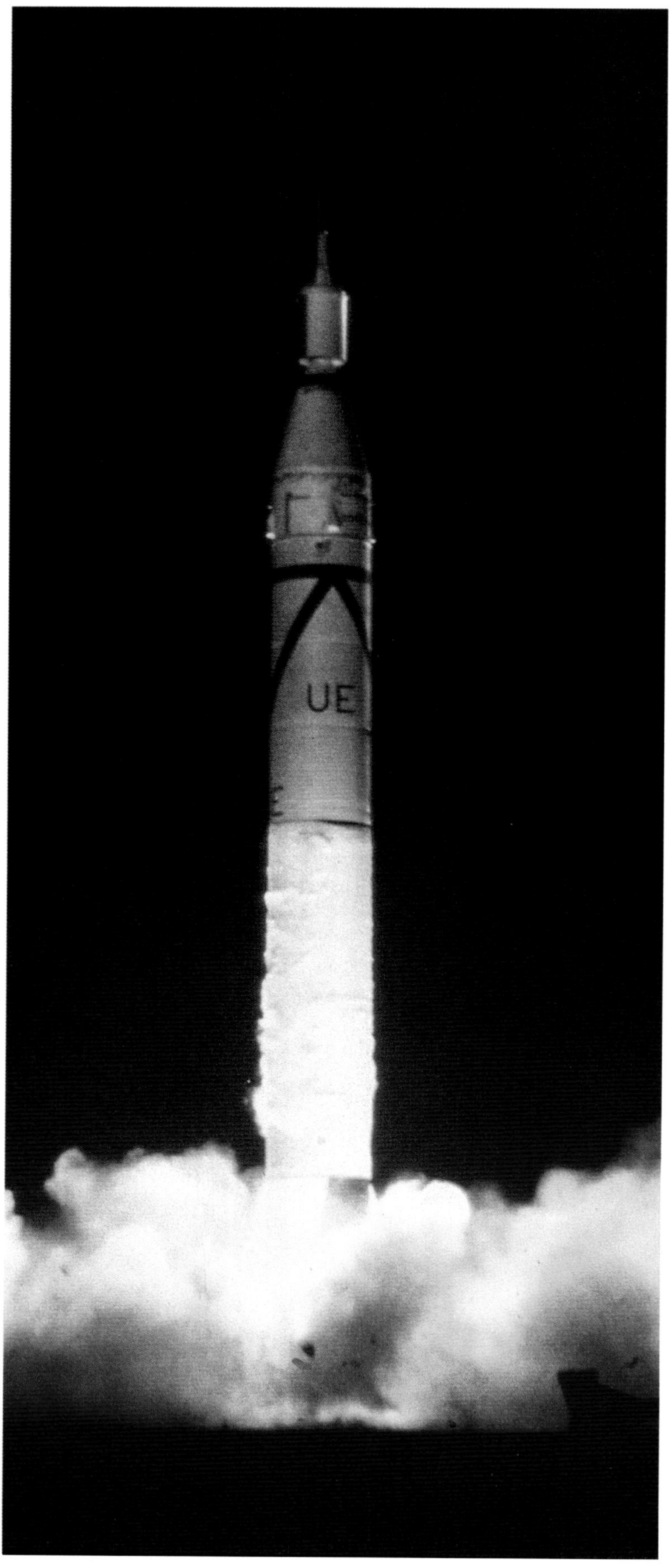


Delays and failures plagued the project, capped by a widely televised launch attempt on 6 December 1957. The rocket lifted a few inches from the pad, hesitated as breathless spectators looked on, then collapsed magnificently in a cloud of flame and smoke. The satellite rolled to a stop a few metres from the gantry, surviving the inferno. It hangs in the National Air and Space Museum today, a scarred but plucky survivor of the American space programme.

In the meantime, the Soviets had orbited Sputnik 2. It housed a small dog named Laika, and weighed over 498 kilograms (1,100 pounds). Laika lived just a few hours before dying from overheating, yet the mission was a coup. Russian Premier Nikita Khrushchev revelled in the USSR's finest hour.

Even the US press indulged in some negative comments about the US attempts to get into space, with headlines like "Kaputnik", "Stayputnik" and even "Flopnik" flogging Vanguard in papers across the nation. President Dwight D Eisenhower, not easily cowed, was indignant.

Meanwhile, at NASA's rocket facility in Huntsville, Alabama, Wernher von Braun and his team watched in smouldering resentment. Long before, von Braun had proposed allowing his engineers and the US Army to make orbit with his already proven booster (even then being used for high-altitude re-entry tests). The idea of letting Germans – even if they were then American Germans – launch the free world's first satellite was difficult for some members of Congress to entertain. Now that the US was being surpassed by the communist USSR, however, maybe it was time to give the former Nazi rocketmen their chance. They were considered, at that point in history, to be the lesser of two evils.

Prior to this, von Braun had been striving to develop the German V2 into a new American launch vehicle. Over the decade since the end of the Second World War, the V2 had spawned a series of rockets, resulting in the Redstone (which eventually powered the first Mercury flights), and the Jupiter-C, which finally lofted Explorer 1 to orbit on 31 January 1958. Explorer 1 was designed by the Jet Propulsion Laboratory in Pasadena, California, and looked itself like a small rocket. It was planned and built in just 84 days, and though launched only months after Sputnik 1, it was far more advanced.

Sputnik was primarily an orbiting propaganda package that proudly announced its presence over the capitalist world every 90 minutes via a radio beep. Explorer weighed a scant 14 kilograms (30 pounds), yet carried instrumentation capable of measuring cosmic rays, micrometeor impacts and temperatures in Earth orbit. It soon made the startling discovery of the Van Allen radiation belts (regions of high-energy particles surrounding the Earth) and it was feared that these would pose a danger to the future of space travel.

In February, Sputnik 3 followed suit with a cosmic ray detector, which failed after launch. With each superpower trying to outdo the other with every successive launch, the space race was officially on. Rocket development now moved to a fever pitch in both countries. Almost as an aside, the Navy did finally get their Vanguard satellite into orbit months later, but by then the US and the Soviet Union were in a pitched battle for technological supremacy.

The goal was to be the first country to send a man into space. The Russians were well ahead with their powerful rockets. Their "Chief Designer", Sergei Korolev, was coaxing tremendous power out of clusters

## ROBOTS BEFORE MEN

Not all the Soviet firsts were manned flights. A long series of large and heavy robotic probes were scouting out the neighbourhood of the moon. Flying between 1959 and 1976, this series of spacecraft provided the first reconnaissance of the nearby solar system. Notable achievements include: Luna 2, the first man-made object to impact on the moon; Luna 3, which returned the first photographs of the lunar farside and Luna 9, which achieved the first soft landing on the moon.

**Above** The Luna-3 probe. Always quite different in appearance than their Western counterparts, Soviet probes tended to be heavy and large, but they often performed impressively.

**Opposite** Explorer 1, launched on a Jupter-C rocket, which was an enhanced Redstone missile. The cylindrical section at the top rotated rapidly to lend stability to the spacecraft once it separated from the booster. It was successfully launched on 1 January 1958.

**Right** Success at last. From Right, Dr Werner von Braun, Dr James van Allen and Dr William Pickering, hold Explorer 1 overhead for an adoring press. They might have found the Sputnik 1, at 83 kilograms (184 pounds), a bit more of a struggle than the 13-kilogram (30-pound) Explorer.

of small rocket engines. In America, von Braun and his team were taking a more technologically advanced (and expensive) incremental approach.

On 9 March 1961, the Soviets hurled a Vostok rocket into orbit, with Yuri Gagarin wedged into the capsule atop it. With his showbiz good looks televised live to the world, he conveyed his sense of wonder at the azure-blue planet outside his window. In one stunning moment the USSR had again surged past the US, not in a jump, but in a huge leap. Up to that point, the Americans had sent a chimpanzee into a suborbital lob in January of that year, and there had been another dozen incremental test flights of the Mercury systems. However, the Russians now had a man in orbit, and within hours the entire world knew. While NASA fumed, Main Street America looked impotently to the skies and wondered, "when will it be our turn?"

# CHAPTER FOUR

# AIMING FOR THE MOON

## THE AMERICAN PUBLIC DIDN'T HAVE TO WAIT LONG. IN TRUTH, MERCURY COULD PROBABLY HAVE FLOWN BEFORE VOSTOK 1 AND ITS HISTORIC FIRST HUMAN PASSENGER YURI GAGARIN, BUT NASA WAS VERY SAFETY CONSCIOUS.

The aerospace medical establishment was wary of all things orbital: questioning whether a man would lose consciousness once he was weightless, whether the g-forces of launch would cause him to blackout and whether he would become dangerously disorientated once the familiar sights of Earth gave way to the dark space above.

The Soviet flights had laid those fears to rest, and, on the morning of 5 May 1961 it was America's turn at last. Alan Shepard sat atop the Redstone booster in Freedom 7 awaiting launch. He was confident and, as the launch controllers fretted and delayed the launch hour after hour, he finally called down from the capsule, where he had been whiling away the last few hours, "Ok, I'm cooler than you are… let's light this candle!" (Andrew Chaikin, *A Man on the Moon: The Voyages of the Apollo Astronauts*, 1995).

The launch director relented, and America's first manned spaceflight was aloft. Then, 15 minutes later, it was over. The first two Mercury flights used the small Redstone booster, barely powerful enough for a short suborbital lob. So, while the astronaut performed his mission as if it were an orbital one, manoeuvring with the thrusters, setting up for re-entry and even firing the retro-rockets, none of it was really needed. The Mercury capsule in these first two flights was essentially a cannonball, following a ballistic trajectory up, over and down.

Just a few weeks after this first manned American flight, President John F Kennedy took a bold step when addressing Congress. He challenged them to follow him to the moon. Despite the huge price tag and risks involved there was broad support for the venture, and the race to the moon was on. America wanted the high ground.

On 21 July 1961, two-and-a-half months after Shepard's flight, Gus Grissom flew a similar mission, and, excepting the fact that his capsule sank into the Atlantic before it could be retrieved, it was a success.

Just two weeks after Grissom's flight, however, Gherman Titov flew another Vostok into orbit, and stayed there for a full day. Now Russian craft had orbited for one-and-a-half days, while the Americans had achieved only 30 minutes in space. NASA was nervous and Congress furious.

Then, on 20 February 1962, John Glenn, seizing his chance to make space history, reclaimed the advantage for the US, orbiting the Earth three times in his Mercury capsule before Mission Control brought him

### A NEAR-DEADLY EXCURSION

When Alexei Arkhipovich Leonov went on his 12-minute spacewalk during the flight of Voskhod 2, he nearly didn't come home. He exited the capsule through an inflatable cloth tube not much longer than a man and his pressure suit began to overinflate. When it was time to return, Leonov, now winded, could not wedge the bulky suit back inside. After a few moments of suspense, he managed manually to deflate the suit enough to crawl back inside the capsule. It was humanity's first excursion outside a spacecraft.

**ABOVE** In this oddly stylized and amazingly inaccurate stamp, the USSR celebrated its most recent triumph: the very first walk in space.

**Above** An early Mercury capsule at the McDonnell Douglas plant. At just over 1,360 kilograms (3,000 pounds), the Mercury spacecraft was the smallest and lightest manned spacecraft ever flown.

home early owing to a faulty emergency sensor. Three more Mercury flights would complete the programme, all on the powerful Atlas booster that had put Glenn into orbit. Next would come Project Gemini, with two astronauts on each flight.

Over the next few years the space race turned white hot. On 18 March 1965, five days before the first flight of the Gemini series, Voskhod 2 was launched and Alexei Leonov became the first person to exit a spacecraft in orbit and "walk" in space. It was a daring mission, using an inflatable airlock that almost doomed Leonov when he had trouble returning to the Voskhod capsule. But Leonov succeeded and once again, the USSR had made news and set records.

On 23 March Gus Grissom and John Young climbed into the Gemini 3 capsule and were hurled into orbit by the new Titan booster. Their mission, to test the spacecraft and its manoeuvring capabilities, was a success, and set the stage for future Gemini flights.

This was followed by nine further Gemini missions, with the objectives of each one becoming progressively more complex and demanding. On 3 June, Ed White made America's first spacewalk, carrying out a much easier excursion than Leonov's.

Gemini 5 followed shortly thereafter, setting the pace of a Gemini launch about every two months.

Gemini 6 and 7 were launched within days of each other in December 1965, and were able to match orbits and rendezvous in space. They did not

**Above** Alan Shepard, America's first man in space, sits inside a Mercury capsule in this undated photo.

## PROJECT MERCURY NAME CHANGE

In 1958, when Mercury was in the planning stages, Robert Gilruth, then director of the Space Task Group at NASA's Langley centre, wanted a name change. He didn't like the name "Project Mercury" and proposed "Project Astronaut" instead. What became of this proposal is unclear, but the name change was never adopted.

Washington, D. C.
December 12, 1958

MEMORANDUM For Dr. Silverstein

Subject: Change of Manned Satellite Project name from "Project Mercury" to "Project Astronaut"

1. Bob Gilruth feels that "Project Astronaut" is a far more suitable name for the Manned Satellite Project than "Project Mercury."

2. If you agree, this should be brought to Dr. Glennan's attention immediately. Present plans call for Dr. Glennan to refer to "Project Mercury" in his policy speech on December 17.

George M. Low

Low:lgs

Thought this might interest you

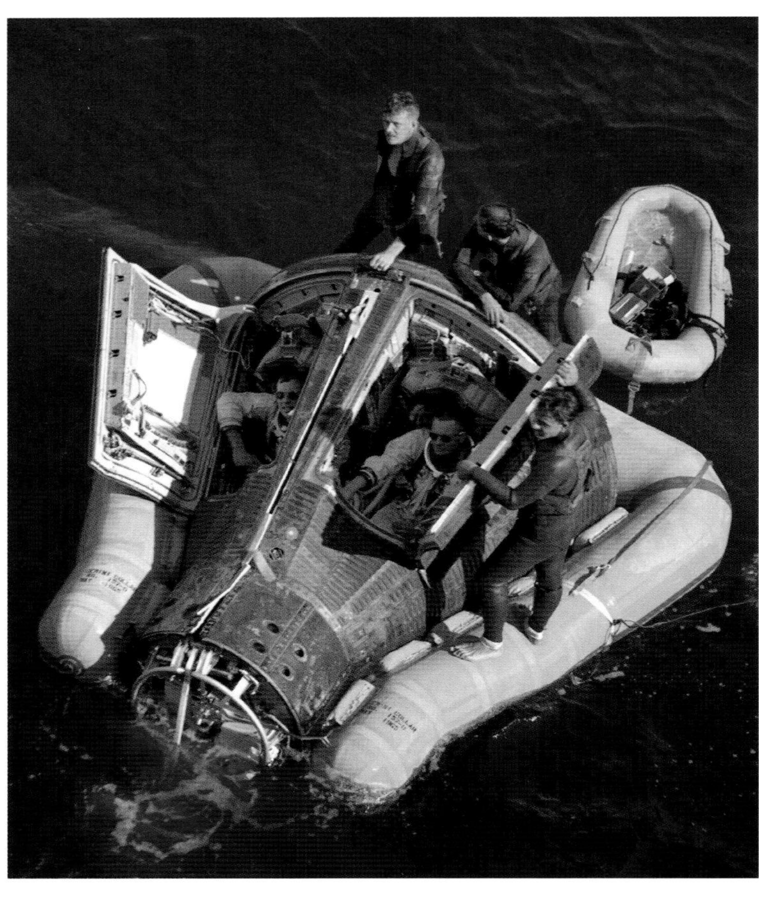

dock, but were able to rendezvous from different orbits and manoeuvre to within a few feet of one another, a critical move for the lunar programme.

Only Gemini 8 flirted with disaster. With Neil Armstrong at the controls, the spacecraft had docked with an unmanned target rocket and was to use its engine to lift both machines to a higher orbit. But the Gemini capsule began to develop a slow roll, so Armstrong disconnected from the target rocket, thinking that it was causing the problem. His capsule then began to spin at an alarming rate until, using his best judgement, he fired the retro-fire thrusters (those normally used for re-entry) and re-entered immediately. It was the closest that NASA had come to a disaster in space up to that time.

The last Gemini mission flew on 11 November 1966, with Jim Lovell and Buzz Aldrin aboard. It was as close to a textbook mission as Gemini achieved, and wrapped up the programme nicely. As 1967 neared, all seemed well with NASA and the US space programme. It was time for Apollo and the moon.

**Left** Gemini 8 after splashdown. Neil Armstrong and Dave Scott can be seen inside the spacecraft, glad to be alive after a near-fatal tumble in orbit.

**Opposite** On 3 June 1964, Ed White makes America's first spacewalk. For about 22 minutes he floated free, fixed only by a tether. He used a small gas thruster gun to do some basic manoeuvres, then got tired and struggled to get back into the Gemini capsule.

## JFK CHARTS THE COURSE

Events moved quickly after Alan Shepard's Mercury flight. With just one manned flight on the books, President John F Kennedy, on 12 May 1961, challenged the US Congress, and the nation as a whole, to reach for the moon:

JFK: I believe that this nation should commit itself to achieving the goal, before this decade is out, of landing a man on the moon and returning him safely to the Earth. No single space project in this period will be more impressive to mankind, or more important for the long-range exploration of space; and none will be so difficult or expensive to accomplish.

# CHAPTER FIVE

# HOW TO GO TO THE MOON

PROJECTS MERCURY AND GEMINI HAD EACH BEEN A TRIUMPH. HOWEVER, OTHER DEPARTMENTS OF NASA WERE WORKING OVERTIME TO TAKE MAN FURTHER THAN HE HAD EVER BEEN BY INVENTING A WAY TO GET TO THE MOON AS PROJECT APOLLO PICKED UP SPEED.

At the same time that a hardware approach was being defined, the physics of the mission were under scrutiny. Early on, von Braun wanted to use one giant rocket, to fly to the moon, land and return, with no risky rendezvous in space. In those days, without onboard computers, meeting up and docking in space seemed an unacceptable risk. With Mercury and Gemini successful, however, and digital computer technology emerging, most agreed that Earth Orbit Rendezvous, or EOR, was the way to go. Modular spacecraft would link up in Earth orbit and fly to the moon and back, using multiple smaller rockets.

Then, an engineer named John Houbolt upset the NASA applecart. He began to lobby for Lunar Orbit Rendezvous, or LOR. First proposed by Hermann Oberth in the 1920s, it was an idea that had met wide resistance within NASA. Two spacecraft would travel to the moon, separate and while one landed the other would stay in orbit. The two ships would then have to find one another and dock to retrieve the landing crew and return home. It scared even the staunchest believers.

Houbolt, however, was undaunted and took his plan to NASA's upper management. After careful consideration LOR was the clear winner, saving both overall mass and fuel. Although it made the engineers

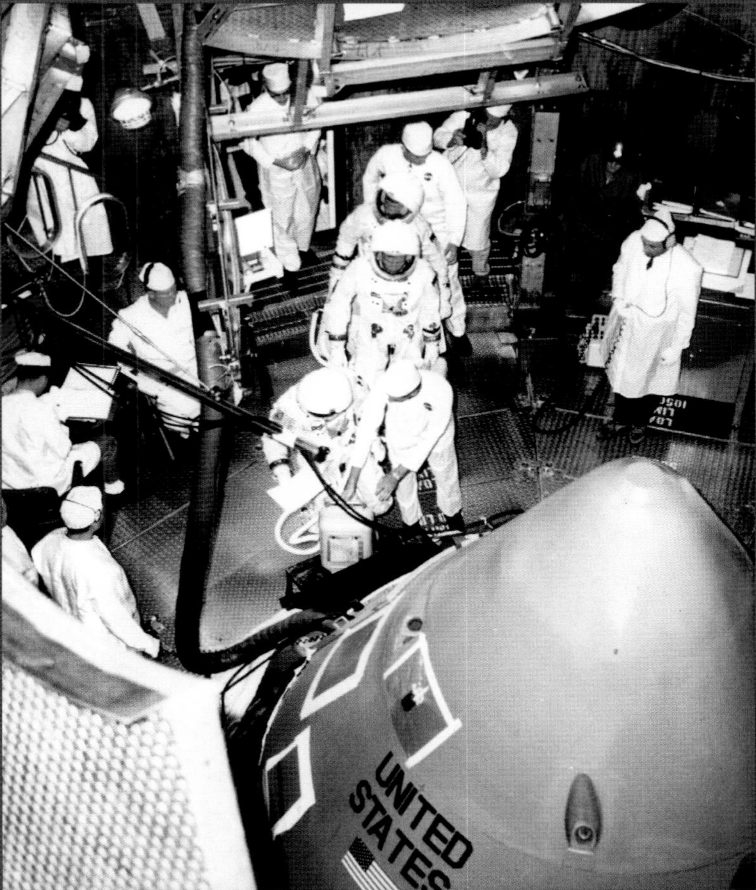

**Above** The logo for the Apollo 1 space flight, complete with the names of the astronaunts written along the edges.

**Top right** Gus Grissom, Ed White and Roger Chaffee are seen entering the Block 1 Apollo capsule in for training. They are wearing early Apollo suits with flammable fabrics that would later be replaced.

**Right** The ill-fated crew of Apollo 1: from left, Gus Grissom, Ed White and Roger Chaffee, a rookie astronaut whose first flight would be Apollo 1. All three died in the Apollo ground-test fire.

## SECOND LIFE FOR GEMINI

Even after the LOR approach had been chosen, the race to beat the Russians prompted some within NASA to consider trying to use the two-man Gemini capsule to circle, or even land on, the moon. This could obviate the need for LOR and use existing, proven hardware. In hindsight, however, it would have saved just a few billion dollars and only cut about six to nine months off the programme while greatly increasing the risk. The Apollo system was the right way to go in the end.

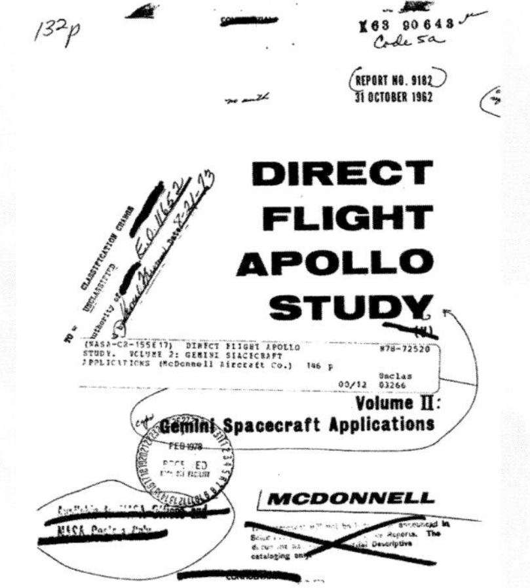

X63 90643

REPORT NO. 9182
31 OCTOBER 1962

DIRECT FLIGHT APOLLO STUDY

(NASA-CR-155E17) DIRECT FLIGHT APOLLO STUDY. VOLUME 2: GEMINI SPACECRAFT APPLICATIONS (McDonnell Aircraft Co.) 146 p

N78-72520

Unclas
00/12 03266

Volume II:
Gemini Spacecraft Applications

MCDONNELL

**Right** The Direct Flight Apollo Study was one of many attempts to rationalize the use of a Gemini spacecraft to go to the moon.

**Opposite** The first stages of Saturn IB rockets, the precursor to the more powerful Saturn V. It was an interim booster, used for the early Apollo test flights

**Below** The charred remains of the Apollo 1 capsule. The original Block I hatch was secured by bolts and opened inwards, effectively dooming the crew when the spacecraft burst into flames during a ground test. Later Command Modules had hatches activated by a single lever and opened outwards.

nervous to think about spacecraft trying to rendezvous in lunar orbit, they had to admit that if the astronauts failed to link their spacecraft together, where they failed to do so made little difference.

With LOR chosen, Apollo moved off the drawing boards and into the physical world. The Apollo Command/Service Modules would be built by North American Aviation (which became North American Rockwell in 1967). The Lunar Module contract went to Grumman Aerospace, and the enormous booster rocket needed to lift both these spacecraft was contracted to Boeing.

Challenges arose quickly. Von Braun's huge F1 engines, intended to power the Saturn V booster, experienced terrible teething troubles. The Lunar Module over at Grumman was grossly overweight, and at North American Aviation, the Command Module was a mess.

Throughout 1967, the first attempt by the US to build a moonship experienced difficulties. The early Command Modules, referred to as the "Block I" versions, were intended to get Apollo into orbit and through the testing phase. Then the newer, improved "Block II" ships would make the trek to the moon.

The Block I ship was dogged with problems, however, most relating to its wiring systems. The Command Module had 24 kilometres (15 miles) of wiring inside, and inspectors continued to find faulty connections and potential fire hazards. NASA was not happy, and Gus Grissom, scheduled to be the commander of the first manned Apollo flight, once hung a lemon over the spacecraft's hatch to express his displeasure. Many in the Apollo crews viewed it as an accident waiting to happen.

On 27 January 1967, during a routine test of the Apollo 1 rocket, the fears ignited into reality. The first Apollo crew, Gus Grissom, Ed White and Roger Chaffee, were strapped into the Apollo 1 capsule. They sat atop a Saturn IB booster at the launch pad in Florida, and were conducting a simulated countdown test. The Command Module was pressurized with pure oxygen – relatively safe in space at 0.3447 bar (two kilograms per centimetre square or five pounds per square inch), but dangerously flammable at ground pressure of about 0.965 bar (6.35 kilograms per square centimetre or 14 pounds per square inch).

A

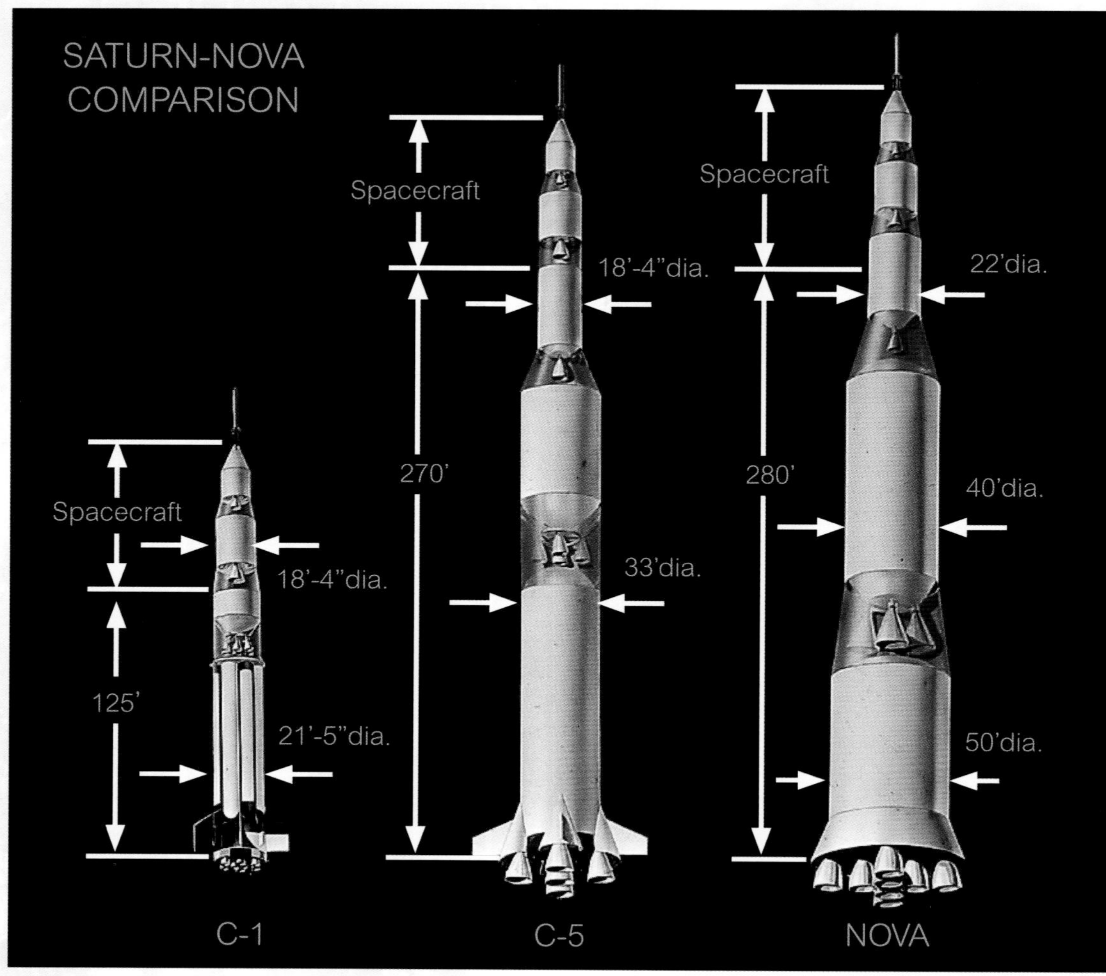


During the battle to choose a preferred path to the moon, the Manned Space Flight Centre (MSFC), in Huntsville, Alabama, home to von Braun's team of engineers, was widely seen as the last bastion of support for EOR. A standoff was predicted, but much to the surprise of all, not least the MSFC engineers, von Braun, who had much earlier foreseen a huge, one-rocket system called Nova as the proper approach to a lunar landing, decided to approve LOR, and the way was clear for the Apollo missions as we know them today.

**Left** A comparison of the various luna booster configurations, with a Saturn I for scale. From left, the Saturn I, the Saturn V and the Nova booster.

After hours of delays and glitches, there was a small spark in the faulty wiring inside the capsule.

Monitors inside Mission Control showed only a bright flash of light. A terse voice called over the voice activated transmission (VOX) circuit, "Fire!" followed by "We have a fire in here!" Technicians at the pad in Florida ran to the capsule and attempted to remove the hatch to no avail: it was held fast by bolts that took long minutes to undo. Flight controllers could only watch helplessly as the fire blew out the sides of the Command Module, forcing the rescue team back. It was a full five minutes before the hatch was removed, and what they found inside was horrifying.

The Apollo programme ground to a halt while investigations attempted to discover the problems, and people, responsible. Ultimately, it was clear that North American Aviation had done much shoddy work on the Command/Service Modules. Some members of Congress even agitated for cancellation of the programme, Walter Mondale prominent among them. But NASA had exercised the good judgement to put Frank Borman, veteran Gemini astronaut, in charge of their part of the investigation, and his continued authoritarian prodding as much as anything else saved the programme. The Apollo Block I capsules were upgraded across the board to Block II specifications, myriad deficiencies were fixed and the programme was allowed to move ahead.

Apollo, after claiming three lives, was once again on its way to the moon.

# APOLLO FACT SHEET

A memo from then-director of NASA's Space Task Group Robert Gilruth about Apollo. He outlines the basic post-LOR decisions regarding the spacecraft, some of the expected difficulties and planned modes of operation. Dated 1962, it was circulated at a time when Gemini was still being referred to as Mercury Mark II.

Apollo Dec 6 or Jan. ca 1962

Spacecraft description

(12)

MANNED SPACECRAFT CENTER

FACT SHEET

APOLLO SPACECRAFT

Robert R. Gilruth

The Project Apollo spacecraft is a three-man vehicle being designed and constructed for this Country's initial expedition to the lunar surface. This lunar expedition has been made a National program under the direction of the National Aeronautics and Space Administration. The Apollo spacecraft is being specifically designed to be launched by the Saturn series of launch vehicles.

The NASA has assigned the management of the Apollo and Saturn programs to the Manned Spacecraft Center and the Marshall Space Flight Center, respectively. These centers will work closely together in the development of this flight hardware to assure complete compatibility and to optimize such compromises which must be made to settle the not unexpected design conflicts. This melding of programs has already begun. Some early Saturn flights which were initially assigned to the sole purpose of launch-vehicle development are scheduled to carry development and prototype versions of the Apollo spacecraft. These flights will not only materially aid in the Apollo development program but will also provide a means for assessing the complete system and the operational problem associated with it.

It is felt that a scheme of successive tests and missions, each of increased difficulty or complexity, is the best means of developing spacecraft for manned flight. This is the traditional method employed in prototype testing of aircraft and is also the method used in the Mercury project. This method is ideally suited to the Apollo spacecraft since it allows for manned flight on early missions of reduced hazard and is in keeping with the development of the Nation's launch vehicle capability. The Saturn C-1 will be suitable for earth-orbital missions. An advanced Saturn will carry the spacecraft to escape velocity and will be suitable for circumlunar and lunar-orbital flights. The lunar-landing mission may be made with some type of rendezvous scheme using Saturn launch vehicles or by the direct approach with a large launch vehicle.

The Apollo spacecraft will be primarily designed for its lunar mission. Nevertheless, it will be well suited for other missions. It will be capable of rendezvous and, therefore, should work well in support of orbital space stations and laboratories. It will be designed to provide adequate accommodations for a 14-day duration mission with the three-man crew. With only minor modifications, it should be able to carry double that number of men on flights of short duration.

# APOLLO TRAJECTORY ILLUSTRATION

This depiction of a Lunar Orbit Rendezvous trajectory is undated, but shows a very preliminary version of the Lunar Module descending to the moon.

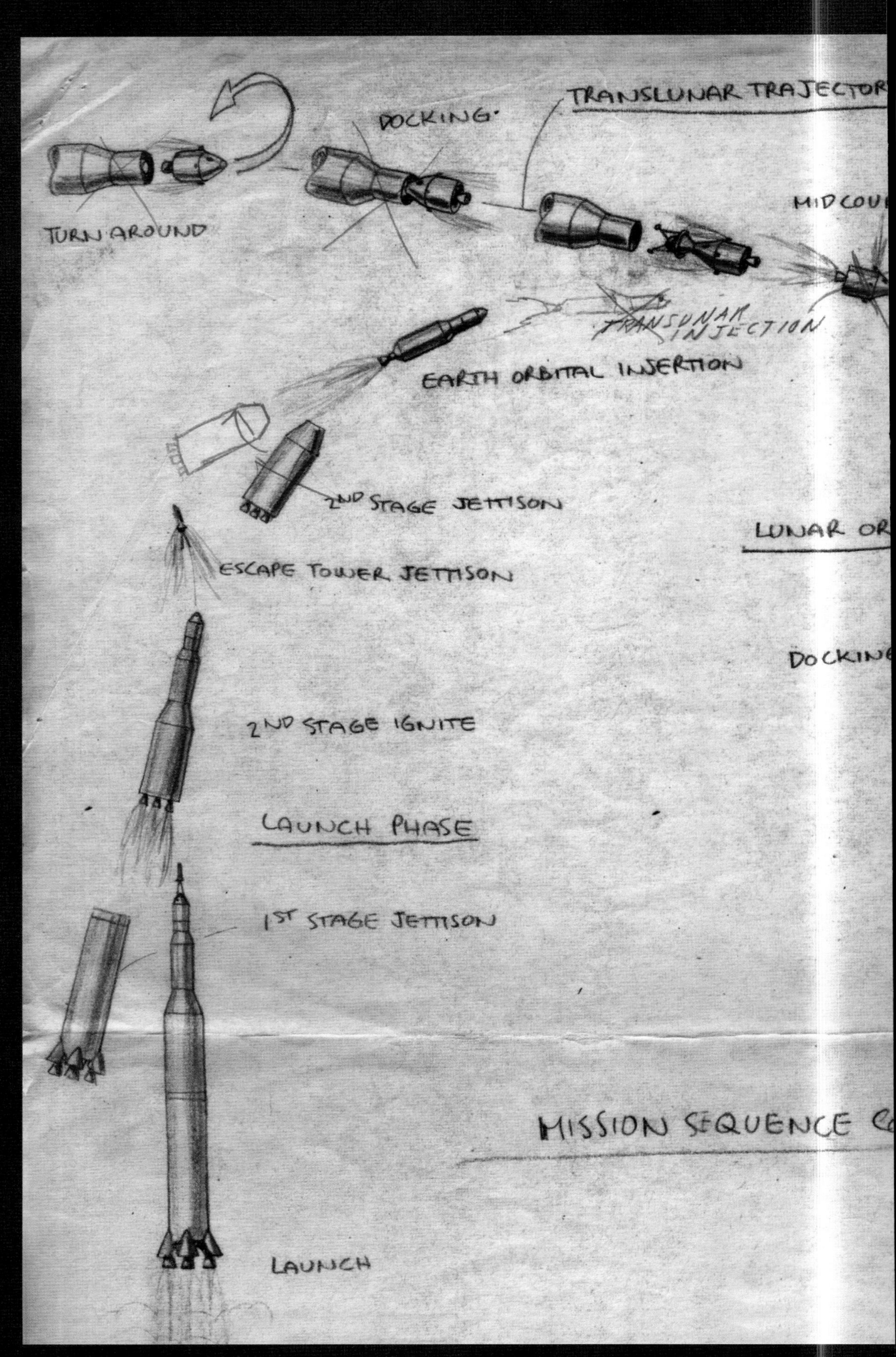

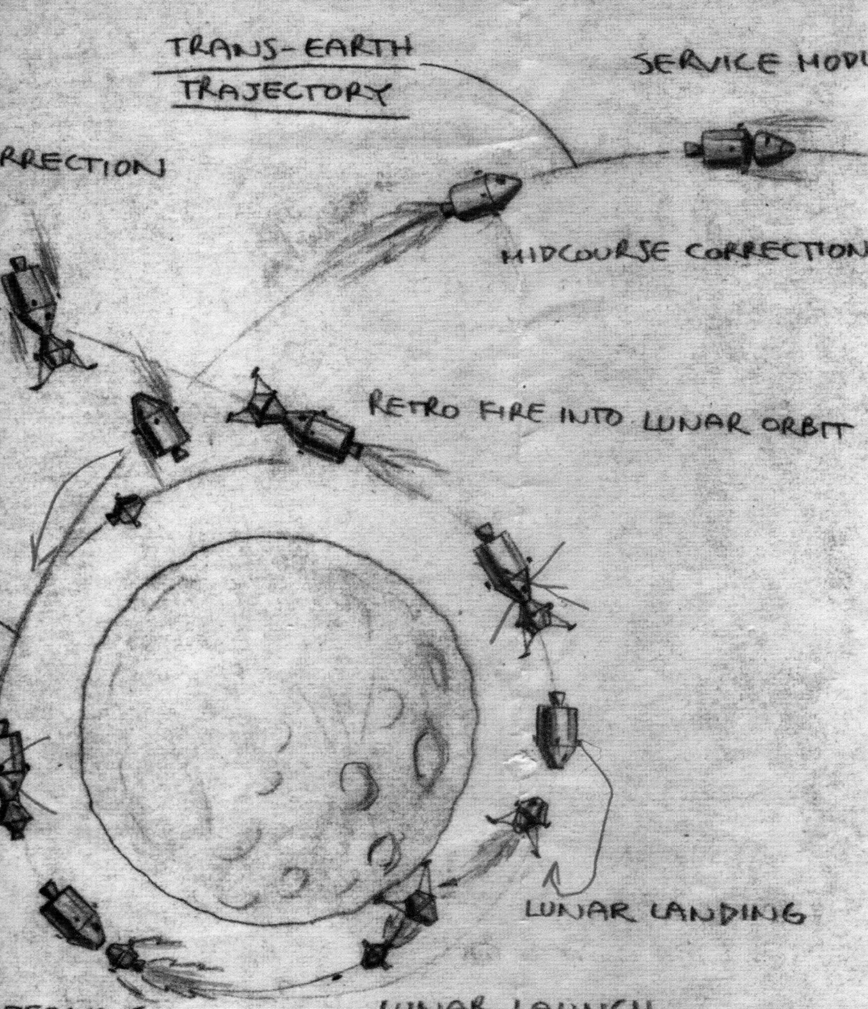
TRANS-EARTH TRAJECTORY
SERVICE MODULE SEPARATION
RRECTION
MIDCOURSE CORRECTIONS
REENTRY
RETRO FIRE INTO LUNAR ORBIT
DROGUE DEPLOY
MAIN CHUTE DEPLOY
AFTERBURNER JETTISON
MAIN CHUTE REEFED
LUNAR LANDING
NDEZVOUS
LUNAR LAUNCH
MAIN CHUTE OPEN
GURATIONS
LANDING & MAIN CHUTE RELEASE

# CHAPTER SIX

# SOVIET DISASTERS

THE SOVIETS HAD NOT BEEN IDLE AS THE US SUFFERED ITS APOLLO 1 TRAGEDY. WHILE PUBLICLY SYMPATHETIC REGARDING THE ACCIDENT, THERE WAS A COLLECTIVE SIGH OF RELIEF THAT PRECIOUS TIME MAY HAVE BEEN GAINED IN THE RACE TO THE MOON.

Then, in April 1967, it was Russia's turn to be visited by disaster. On the 23rd of that month, Vladimir Komarov was launched in the Soyuz 1 spacecraft, the Russian equivalent of the Apollo Command/Service Module. Komarov had been very concerned about the integrity of his ship, which, like Apollo 1, was the first of its kind and plagued with hundreds of deficiencies. Pressure from the Soviet leadership prevailed, however, and the Soyuz I flew on schedule.

The problems began almost immediately. Soon after making orbit, one of two solar panels failed to deploy, leaving the spacecraft low on power. Then, the manoeuvring system began to malfunction, and Komarov was increasingly unable to control the orientation of the craft. It began to tumble in space.

Near the 18-orbit mark it was determined that the flight should be aborted. Komarov's wife was brought to the control centre to have a short conversation with her husband, now motion-sick from the gyrations of his ship. He made it clear that he was not optimistic about his chances, and said goodbye with finality. Then, reportedly cursing the Soviet engineers and programme at large, he attempted to initiate an emergency re-entry using manual control.

He did successfully deorbit, but as he descended the parachute shrouds tangled, and Soyuz 1 hit its home soil at about 145 kilometres (90 miles) per hour. After the ensuing fire, there was not much left of the USSR's first moonship.

**Below** A Soyuz launch vehicle. It has an escape tower, similar to the Apollo version. The Soyuz spacecraft is nestled inside the fairings that make up the top stage of the rocket.

## THE LK LANDER

The Soviet Union's vessel for landing on the moon was the LK lander. Smaller than the American Lunar Module, it would carry only one cosmonaut to the lunar surface. It was also simpler in design than the US lander in that it had no crew tunnel, so, when docked, the cosmonaut would have to exit the Soyuz spacecraft and spacewalk to the LK. Once he returned from the moon, the opposite manoeuvre would occur, only this time with an assortment of lunar rocks in tow. The LK's ability to carry out a lunar landing remained untested.

**Below** The Soviet Lunar lander, known as the LK or Lunniy Korabl ("Lunar Craft").

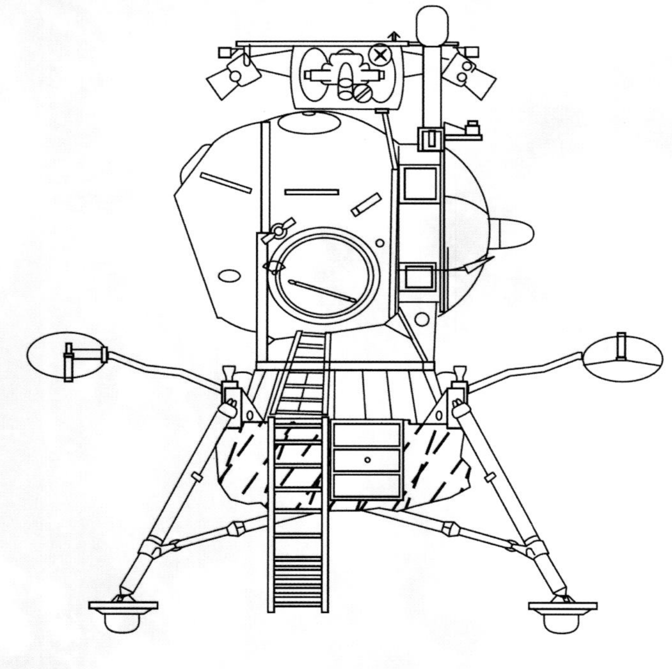

In an ironic and tragic twist, both programmes slowed to a standstill as the issues were resolved. Both had succumbed to the hubris inspired by early orbital successes, and both had paid the ultimate price for the slapdash engineering that was a political expedient. The US and the USSR were delayed almost 18 months each in their quest for the moon.

All the while, however, the other systems needed to achieve the dream continued to evolve. The Soviet answer to the US Saturn V was the N-1, which was similar to von Braun's Saturn V in overall size and appearance, but there the similarities ended. Rather than develop huge and trouble-prone engines as the Americans had chosen to do, the Soviets opted for 30 smaller engines to hurl the heavy Russian lunar spacecraft to the moon. It would save weight, money and time, or so they hoped.

The N-1 was a monster. Almost 107 metres (350 feet) tall and producing almost 4.5 million kilograms (10 million pounds) of thrust, whereas the Saturn V produced 3.4 million kilograms (7.5 million pounds), the N-1 was the largest rocket design ever attempted.

To make an already difficult project worse, "Chief Designer" Sergei Korolev, determined and forceful, died in January 1966. His second-in-command, Vasily Mishin, was assigned to complete the N-1 project, but had neither the political adroitness nor the leadership qualities of his mentor. Still, the N-1 moon programme limped along.

Finally, on 3 July 1969, with Apollo 8 having orbited the moon just six months earlier and the Apollo 11 mission scheduled to launch in about two weeks, an improved N-1 was set to launch. This may not have been another test, but has been suspected of being an all-out attempt to beat the Americans to a lunar landing. On top of the rocket was the USSR's new (and untried) lunar lander. By some accounts, a few miles away was a smaller rocket with a crew of cosmonauts inside a Soyuz spacecraft, who would launch after the N-1 had made orbit, then rendezvous and proceed to the moon, beating the Americans by at least a week.

As the countdown concluded, the mighty rocket struggled off the pad, all 30 engines alight. Then, just a few hundred metres up, the second stage received an erroneous signal that the first stage had finished firing, and it too ignited. Soon, the entire 35-storey rocket exploded in a huge fireball, crashing to the ground in a massive pyre. When the smoke cleared, a crater marked the final resting place of the N-1. The second-best technology for a manned lunar landing lay smouldering for days, and the failure was kept a state secret for decades. There would be further attempts to revive the N-1, but none would succeed. The Soviet dream of beating the United States to the moon died in one all-consuming explosion.

**Opposite right** A Soyuz rocket poised for liftoff at the Baikonur launch complex.

**Top** A view of the Soviet (now Russian) Soyuz spacecraft. Designed in the early 1960s as the answer to Apollo, the three-man Soyuz flew to the moon but never with a crew. Over the years, though, the design proved to be incredibly robust and it continues to fly to the International Space Station to this day.

**Above** The N-1 rocket. Larger and more powerful than von Braun's Saturn V, the N-1 was test launched many times but was never wholly successful. Finally, in an attempt to beat Apollo 11, an N-1 launch attempt resulted in an enormous explosion, killing many of the USSR's leading space scientists. While further efforts were made to develop the rocket, it never flew a successful mission.

**Left** A stamp bearing the heroic image of Vladimir Komarov. He died during the descent of Soyuz 1, when its parachutes failed to deploy properly.

## THE "CHIEF DESIGNER" PASSES ON

Sergei Korolev was known to the Russian people only as the "Chief Designer" until after his death. He was part of a Stalinist purge in 1938, and imprisoned in Siberia for six years. These years of hard labour contributed to his early death in 1966 at the age of 59. Once "redeemed" and in charge of much of the Soviet space effort, Korolev was able to lead the way to the successful Vostok and Voskhod flights in the early 1960s. He died before his dream of a lunar landing could be realized, and his demise doomed the Russian lunar programme.

# *PRAVDA* – 22 JANUARY 1969

The 22 January 1969 edition of *Pravda* in the USSR. Soyuz 4 and Soyuz 5 were launched within a day of each other and were able to rendezvous in orbit where two of the cosmonauts from Soyuz 5 spacewalked to Soyuz 4. It was a threadbare parry to the triumph of Apollo 8 just weeks earlier.

Пролетарии всех стран, соединяйтесь!

Коммунистическая партия Советского Союза

ЛЕНИНГРАДСКАЯ ПРАВДА

ОРГАН ЛЕНИНГРАДСКОГО ОБЛАСТНОГО И ГОРОДСКОГО КОМИТЕТОВ КОММУНИСТИЧЕСКОЙ ПАРТИИ СОВЕТСКОГО СОЮЗА, ОБЛАСТНОГО И ГОРОДСКОГО СОВЕТОВ ДЕПУТАТОВ ТРУДЯЩИХСЯ

Год издания 51-й № 18 (16415) | Среда, 22 января 1969 года | ЦЕНА 2 КОП.

# РОДИНА СЛАВИТ ГЕРОЕВ!

Космонавты полковник В. А. ШАТАЛОВ, полковник Б. В. ВОЛЫНОВ, А. С. ЕЛИСЕЕВ и полковник Е. В. ХРУНОВ на космодроме. Телефото ТАСС

## УДАРНАЯ ВАХТА ПЯТИЛЕТКИ

НАВСТРЕЧУ 100-летию СО ДНЯ РОЖДЕНИЯ В. И. ЛЕНИНА

БОЛЬШЕ, ЛУЧШЕ, ДЕШЕВЛЕ!

## НА ОСНОВЕ ТЕХНИЧЕСКОГО ПРОГРЕССА

ОБЯЗАТЕЛЬСТВА ТРУДЯЩИХСЯ МОСКОВСКОГО РАЙОНА

## ТРУДОВЫМ ДЕЛАМ—КОСМИЧЕСКИЙ РАЗМАХ

## СТРОИТЬ РИТМИЧНО

НАМЕЧАЕТ ГЛАВЗАПСТРОЙ

## ДВОЕ ШАГАЮТ НАД БЕЗДНОЙ...

*Техника космического перехода*

Н. АНДРЕЕВ, инженер (ТАСС)

## Кировцы идут вперед

ВСЕ РЕЗЕРВЫ — В ДЕЙСТВИЕ

## ПОБЕДА У СТЕН ЛЕНИНГРАДА

НАУЧНАЯ КОНФЕРЕНЦИЯ В СМОЛЬНОМ ЗАКОНЧИЛА РАБОТУ

РАБОТЫ НАШЕГО ГРАФИКА

## ЛЮБИМАЯ ТЕМА

НА ЛИСТЕ — изображение старинного парусника, на который как бы накладывается человеческая фигура, стремительным полетом несущаяся в пространстве. Лист называется: «От мореходов до космонавтов». В символической форме он отображает извечное тяготение человека к открытию нового, неизведанного. Когда-то, плавая на парусниках, люди открывали земные материки, а сегодня, поднявшись над Землей, открывают для себя космос...

Автор этого произведения — ленинградский график Илларион Некрасов. Уже несколько лет, как «космическая» тема стала одной из главных в его творчестве. Свои работы, в которых фантастика, воображение художника, сочетаются с вполне научной действительностью, он демонстрировал на всесоюзных и международных выставках.

— Сейчас задумал работу, — говорит художник, — где хочу показать человека, высадившегося на чужой планете, находящейся очень далеко от Земли. Конечно, это будет фантазия, но должен сказать, что в теме космоса я уже не раз чувствовал, как реальность буквально наступала фантазии на пятки...

## АЛЛЕЯ НА БАЙКОНУРЕ

Городок космодрома... Улицы его носят и традиционные, какие встретишь повсюду, названия — Театральная, Коммунальная, и связанные с героикой труда большинства его жителей — улица имени Гагарина, площадь Королева, улица Космонавтов... Есть и одна особенная аллея. Каждый из космонавтов посадил в ней по дереву. Последнее в ряду, самое маленькое, — Георгия Берегового. И вот сейчас, в январские холода, аллею удлинили еще...

КОММЕНТИРУЕТ ЛЕНИНГРАДСКИЙ УЧЕНЫЙ

# «ОЧЕНЬ ЦЕННЫЙ ЭКСПЕРИМЕНТ...»

**ПОЛЕТ космических кораблей «Союз-4» и «Союз-5» по-прежнему в центре всеобщего внимания. Вчера корреспондент «Ленинградской правды» В. Захарько обратился на кафедру авиационной медицины Военно-медицинской академии имени С. М. Кирова с просьбой прокомментировать результаты этого орбитального полета.**

— ШТУРМ космоса, начатый советскими людьми, непрерывно набирает темпы, — говорит руководитель кафедры, доктор медицинских наук, профессор Г. И. Гурвич. — Опыт показал, что наиболее полно решать проблемы исследования космического пространства можно лишь при условии, когда в нем длительное время будет находиться человек. А это в свою очередь возможно только при создании на орбите космических обитаемых станций, с доставкой на них сменных экипажей, различной аппаратуры, других грузов. Вот почему произведенная стыковка кораблей является выдающимся достижением, открывающим новый этап в освоении космоса, в развитии космической медицины.

Данные медицинских наблюдений за космонавтами, и особенно за выходившими в открытый космос А. Елисеевым и Е. Хруновым, наметят пути дальнейшего совершенствования кораблей, регенерационных скафандров, помогут создать лучшие условия для деятельности человека в космическом пространстве. Огромную ценность для медиков представляют данные о нервно-эмоциональном напряжении, которое испытывали участники полета.

Первый врач-космонавт Б. Егоров работал в условиях довольно ограниченного размерами корабля «Восход-1». Орбитальные лаборатории предоставят неизмеримо больше возможностей для научных экспериментов всех членов экипажей, и в том числе медиков. Они смогут детально, с помощью различной аппаратуры проводить исследования, непосредственно и всесторонне изучать реакцию космонавтов на невесомость, изменяющееся барометрическое давление, температуру и многие другие факторы полета.

В таких лабораториях медики получат важнейшие сведения о приспособляемости человеческого организма к необычным, неземным условиям. Все эти материалы послужат не только делу прогресса в освоении космоса. Нет сомнений, что они смогут также и облегчить, улучшить профилактическую и лечебную работу среди всего населения.

— Уникальный эксперимент отважных советских космонавтов, — сказал в заключение Г. И. Гурвич, — имеет важнейшее значение для многих областей наук и особенно для медицины.

ВСПОМИНАЯ ОДИН ЭПИЗОД...

# МНОГО ЛИ КОСМОНАВТУ НАДО?

ИМЯ Евгения Хрунова — одного из четверки отважных — известно сейчас всему миру. И тем интереснее вспомнить сегодня небольшой эпизод, который приведил как-то в одном из своих публичных выступлений наставник советских космонавтов Е. Петров. Тогда речь шла просто о Жене — теперь мы знаем: это был Хрунов...

**К ОДНОМУ из наших космонавтов приехал товарищ — летчик-истребитель из далекого гарнизона. Встретились бывшие однополчане. Пошли расспросы, рассказы. Гость сообщил полковые новости... И тут же, как бы между прочим, осведомился:**

— Ну, а как, Женя, твои дела?

— Без изменений. Чины те же. Да я за ними и не гонюсь. Главное — живу в своей стихии. С головой окунулся.

Майор обратил внимание на полки с книгами в комнате товарища. Каких только здесь не было! Резолюции партийных съездов, история, сплавы металлов, искусство, электроника, медицина, ракеты, метеорология, спорт, поэзия, астрономия, математика, психология, приборостроение, география, физика... Гость недоверчиво спросил:

— И все это тебе нужно?

— Конечно, — ответил хозяин.

Майор не поверил.

— Ну, я понимаю, Циолковский, Кибальчич, «Туманность Андромеды», современное ракетостроение — это, так сказать, твой хлеб. Но Макаренко, Репин, Павлов, Станиславский — какое эти книги имеют отношение к космосу?

В ответ космонавт рассказал приятелю, как однажды пришлось ему побывать в институте, имеющем близкое отношение к космонавтике. Разговорились о профессиональных делах. Неожиданно перешли к искусству. Один из научных сотрудников спросил космонавта:

— А что вы, Евгений Васильевич, скажете насчет живописи Пикассо? Тона — прямо-таки фантастические. Кажется, что художник из космоса взглянул на нашу планету. Здорово!

Космонавт для приличия согласился, что у Пикассо действительно тона получаются «здорово», но сам понятия не имел о живописи Пикассо. Пришел домой расстроенный: ведь с ним говорили, как равные с равным, а он оказался невеждой. И, может, именно тогда впервые не на словах, а на деле Евгений понял, как много ему надо знать. На космонавта смотрят, как на человека высокообразованного; в арсенале человеческих знаний столько наук, имеющих прямое и косвенное отношение к его профессии. Ему нужны и психология, и электроника, и спорт, и медицина, и металловедение, и многое, многое другое.

— Вот теперь сам посуди, много ли нам, космонавтам, надо? — улыбаясь, спросил хозяин гостя.

И тот согласился.

— Да, много!

«Над планетой». Рис. художника А. Соколова

## ВСЕ ЧЕТВЕРО — ЗАСЛУЖЕННЫЕ МАСТЕРА СПОРТА

*ЧЛЕНАМ экипажей космических кораблей «Союз-4» и «Союз-5» летчикам-космонавтам В. А. Шаталову, Б. В. Волынову, Е. В. Хрунову и А. С. Елисееву Комитет по физической культуре и спорту присвоил звания «Заслуженный мастер спорта СССР» и наградил их, как сообщает ТАСС, памятными медалями «За выдающееся спортивное достижение».*

## САЛЮТ В ЧЕСТЬ ОТВАЖНЫХ

ОТ НАЧАЛЬНИКА ГАРНИЗОНА ГОРОДА ЛЕНИНГРАДА

В ознаменование великой победы советского народа, выдающегося подвига ученых, инженеров, техников и рабочих, обеспечивших в Советском Союзе запуск и стыковку космических кораблей «Союз-4» и «Союз-5», в городе Ленинграде в 20 часов 22 января 1969 года будет произведен салют ДВАДЦАТЬЮ артиллерийскими залпами.

Десятки эскизов в карандаше и глине, многочисленные пробы и долгие часы раздумья потребовались ленинградскому скульптору Л. МИХАЙЛЕНКУ, прежде чем фигура советского солдата обрела выразительность и ясность пластического решения. Эта скульптура станет завершающим элементом композиции на Пулковских высотах, посвященной героической обороне Ленинграда.

Фото О. Петринова

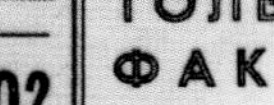


● ВЧЕРА опереттой «Раскинулось море широко» на сцене Театра народного творчества начал свои гастроли в нашем городе самодеятельный коллектив Дворца культуры Ульяновского автозавода. Героическая оперетта о команде небольшого сторожевого катера «Орленок» и разведчице Елене особенно дорога ленинградцам: она была написана и впервые поставлена в блокадном Ленинграде.

● ЖИТЕЛИ Пхеньяна получат возможность пользоваться движущимися лестницами ленинградской конструкции. Разработку технической документации на изготовление семи эскалаторов для КНДР начали инженеры Специального конструкторского бюро эскалаторостроения. По конструкции они будут аналогичны тем, которые действуют на станциях Ленинградского метрополитена.

● НАЗИЕВСКИЙ опытно-промышленный завод изготовил первые десятки тысяч пакетов с высококонцентрированными торфоминерально-аммиачными удобрениями, которые рекомендуется использовать при выращивании плодовых, ягодных, декоративных и лесных культур, однолетних и многолетних цветов, тепличных и комнатных растений, овощей, картофеля. Эти удобрения способствуют повышению урожаев и ускоряют рост растений.

● ПЕРВЫЕ 40 километров прошли из южнополярной обсерватории Мирный по ледяному плато участники объединенной советско-французской гляциологической экспедиции, направляющиеся на санно-гусеничном поезде к внутриконтинентальной станции Восток. Об этом вчера радировали из Антарктиды в Ленинград. Поезд, состоящий из 10 тягачей с санями, пройдет по маршруту Мирный — Восток — Мирный, преодолев около трех тысяч километров.

## «СПАСИБО, РОДНЫЕ ТОВАРИЩИ!»

**Поэтесса — член бригады коммунистического труда**

В ОДИН из январских дней 1943 года на фабрику № 2 «Пролетарская победа» пришла О. Берггольц. Замолкли станки и машины. В окружении истощенных работниц стояла она, продрогшая от холода, в стоптанных туфлях и читала стихи... А когда кончила, к ней подошли женщины:

— Видим, Ольга Федоровна, у вас плохо с обувью. Мы сошьем вам сапожки...

— Большое спасибо, мои дорогие, — поэтесса была растрогана до слез.

Позднее Ольга Федоровна писала об этом:

В ту зиму
по фронтам меня носило, —
По улицам, где не видать
ни зги.
Но мне фонарь дала
«Электросила»,
А на «Победе» сшили сапоги...

На днях в квартире Ольги Берггольц раздался телефонный звонок. Обувщицы с фабрики № 2 «Пролетарская победа» сообщили, что ей присвоено звание ударника коммунистического труда. Вскоре закройщица Т. Б. Анисимова приехала к поэтессе домой и вручила ей алую книжечку.

«Спасибо, родные товарищи, за огромный почет! Всей жизнью и работой постараюсь оправдать это звание», — сделала Ольга Берггольц благодарственную запись в бригадном дневнике. — Особенно дорого мне, что это произошло в драгоценные для всех дни — 25-летия полного освобождения Ленинграда от фашистской блокады и победоносного полета наших космонавтов...».

Поэтесса подарила обувщицам книгу стихотворений. Написала автограф: «Моей (отныне моей) бригаде коммунистического труда... От всего сердца Ольга Берггольц».

О. ГОРНАЯ

ХОККЕЙ

## СКА — В ЧЕТВЕРТЬФИНАЛЕ

ВСТРЕЧА СКА (Ленинград) — «Автомобилист» (Свердловск) вызвала повышенный интерес у любителей хоккея по нескольким причинам. Во-первых, это была встреча команд первой группы (а такого ленинградцы уже давно не видели!), разделенных ныне не слишком справедливой системой розыгрыша. Во-вторых, этот матч можно было назвать еще матчем престижа: многие ленинградские болельщики считают, что именно свердловчане заняли то место в финальной шестерке, которое «предназначалось» для СКА. В-третьих, настоящие ценители хоккея помнили, что «Автомобилист» — самая, пожалуй, трудная для ленинградских армейцев команда в психологическом отношении. Но главная особенность вчерашней встречи состояла в том, что это был кубковый матч — ⅛ финала!

На 1-й минуте ленинградцы оказались в большинстве и обрушили на ворота гостей шквал атак. Но лишь в конце периода им удалось забросить шайбу. Это сделал С. Солодухин.

Во втором периоде свердловчане отквитали шайбу, а затем повели в счете.

«Скорость, скорость и скорость!» — под этим девизом провели заключительный период ленинградцы. Это и решило исход борьбы — Н. Григорьев, В. Кустов и Д. Копченов забрасывают три безответные шайбы.

Победив со счетом 4:2, армейцы Ленинграда вышли в четвертьфинал.

А. ЦЕЛЯК

## ПОГОДА

**В БЛИЖАЙШИЕ два дня ожидается небольшое ослабление мороза. Сегодня в течение суток — минус 12—18, завтра днем — 7—12. Переменная облачность, местами небольшой снег и изморозь. Ветер южный и юго-западный, 5—8 метров в секунду. В Ленинграде температура днем 12—14, ночью 10—12 градусов мороза.**

Редактор М. С. КУРТЫНИН

ИНТЕРВЬЮ ПО ПРОСЬБЕ ЧИТАТЕЛЕЙ

# ПРИШЕЛЕЦ ИЗ ГОНКОНГА

**В ПЕЧАТИ все чаще упоминается об эпидемии так называемого гонконгского гриппа, который сейчас свирепствует в Соединенных Штатах Америки и угрожает европейскому континенту. Расскажите, пожалуйста, об этом заболевании и о том, какие меры предпринимают наши органы здравоохранения для предупреждения и лечения этой болезни?**

**П. МАКЕЕВ**

**В НАШЕМ городе около двух лет действует Всесоюзный научно-исследовательский институт гриппа. Каких успехов в борьбе с болезнью удалось добиться коллективу этого нового медицинского учреждения?**

**Т. ИКОНОВА**

□

НАШ корреспондент Г. Журавлева встретилась с заведующим клиническим отделом Всесоюзного научно-исследовательского института гриппа доктором медицинских наук Д. М. Злыдниковым и попросила его ответить на вопросы читателей.

— Грипп — одна из самых распространенных и массовых инфекций, известных на земном шаре. Достаточно сказать, что в 1918—1919 годах пандемия «испанки» охватила почти все страны мира и унесла около 20 миллионов человеческих жизней. Другая вспышка — «азиатского гриппа», возникшая в 1957—1959 годах, охватила около двух миллиардов человек, т. е. более двух третей населения земного шара. Однако с гриппом врачи встречаются не только во время эпидемий и всеобщих заболеваний — пандемий. В другие более спокойные периоды грипп ведет себя относительно безобидно.

Долгое время возбудитель гриппа был неизвестен. И лишь в 1933 году английские микробиологи доказали, что возбудитель гриппа человека — особый вирус. Вирусную природу гриппа в нашей стране обосновали советские ученые А. А. Смородинцев и Л. А. Зильбер. Тщательные наблюдения показали, что одно и то же заболевание «грипп» могут вызывать сходные вирусы. Условно их обозначили буквами латинского алфавита А, В и С. Дальнейшие исследования в этой области принесли новое открытие: господствующие вирусы гриппа А и В не остаются постоянными и неизменными. Во время каждой новой вспышки ученые обнаруживают вирусы как бы в новом обличье. Именно эта постоянная изменчивость вируса гриппа и является главной причиной трудностей, возникающих перед учеными при изыскании радикальных средств против гриппа.

А теперь несколько слов об относительной «безобидности» вируса в периоды между грозными пандемиями. Ослабленный в поединке с защитными механизмами человека и медицинскими препаратами, вирус приспосабливается к новым условиям. Постепенно он изменяет свои антигенные свойства и как бы накапливает силы. В конце концов эволюция вируса рождает новые штаммы (видоизмененных возбудителей). Эти-то новые штаммы и вызывают обычно тяжелые эпидемии и даже пандемии гриппа.

**ВОПРОС:** Какими средствами борьбы с гриппом располагает современная медицина?

**ОТВЕТ:** Я уже сказал, что вирус гриппа непрерывно эволюционирует и изменяется, что осложняет работу по изысканию радикального оружия. Есть еще одно обстоятельство, затрудняющее борьбу с истинным гриппом. Под маской гриппозного вируса нередко скрываются совсем другие возбудители, которые порою вызывают заболевания, очень сходные с истинным гриппом. Все они способны при благоприятных условиях вызывать тяжелые осложнения, такие, как пневмония, менингит и другие. Достижения современной медицины помогли ученым распознавать эти «невидимки», изобрести ряд средств для успешной борьбы с ними.

Вирусный грипп даже в тяжелой форме продолжается не более пяти—восьми дней. В это время организм, реагируя на внедрение вируса, мобилизует свои силы на выработку антител, способных нейтрализовать токсическое (отравляющее) действие вируса и убить его. Антитела и создают иммунитет (невосприимчивость) в организме к повторным заболеваниям на два-три года.

Вызвать подобный иммунитет искусственным путем, вводя в организм человека живой, ослабленный вирус, — эта идея легла в основу работ известного в нашей стране и за рубежом вирусолога А. А. Смородинцева. Под его руководством создана противогриппозная вакцина, применение которой значительно сокращает заболеваемость гриппом. Сейчас во Всесоюзном НИИ гриппа продолжается работа над усовершенствованием прежних и созданием новых противогриппозных вакцин.

Ученые доказали, что вирус гриппа может жить и размножаться только в клетках организма: в эпителиальной ткани носа, носоглотки, трахеи, бронхов. Как реагируют эти клетки на внедрение нежданных пришельцев? Они вырабатывают новое защитное белковое соединение — интерферон, который вступает в единоборство с опасным врагом. Интерферон так же, как и антитела, — важнейший защитный механизм нашего организма в борьбе с вирусом. Медики учли эту ценную способность зараженных тканей организма противостоять заболеванию и научились стимулировать выработку интерферона искусственным путем.

До недавнего времени медики считали, что в борьбе с вирусом гриппа невозможно применение каких-либо химических препаратов. Но в 1963 году в США был синтезирован солянокислый амантадин, обладавший выраженным профилактическим действием против гриппа. В нашем институте была проведена широкая клиническая проверка амантадина. Выяснилось, что большая часть людей, принимавших амантадин с профилактической целью, не заболели гриппом.

В содружестве с нашим институтом изучением и изготовлением отечественного амантадина занимается Рижский институт органического синтеза Академии наук Латвийской ССР. Сейчас наши медики получили на вооружение принципиально новое средство для предупреждения гриппа. В этом году оно проходит широкую проверку среди населения города.

**ВОПРОС:** Читатели нашей газеты интересуются «гонконгским гриппом», эпидемия которого свирепствует сейчас в Соединенных Штатах Америки. Как протекает этот грипп и чем отличается от своих предшественников?

**ОТВЕТ:** Тщательное изучение клиники заболевания и самого вируса «Гонконг» показало, что он сходен с возбудителем «азиатского гриппа».

Эпидемия гриппа «Гонконг» началась в городе, именем которого он и назван. В Соединенных Штатах Америки грипп нанес большие потери. Смертность от заболевания там очень высока. Но статистика свидетельствует: болезнь в тяжелой форме протекает в основном среди бедняков, безработных, особенно в негритянских кварталах.

Приостановить распространение инфекции можно с помощью комплекса лечебно-профилактических мероприятий. А в США, как и в любой капиталистической стране, где всякая медицинская помощь является платной, такие мероприятия проводятся весьма слабо.

Клиника «гонконгского гриппа» ничем не отличается от клиники обычного гриппа: высокая температура, головная боль, слабость, ломота в теле. У людей, ослабленных хроническими заболеваниями, иногда появляются осложнения на легкие и другие органы.

В нашем городе созданы специальные оперативные группы и комиссии по борьбе с начавшейся эпидемией. Исполком Ленинградского городского Совета и органы здравоохранения города предприняли ряд организационных и других мер, чтобы избежать широкого распространения болезни.

На вооружении медиков имеются в достаточном количестве противогриппозные вакцины, сыворотки, специфический противогриппозный донорский гамма-глобулин, антибиотики и т. д.

Однако для предупреждения гриппа не всегда достаточно одних медицинских средств. Население должно соблюдать правила индивидуальной защиты, избегать контакта с больными, чаще проветривать помещения, гулять на свежем воздухе, постоянно закаливать свой организм.

В Павловском парке. Фото Б. Аразина

## ТЕАТР

Академический театр оперы и балета им. С. М. Кирова в помещении Дворца культуры им. Ленсовета: 2-й спектакль 3-го абонемента «Каменный цветок». **Академический театр драмы им. А. С. Пушкина:** новый спектакль «Много шума из ничего». **Академический Малый театр оперы и балета:** «Лебединое озеро». **Академический Большой драматический театр им. М. Горького:** «Мещане». **Академический театр комедии:** «Цилиндр». **Театр музыкальной комедии:** «Моя прекрасная леди». **Театр им. Ленинского комсомола:** «Соломенная шляпка». **Театр им. В. Ф. Комиссаржевской:** «Миллионерша». **Театр им. Ленсовета:** новый спектакль «Последний парад». **Театр драмы и комедии:** «Дурочка». **Малый драматический театр:** «Вся ворона». **Оперная студия Консерватории:** «Фауст». **Театр юных зрителей:** «После казни прошу». **Филармония** — Большой зал: вечер русской песни и романса. Исп. Л. Филатова. **Филармония** — Малый зал: 4-й концерт 10-го абонемента. Выступает квартет ЗБГ. **Большой концертный зал «Октябрьский»:** поет Эмил Димитров (Болгария). **Ленинградский концертный зал:** поет Ж. Таупэ. **Дворец культуры им. А. М. Горького:** «Я, бабушка, Илико и Илларион», спектакль Большого драматического театра им. М. Горького. **Выборгский дворец культуры:** выступает Ленинградский мюзик-холл. **Дворец культуры им. С. М. Кирова:** концерт ансамбля «Дружба». **Цирк:** программа «Снежные мелодии». Нач. в 20 час.

## КИНО

К 25-летию со дня полного освобождения Ленинграда от вражеской блокады. **«Два капитана»:** Аврора; **«Два бойца»:** Балтика; **«Щит и меч»** (фильм 1-й): Слава; (фильм 2-й): Ладога; (фильмы 3-й и 4-й): Дом культуры «Кировец». **«Удар! Еще удар!»:** Дворец культуры им. Ленсовета; **«Просто девочка»:** Родина, Дом культуры им. Володарского; **«Жила-была девочка»:** Дворец культуры им. 1-й Пятилетки; **«Сильные духом»:** Стереокино; **«Она защищает Родину»:** Дворец культуры им. В. И. Ленина; **«Балтийское небо»:** Дом культуры работников связи.

* * *

**«Братья Карамазовы»** (1-я и 2-я серии): Ленинград. **«Мертвый сезон»** (1-я и 2-я серии): Аврора, Балтика, Водник, Выборгский, Гигант, Зенит, Ладога, Мир, Молодежный, Москва, Нарвский, Октябрь, Победа, Прибой, Призыв, Прогресс, Родина, Слава, Спартак, Художественный, Юность; во дворцах культуры им. В. И. Ленина, им. Ленсовета, им. 1-й Пятилетки; в домах культуры им. Ильича, им. Володарского, им. Цюрупы, пищевой промышленности, им. 1 Мая.

* * *

**«Случай из следственной практики»:** Дружба, Совет, Экран; **«Ошибка Оноре де Бальзака»:** Арс, Заря, Нева, Дворец культуры им. А. М. Горького; **«Армия Трясогузки снова в бою»:** Дружба, Озерки; **«Доживем до понедельника»:** Арс; **«Ташкент — город хлебный»:** Нева, Стрела; **«Шестое июля»:** Ленинград; **«Трембита»** и **«Аппассионата»:** Луч; **«Дом и хозяин»:** Свет; **«Ленин в Октябре»:** Совет; **«Моя любовь»:** Стрела; **«Беспокойное хозяйство»:** Рассвет; **«Строго засекреченные премьеры»:** Гигант, Радуга, Родина, Смена, Стереокино, Спутник, Титан; **«Сангам»** (1-я и 2-я серии): Баррикада, Заневский, Максим, Молния, Москва, Север, Спорт, Титан, Дворец культуры им. Газа, Дом культуры им. Карла Маркса, клуб Политехнического института им. Калинина; **«Небо начинается на 3-м этаже»:** Заневский, Колизей, Москва, Радуга, Спутник, клуб завода «Вулкан»; **«Воздушные приключения»** (1-я и 2-я серии): Колизей; **«Шкатулка с сюрпризом»:** Дружба, Звездочка; **«Как избавиться от Гелении»** и **«Угловая комната»:** Сатурн; **«Происшествие в порту»:** Дом культуры им. Капранова; **«Под созвездием Девы»:** Салют; **«Оскар»** и **«Полный вперед»:** Зимний; **«Ход конем»:** Художественный; **«Незаконнорожденный»:** Молодежный; «Язык животных»: Нева, Ленинград; «Ташкент — землетрясение»: Свет.

## РАДИО

**СРЕДА, 22 ЯНВАРЯ**

8.45 — Беседа о гриппе. 9.15 — Очерк М. Горького «9 января». 9.50 — Обзор ленинградских газет. 10.05 — Обзор газеты «Ленинские искры». 10.15 — «Гусдина консерватория». 10.40 — Очерк Черкасского «Смотритель маяка». 11.15 — Ленинградский выпуск «Последних известий». 11.25 — Концерт Русского народного оркестра им. Андреева. 11.55 — Пятиминутка технических новинок. 12.15 — Фантазии для оркестра на темы песен советских композиторов. 12.30 — Передача, посвященная встрече героических экипажей космических кораблей «Союз-4» и «Союз-5». 16.00 — Хоровые поэмы. 16.15 — «Голос Ленина». 16.30 — Для школьников, изучающих французский язык. 17.00 — «Юность». 18.00 — Ленинградский выпуск «Последних известий». 18.15 — «Любите ли вы это?». Г. Перелл. «Пазыйм» и «Чжойпа». 18.40 — Ленинский университет миллионов. «Работа В. И. Ленина «Государство и революция» и современность». 19.00 — «Последние известия». 19.20 — «Трибуна партийного работника». 19.35 — Музыкальная передача «Хроника великих дней». 20.25 — Радиоочерк «Рабочие люди». 20.45 — Международный дневник. 21.00 — «Невская волна». 22.00 — «Последние известия». 22.30 — Литературная передача «По вашим письмам». 23.30 — Поемы В. Бунчиков и В. Нечаев.

## ТВ

**СРЕДА, 22 ЯНВАРЯ**

**1-я программа.** 9.55 — Программа передач. 10.00 — Теленовости. 10.15 — Для младших школьников: «Занимательная азбука». 10.45 — Успехи советского народа в освоении космоса. 12.45 — Передача, посвященная встрече героических экипажей космических кораблей «Союз-4» и «Союз-5» тт. Шаталова В. А., Волынова Б. В., Хрунова Е. В. и Елисеева А. С. 17.00 — Теленовости. 17.15 — Телевизионный фильм «Возвращение Одиссея». 18.00 — Для школьников: «Мое Отечество» в выставке детских рисунков. 18.30 — «Твоя ленинская библиотека» «Три источника и три составных части марксизма». 19.00 — Л. Леонов. «Барсуки» — телеспектакль. 2-я часть. 20.30 — «Время» — информационная программа. 21.15 — Концерт классической музыки. 21.45 — Киноочерк «Союз равноправных». 22.15 — «В эфире — «Молодость». 23.15 — «Новости», «Комментарий», программа передач. **2-я программа.** 18.35 — Новости. 18.40 — Киноочерки «Здравствуй, Венера!» и «Ждите нас, звезды!». 19.20 — «Волшебный сундук» — мультфильм для детей. 19.30 — Для старшеклассников: «Тебе, юность!». 20.15 — «Ленин, время и мы». 21.00 — Концерт Краснознаменного ансамбля песни и пляски Советской Армии. 22.00 — Новости. 22.50 — «Стадион». «События. Факты. Мнения». **3-я программа.** 10.00 — 10.35 и 11.05 — 11.50 — Для учащихся 9-х классов: химия. «Классификация химических реакций». 12.10 — 12.35 и 13.05 — 13.30 — Для учащихся 5-х классов: география. «Рельеф дна мирового океана». 14.00 — Для учащихся 10-х классов: обществоведение (факультативный курс). «Мышление и его законы». Передача 2-я. 21.00 — Для абитуриентов: математика. Консультация 3—4-я. «Решение конкурсных задач на преобразование иррациональных выражений. Анализ домашнего задания № 3—4».

Наш адрес: Ленинград, Д-23, Фонтанка, 59.
Телефон для справок по редакции 15-39-64.

Типография имени Володарского

М 07037 Зак. № 2036

# A MOST COMPLEX MACHINE

ALTHOUGH AT THE TIME THE APOLLO 1 FIRE DEALT THE US PROGRAMME A STAGGERING BLOW, IN THE END IT MAY HAVE ACTUALLY SAVED MORE LIVES THAN IT COST.

Awful as it was, the accident exposed weaknesses in the Command Module, its builders and even in NASA management. Some employees were released from NASA, and more were chastened. North American Aviation was put under intense scrutiny, and the astronauts took it upon themselves to become more invovled in the design and manufacture of this, the most complex machine in the history of flight.

All along, von Braun and his team had been labouring steadily on the Saturn V booster. This magnificent rocket, like all of Apollo, was an undertaking on a scale unimaginable just a few years previously. At 111 metres (363 feet) in height and with 3.4 million kilograms (7.5 million pounds) of thrust, the rocket had the power to lift all the spacecraft launched to date by the US in one go, yet just enough to get one Apollo system to the moon.

Designing the Saturn was a long and intricate process, and much of the effort focused on the immense first stage engines. While the upper stages would burn a mixture of liquid hydrogen and liquid oxygen, both highly efficient propellants, the first stage used liquid oxygen and kerosene to lift itself clear of the pad. This was a less powerful mixture of propellants, so

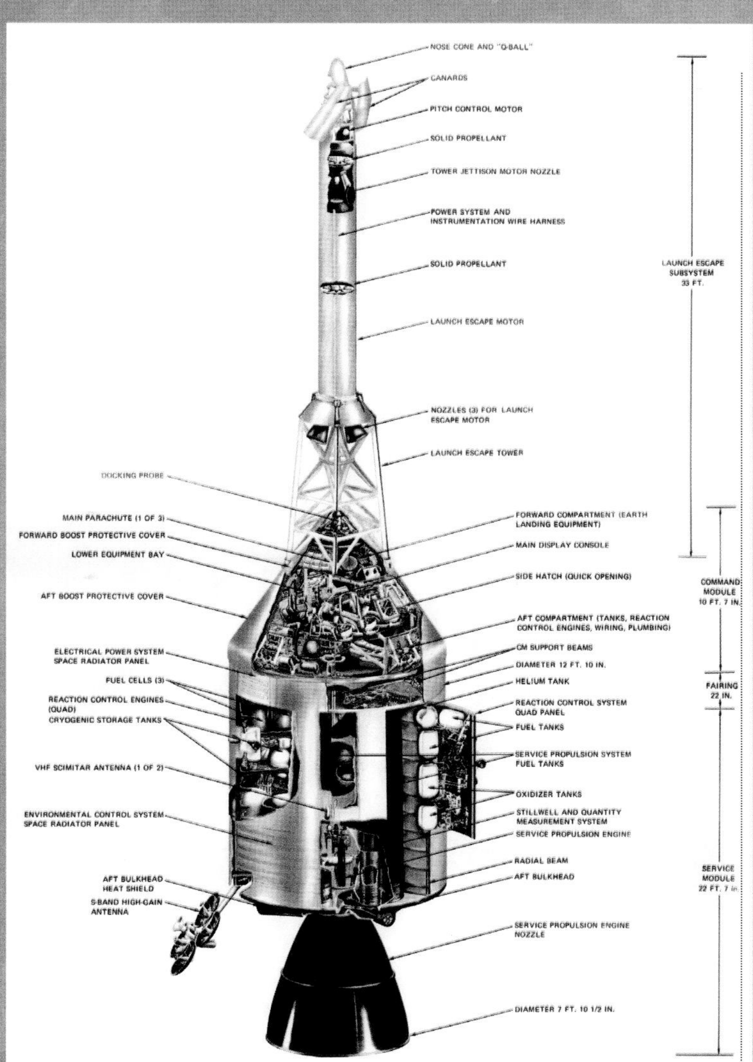


## BY THE NUMBERS: THE COMMAND/SERVICE MODULE

**The Command/Service Module, first cis-lunar transport vehicle:**
**Height:** 9.75 metres (32 feet)
**Diameter:** 3.96 metres (13 feet)
**Weight:** 30,333 kilograms (66,871 pounds)

**Propulsion:**
**Main Engine (Service Propulsion System):** 113,400 kilograms (20,500 pounds) thrust

**Manoeuvring Engines:**
**Command Module:** 12 engines – 42 kilograms (92 pounds) thrust each
**Service Module:** 16 engines – 45 kilograms (100 pounds) thrust each

**Propulsion fuel:**
**Service Propulsion System:** Hypergolic, hydrazine and nitrogen tetroxide
**Manoeuvring:** Hypergolic, hydrazine and nitrogen tetroxide

**Endurance:** 14 days

**Heat shielding:** Phenolic honeycomb, ablative

**Auxiliary power:** Three fuel cells, hydrogen and oxygen fuelled, electricity and water produced.

**Designer:** Maxime Faget, NASA (1921–2004); also designed the Mercury capsule and the Space Shuttle.

**Manufacturer:** North American Aviation (Later North American Rockwell)

**Left** The Apollo Command/Service Module. Capable of carrying three astronauts to the moon and back, it was a masterpiece of engineering sophistication and simplicity. The rocket aatop the capsule, the escape tower, was blown free of the spacecraft shortly after launch, when it was no longer needed. It was designed to lift the capsule of a manufacturing booster prior to or just after launch.

the engines would need to be massive on a scale never before attempted.

Built by Rocketdyne in Canoga Park, California, each of these F1 engines was the size of a large sport utility vehicle stood on its end. The enormous rocket nozzles were surrounded by hundreds of metres of large tubing through which the fuel was pumped to both cool the nozzle and pre-heat the fluids. Everything about the F1 engine was gigantic, exotic and new. Yet, they were still rocket engines like any other, consisting of metal chambers that converted chemicals to a high-energy explosion in a (hopefully) controlled manner.

Testing was conducted as rocket engines have always been tested, by building them, firing them and watching them explode. Engineers would then figure out what went wrong, fix it and test again. Over time, the explosions were less frequent and the successful burn periods longer as the F1s were transformed from a wild vision to a reliable reality. It is remarkable to think that all this was being carried out just 15 years after the V2 flew only 322 kilometres (200 miles) with a small payload.

**Opposite** Von Braun and his mightiest creation, the first or SIC stage of the Saturn V rocket. The five F1 engines behind him were a source of lengthy and unremitting developmental difficulties, but ultimately proved to be tough, reliable and powerful.

**Below** Two Saturn V first stages in final assembly. The five main engines produced over 3.4 million kilograms (7.5 million pounds) of thrust. It remains the most powerful rocket to fly successfully.

There were problems, however, and none was worse than those encountered when designing the huge combustion chambers where the fuels mixed and burned. The combustion chambers were so large that the fuels mixed and ignited unevenly, resulting in what the engineers inelegantly termed the "pogo effect". The rocket would bounce and shudder as the first stage pushed it skyward, generating massive stresses within its airframe. Solutions were tried and tested and improvements made, but eventually much of the pogo effect was simply accepted. This was NASA at its boldest.

The upper stages were less vexing, yet each presented unique challenges, with the final stage, the SIVB, being the most complex. With just one engine, it would have to fire, shut down and fire again to get the spacecraft headed towards the moon. Reusability was not a trademark of rocket engines in the 1960s, but testing was the watchword, and eventually the SIVB stage was wrestled into compliance.

Before NASA could send the Saturn V moonward, it had to be sure that the Command/Service Module was fit for spaceflight. This trial would be up to the crew of Apollo 7, in a daring test flight – NASA's first manned mission since the loss of Apollo 1.

**Opposite** The Command/Service Module atop a Saturn V, ready to launch. The small rocket atop the Command module is the escape tower, which would be used to loft the Command Module away from the booster in the event of an emergency.

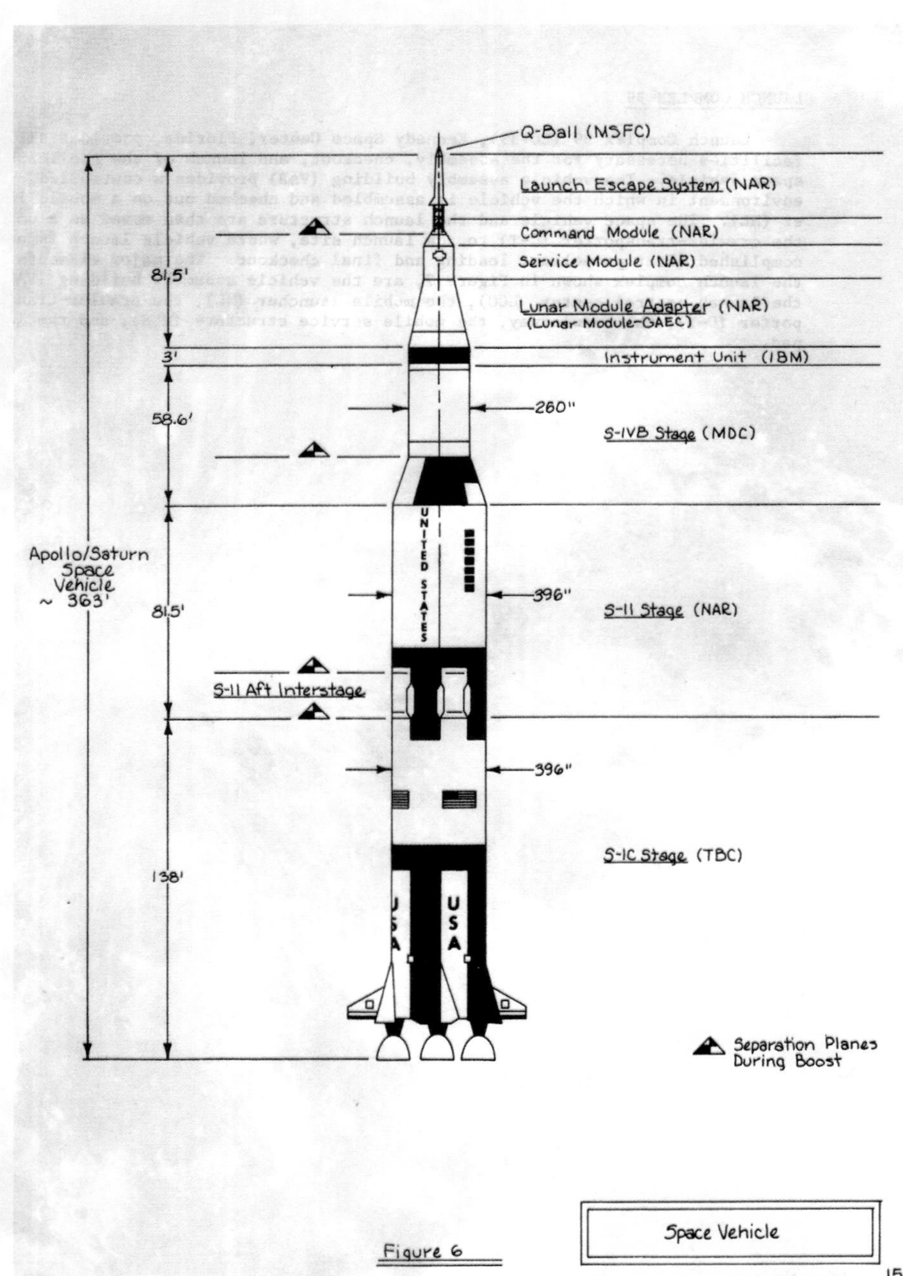


**Left** A diagram of the Saturn V launch vehicle. At 110.64 metres (363 feet) in height, it was the largest rocket ever successfully flown. Only the Command Module, second item from the top, would return from the moon missions.

## BY THE NUMBERS: THE SATURN V

**First moon-rated launch vehicle:**
**Height:** 111 metres (363 feet)
Diameter: 10.1 metres (33 feet)

**Stages:** 3

**Thrust:**
**Stage 1 (SIC):** 3.4 million kilograms (7.5 million pounds)
**Stage 2 (SII):** 453,600 kilograms (1 million pounds)
**Stage 3 (SIVB):** 102,060 kilograms (225,000 pounds)

**Propulsion:**
**SIC:** Five F1 rocket engines, liquid oxygen and kerosene fuelled
**SII:** Five J2 engines, liquid oxygen and liquid hydrogen fuelled
**SIVB:** One J2 engine, liquid oxygen and liquid hydrogen fuelled

**Endurance:** Ascent to orbit; SIVB stage through trans-lunar injection

**Auxiliary power:** Batteries

**Designer:** Wernher von Braun, Marshall Spaceflight Centre (1912–1977), and others.

**Manufacturer:**
**SIC:** Boeing Company
**SII:** North American Aviation
**SIVB:** Douglas Aircraft Company

SATURN V

# THE CONTROL PANELS OF THE APOLLO "BLOCK II" COMMAND MODULE

Inside this ship were 24 kilometres (15 miles) of wiring and over 566 switches! While each crew member had a specific area of specialization, each was expected to have at least a functional knowledge of each and every component.

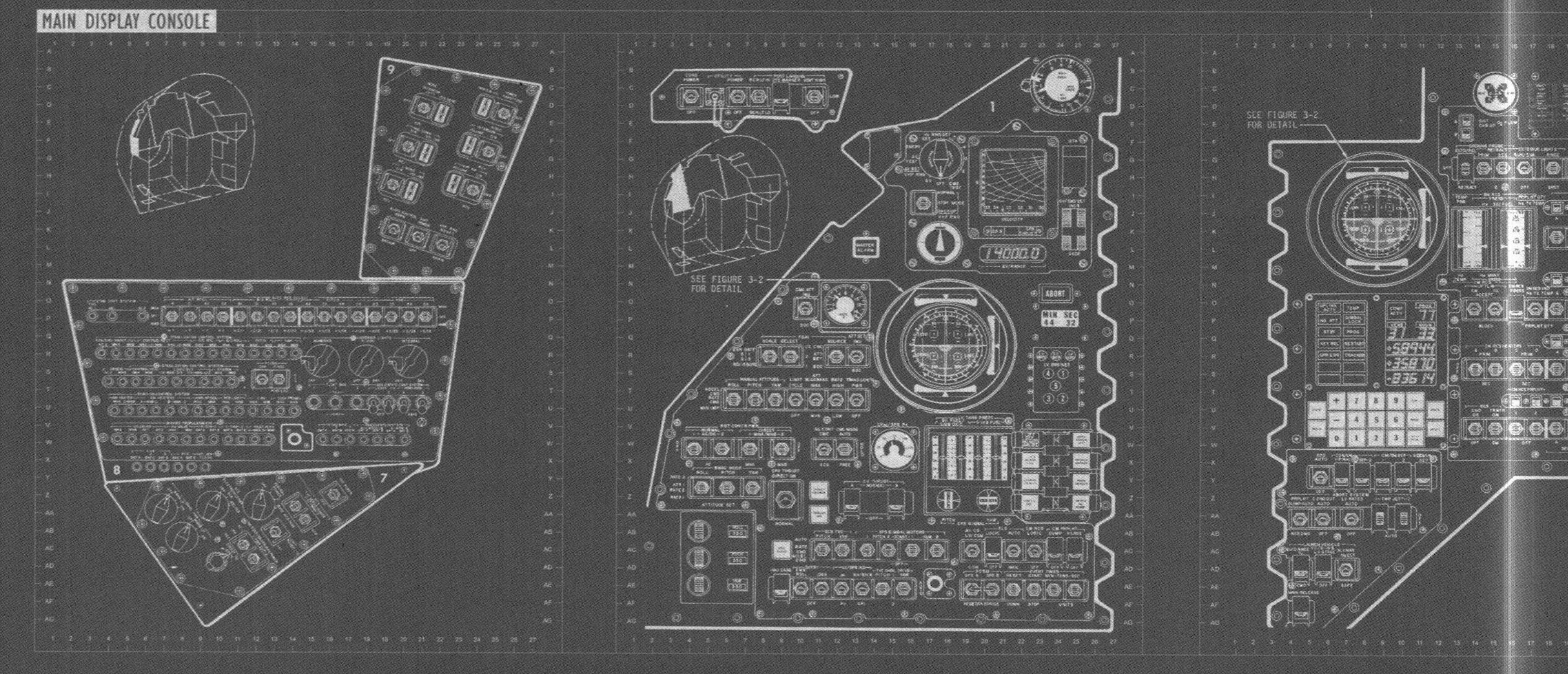

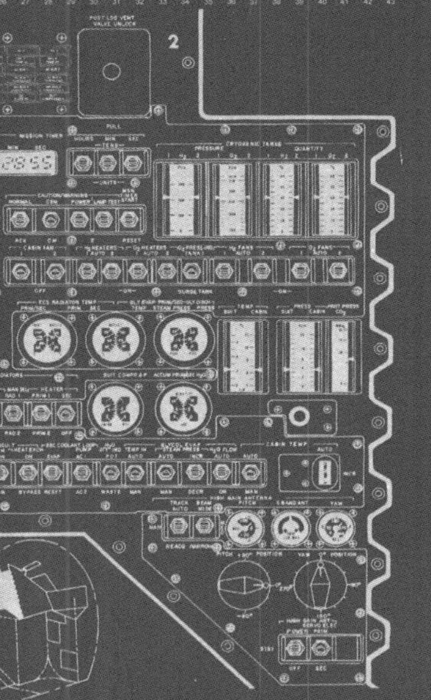

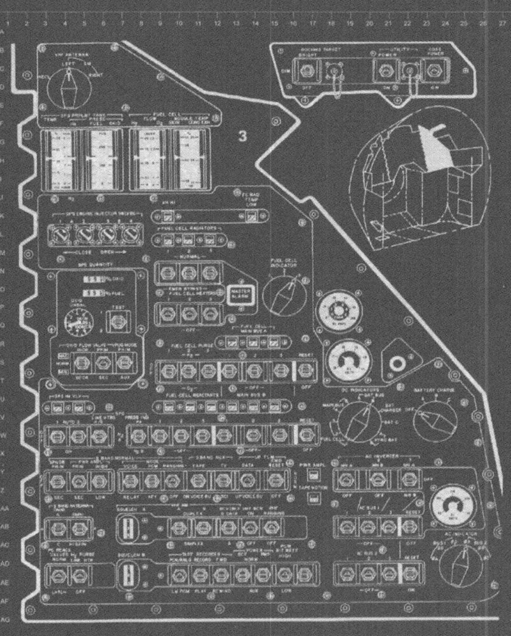

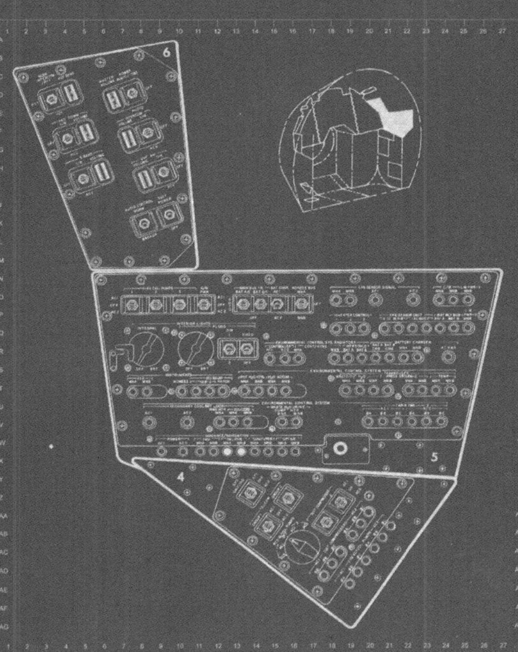

# THE FLIGHT OF THE PHOENIX

WALLY SCHIRRA, MISSION COMMANDER OF THE APOLLO 7 MISSION, HAD WANTED THE CALL SIGN FOR HIS MISSION TO BE PHOENIX, AFTER THE MYTHICAL BIRD THAT ROSE FROM THE ASHES OF DEFEAT.

It seemed a fitting tribute to his friend, Gus Grissom, and the Apollo 1 fire. NASA, however, would not allow it – there was no Lunar Module on this flight for the Command/Service Module to rendezvous with, so a separate call sign was not needed. They would fly, simply, as Apollo 7.

On 11 October 1968, at 11:02:45 am Eastern Standard Time (EST), the first manned Apollo flight began. It would be the only Apollo mission to launch from Pad 34, and the only mission other than the later Skylab and Apollo-Soyuz flights to use a Saturn IB, for Schirra and crew did not need to achieve the ultra-high velocity needed to escape Earth's gravity and head off to the moon. Apollo 7 was an engineering test flight, one for which Schirra was well qualified. As a veteran of a Mercury flight as well as a Gemini mission, he was in his element. The mission was simply to spend 11 days in Earth orbit and test the new Apollo Command/Service Module combination.

With Schirra were two rookies – Donn Eisele, Command Module Pilot and Walter Cunningham, Lunar Module Pilot.

**Above** The patch for the Apollo 7 mission. Note the lack of a Lunar Module; this flight was a test of the Command Module only; the Lunar Module was not yet ready to fly.

## THE SATURN IB

The Saturn IB was an early development of the Saturn series. It featured the new SIVB upper stage, and was used primarily to test Apollo components in Earth orbit. Built by the Chrysler Corporation, it was 68 metres (224 feet) high, almost 48 metres (150 feet) shorter than the Saturn V, and the first stage had only about as much thrust as a single F1 engine.

**Right** The crew of Skylab 1 blasts off in a Saturn IB. The scaffolding underneath the rocket, known as the "milk stool", was required to launch the rocket from the Apollo launch complex and was designed for the larger Saturn V.

## THE CREW OF APOLLO 7

The official NASA photograph of the crew of Apollo 7. From left, Donn Eisele, Command Module Pilot; Wally Schirra, Mission Commander and Walter Cunningham, Lunar Module Pilot. The image opposite shows the back of the photograph.

MANNED SPACECRAFT CENTER

HOUSTON, TEXAS

OFFICIAL PHOTOGRAPH

COLOR (PORTRAIT)

22 MAY 1968 S-68-33744

KENNEDY SPACE CENTER, FLORIDA

APOLLO 7 CREW------The prime crew of the first manned Apollo space mission, Apollo 7 (Spacecraft 101/Saturn 205), left to right, is Astronauts Donn F. Eisele, senior pilot; Walter M. Schirra Jr., command pilot; and Walter Cunningham, pilot.

PHOTO CREDIT—NASA OR NATIONAL AERONAUTICS AND SPACE ADMINISTRATION

This photograph is released for non-commercial, non-copyrightable public information use. Written permission must be received from NASA-MSC if this photograph is used in advertising, posters, books, etc., and layout must be submitted to NASA-MSC for approval prior to release. NASA-MSC also requests written notification of any uses of this photograph in scientific-engineering projects.

## CAREERS ENDED

Sadly, the flight of Apollo 7, while broadly successful, ended the careers of the three-man crew. Wally Schirra, who had flown brilliantly in the Mercury and Gemini programmes, was too cantankerous for Mission Control (presumably largely because of the squabble over whether to re-enter with or without helmets), and the remaining crewmen suffered owing to their commander's perceived mutinous behaviour. None ever flew again, and they moved on to other endeavours. Schirra remained the most visible, becoming an Apollo consultant to Walter Cronkite on CBS News.

**Above** The crew of Apollo 7, from an original NASA PR photo taken after splashdown. From left, Wally Schirra, Donn Eisele and Walt Cunningham are sick but glad to be home.

It was the first space flight for both of them, and Cunningham did not even have a Lunar Module to fly, but there were plenty of other tests to attend to. This was the first manned flight of North American Rockwell's new Block II Command Module, and whether it was discussed or not, the Apollo 1 fire was still fresh in many minds.

The Saturn IB that launched Apollo 7 skyward was an odd amalgamation. This booster was a stepping-stone in the development of the Saturn V. Its first stage had eight fuel tanks and engines, each essentially a Redstone rocket from earlier days, surrounding a single, ninth Jupiter rocket tank in the centre. The entire first stage had the thrust of one of the Saturn V's engines.

The second stage, the SIVB, was generally similar to those used on later Apollo flights (used then as a third stage). Atop this was the housing for the Lunar Module. On this flight, however, it was empty save for a few metal trusses, which held a docking target for rendezvous practice.

Major tests planned for Apollo 7 to undertake included the environmental control system, or ECS, rendezvous and docking manoeuvres and the service propulsion system, or SPS. The latter was a name for the single rocket engine aft of the Command Module that would slow them into lunar orbit and, critically, break them out of it to return home. On this flight it fired and stopped with Swiss-watch-like precision eight times, and everyone was pleased – and relieved.

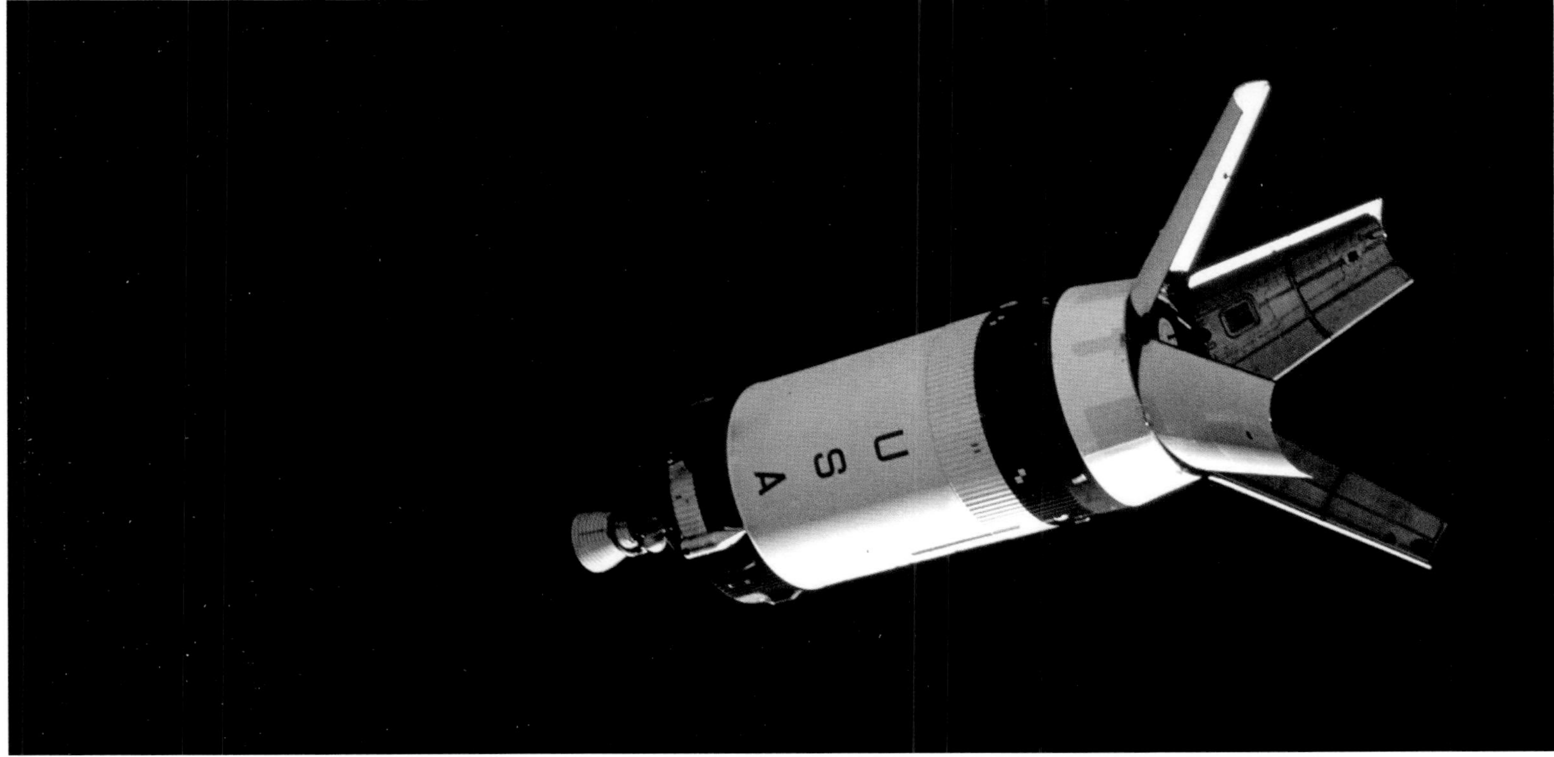


Not so pleasing was the health of the crew. Within a day, Schirra had developed a head cold which soon spread to his crewmates. While a cold is no picnic here on Earth, in space, in a small, cramped capsule, it soon became a nightmare for the crew. Without gravity, the mucus build up, which would normally drain, simply sat in their heads, clogging their ears and making them miserable.

Another frustration was the windows, which developed a problem that could impede rendezvous and docking in later flights. Some became fogged, and there was no way to clean them in space. They would simply remain obscured for the duration. The issue was later traced to a window-sealing compound, and was fixed for Apollo 9.

On 22 October the Command Module deorbited and hurtled into the Atlantic Ocean. Inside were three grumpy, sick astronauts. There had been an argument – one of many – between Schirra and the ground about the need to wear helmets during re-entry. Houston wanted them on, but Schirra insisted they not wear them for fear of burst eardrums. Being the commander on-scene, Schirra won the battle, but NASA management later decided the war.

In one final indignity, when they splashed down, the capsule went immediately into "Stable-2", which is NASA terminology for upside down. The sniffling crew hung from their restraint straps, bobbing in what Schirra would later call "a lousy boat", until eventually righted by floats on the nose of the craft. The recovery team arrived quickly, but not soon enough for the three men inside.

Apollo 7 was ultimately a rousing success – despite a near-mutiny over minor matters – and lifted the programme from the malaise of the fire. Schirra and crew had mastered both the machines and the public relations battle over the fate of Apollo.

Soon, Apollo 8 would aim for the moon.

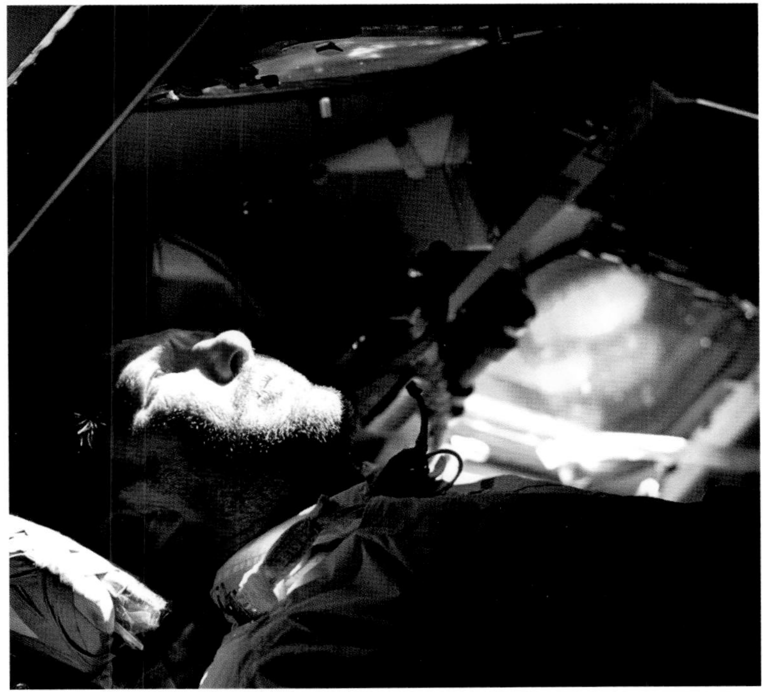

**Opposite** The launch of Apollo 7 on a Saturn IB, on 11 October 1968, at 11:02 am, EST.

**Top** A dramatic view of Mission Commander Wally Schirra after days in orbit aboard Apollo 7.

**Above** The Saturn SIVB stage as seen from the Command Module. In later Apollo flights, this stage would hold the Lunar Module inside the "petals" of the shroud. On Apollo 7, the stage was empty, save for a small trusswork and docking target for practice.

# CHAPTER NINE

# INTO THE VOID

## IT WAS AUGUST 1968, AND FRANK BORMAN AND HIS CREW JAMES LOVELL AND BILL ANDERS WERE BUSY PREPARING FOR THEIR FLIGHT ON APOLLO 9.

It was a bit of a surprise, then, when these men were called into a meeting with NASA management and told that the rocket they were to ride had switched from a Saturn IB to a Saturn V, their mission had been bumped from Apollo 9 to Apollo 8 and – most remarkably – their target had been reset from Earth orbit to the moon.

The Apollo 7 Command/Service Module had performed well, so there was really no need for another Earth orbital test-flight as originally planned, and, while the huge Saturn V booster had only been flown twice, it was considered to be generally sound. Two other factors were really at the crux of this decision, however. First, there was increasing suspicion that the Soviets were planning a lunar flyby in order to steal Apollo's thunder. Second, the American Lunar Module, being built at Grumman Aerospace, was overweight. It would not be ready to land until mid-1969.

It was, it seemed, now or never with regard to the moon. America had to get there first, even if it meant flying barely tested equipment. The Saturn V still had issues, not least of which was an alarming tendency to burn fuel unevenly and shake violently. The Command Module had flown a crew only once on Apollo 7. It was a daring gambit, one that had been rapidly forced through NASA management and won grudging approval. Borman, Lovell and Anders, however, couldn't say "yes" fast enough – such was the nature of the Apollo astronauts.

So it was that on 21 December 1968, a few minutes before 1:00 pm local time, Apollo 8 rose from Pad 39A. The crowd viewing the launch included many luminaries, notably Charles Lindbergh and his wife, watching with awe the logical conclusion of his record-setting trans-Atlantic flight of 1927.

Aboard Apollo 8 was everything needed for the daring trip to the moon and back – except for a lander. The Lunar Module, which would become so critical two years later on Apollo 13 as a lifeboat (see page 42), was still deep in development at Grumman Aerospace, and would not be ready for months. NASA had sufficient confidence in the existing command ship to move forward, however. Fortunately, the faulty oxygen tank that would later threaten the crew of Apollo 13 was further down the assembly line, awaiting installation (see page 40). This mission would depend entirely on Command/Service Module #103.

**Above** The crew of Apollo 8, from left: Jim Lovell, Lunar Module Pilot; Bill Anders, Command Service Module Pilot and Frank Borman, Mission Commander.

**Left** The mission patch for Apollo 8. Broadly representative of the trajectory they would fly to the moon, the large red figure 8 shows what would actually be a "free-return" trajectory, to be used only in an emergency and if they were not entering lunar orbit!

## RISKY BUSINESS

Apollo 8 headed off to the moon without a Lunar Module because none were ready to go. Instead, they had the Apollo Lunar Test Article or LTA, a framework of metal trusses, snuggled inside the upper housing of the SIVB stage to simulate a Lunar Module. So when they separated the Command/Service Module from this upper stage, they headed off to the moon without a Lunar Module. Their only life support systems were in the Command Module; had they experienced problems similar to Apollo 13, when the oxygen tank in the Service Module exploded, they would have suffocated long before reaching the moon.

**ABOVE** The Apollo 8 Command/Service Module and Lunar Module housing being mated to the Saturn V "stack" at the Kennedy Space Center in Florida.

The Saturn V performed flawlessly. Within a few minutes, the Saturn's SIVB stage shut down and coasted into a parking orbit. It was at this point that the flight plan deviated from the familiar as, for the first time, this crew would leave Earth orbit and head off to another body – the moon.

After another burn of the SIVB stage, Apollo 8 was moving at over 10,500 metres (35,000 feet) per second. About 60 hours into the flight, although they could not feel it, the crew left the familiar pull of the Earth and began to fall towards the moon – they were in the clutches of the lunar gravity well. The smallest error in planning and calculation would result in Apollo 8 either missing the moon and flying past it into deep space forever, or slamming into its surface. Their preferred destination was a 97-kilometre- (60-mile-) high lunar orbit, but anything close was better than the alternatives.

Among the many other firsts of this mission was mankind's first view of his own world from deep in space, and what a view it was. Bill Anders, the Command Module Pilot, was pragmatic as he spoke to Ground Control: "It was the only colour we could see in the universe... We're living on a tiny little dust mote in left field on a rather insignificant galaxy. And basically this is it for humans. It strikes me that it's a shame that we're squabbling over oil and borders."

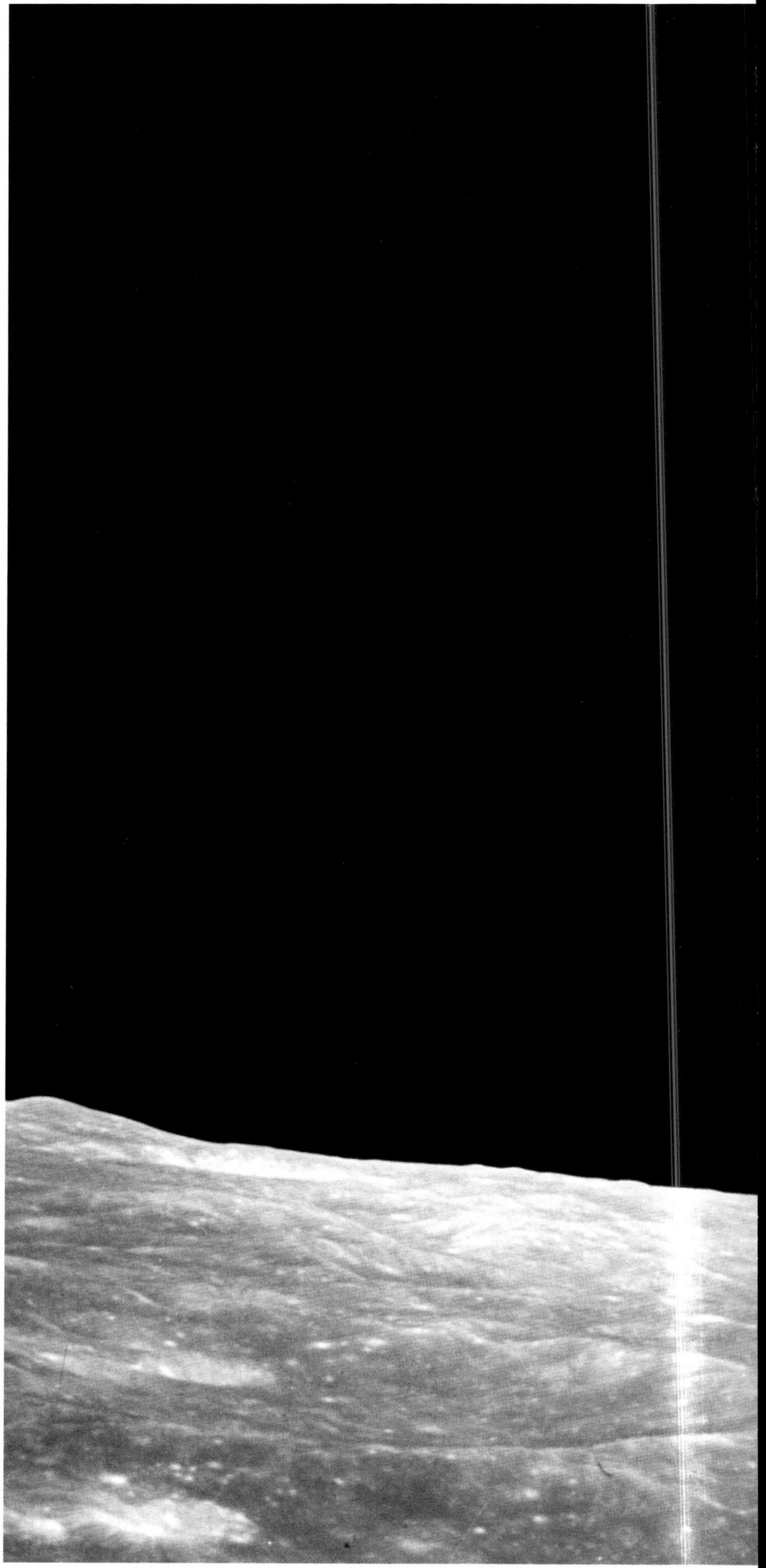

Jim Lovell was a bit more expansive: "It gives you in an instant... [an idea of] how insignificant we are, how fragile we are, and how fortunate we are to have a body that will allow us to enjoy the sky and the trees and the water... It's something that many people take for granted when they're born and they grow up within the environment. But they don't realize what they have. And I didn't till I left it."

Frank Borman, Mission Commander, was too busy to rhapsodize about the Earth, for the moon was near. As they went behind it – the first beings to be totally out of communication with Earth – they would have to fire up the Service Module engine to slow the ship enough to be captured into lunar orbit, or they would shoot past it into deep space, and never see home again.

**Far left** Earthrise from Apollo 8.

**Left** NASA used the Swedish Hasselblad 2¼ inch still camera for all Apollo missions. Some, like this one shown here, were outfitted for use inside the spacecraft, while others were toughened for use on lunar Extra-Vehicular Activity (EVAs).

## SICK IN SPACE

Before every manned launch it was NASA tradition to treat the astronauts to a special breakfast. Steak, eggs and lots of coffee were on the Apollo 8 menu, and Frank Borman had seconds, a fact that he may have regretted a few hours later. Whether it was the food or the Seconol he took to get to sleep, the capsule was soon full of drifting vomit and worse. The crew managed to clean things up, but Borman was very careful about what he ate and when for the rest of the mission.

**Above** The crew of Apollo 8 enjoying the prelaunch breakfast, little knowing what the result would be for Borman!

# APOLLO 8 PRESS KIT

This press kit, released six days prior to the launch of Apollo 8, detailed the minutiae of the ambitious flight. It notes that a "full duration lunar orbit mission" – meaning a successful one – would last ten orbits, and that's exactly what they accomplished.

**NEWS**

NATIONAL AERONAUTICS AND SPACE ADMINISTRATION
WASHINGTON, D.C. 20546

TELS. WO 2-4155
WO 3-6925

**FOR RELEASE:** SUNDAY
December 15, 1968

RELEASE NO: 68-208

**PRESS KIT**

**PROJECT:** APOLLO 8

**contents**



-0-

12/6/68

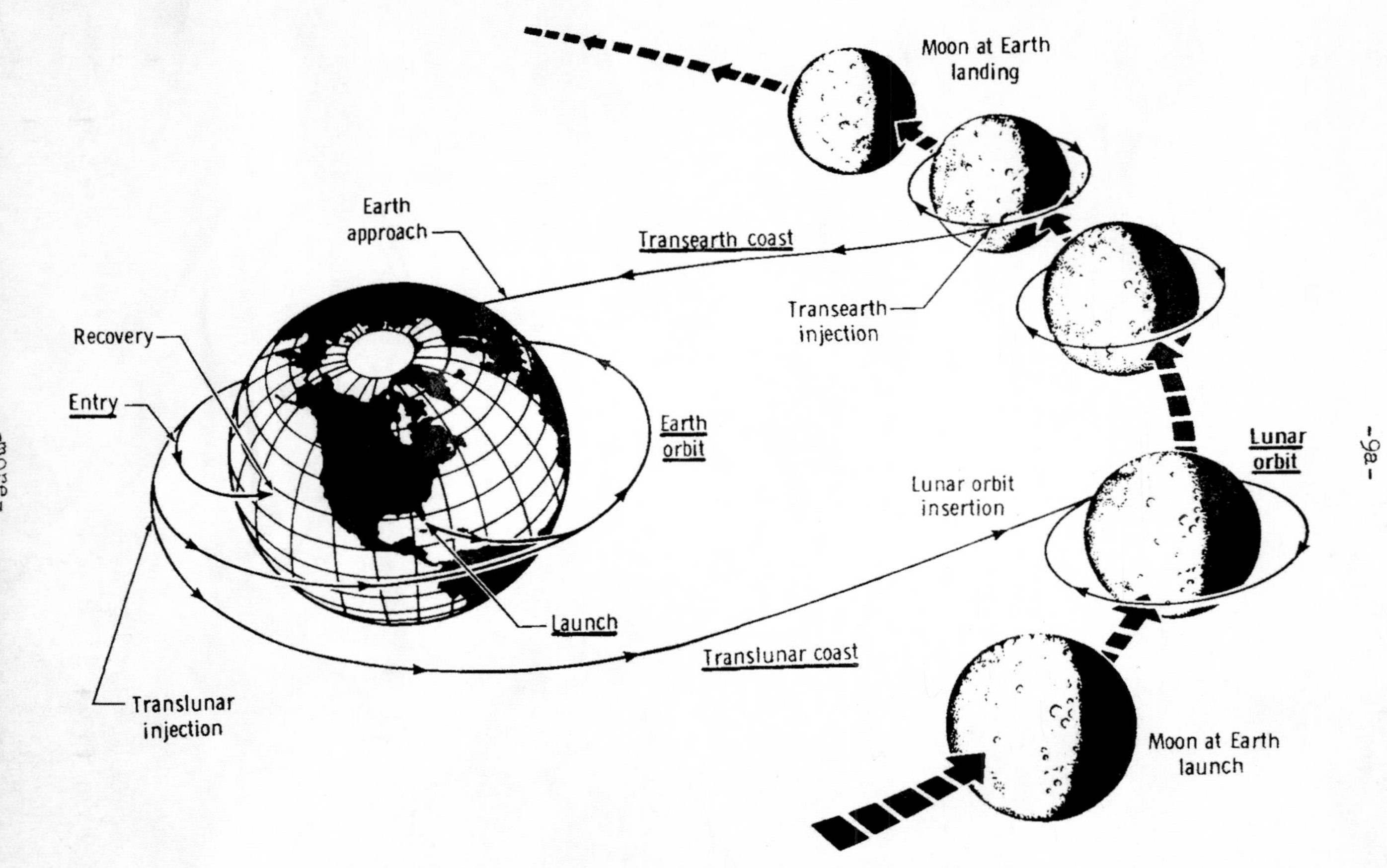
Moon at Earth landing
Earth approach
Transearth coast
Transearth injection
Recovery
Entry
Earth orbit
Lunar orbit
Lunar orbit insertion
Launch
Translunar coast
Translunar injection
Moon at Earth launch
-more-
-9a-

# CHAPTER TEN

# CHRISTMAS IN SPACE

AS APOLLO 8 SPED BEHIND THE MOON IT WENT INTO A STATUS KNOWN AS LOSS OF SIGNAL OR LOS. WITH THE MOON INTERPOSED BETWEEN EARTH AND THE TINY COMMAND/SERVICE MODULE, RADIO CONTACT WAS IMPOSSIBLE.

It was the first time a space mission – US or otherwise – had a planned total communication blackout (other than for a few minutes during re-entry).

The technicians at Mission Control expected it; still, there was a bit more toe-tapping and a few more cigarettes were lit than usual. Nerves were on edge, for if the Service Propulsion System – the rocket engine on the Service Module – did not fire, Apollo 8 would be lost. They had no Lunar Module with its spare engine, so there would be no second chances.

The minutes passed as Mission Control awaited a signal from the spacecraft. They would not even need to speak to the astronauts to know if all was well, as just the appearance of radio telemetry from the ship at a specific time would mean that the engine had done its job. Then, right on time, data from Apollo 8 came flowing in, and everyone sighed in relief. Far off, in the spacecraft, the crew described SPS burn as "the longest four minutes of our lives".

Now locked in lunar embrace, Apollo 8 would stay for ten orbits. The moon filled their viewports, a panorama of cool greys and charcoal blacks. It was a mesmerizing sight, and the crew found it difficult to tear themselves away from the windows to do their chores. Lovell was the first to describe what he saw:

**LOVELL:** The Moon is essentially gray, no color; looks like plaster of Paris or sort of a grayish beach sand. We can see quite a bit of detail. The Sea of Fertility doesn't stand out as well here as it does back on Earth. There's not as much contrast between that and the surrounding craters. The craters are all rounded off. There's quite a few of them, some of them are newer. Many of them look like – especially the round ones – look like hits by meteorites or projectiles of some sort. Langrenus is quite a huge crater; it's got a central cone to it. The walls of the crater are terraced, about six or seven different terraces on the way down.

Later, during the fourth orbit, the crew witnessed a first in human history – Earthrise. The home planet climbed slowly up from behind the monochrome of the lunar limb, dazzling with its blues, browns and white clouds. It was a stunning view that would stay with them for the rest of their lives.

On Christmas Eve, during their ninth orbit and as their stay was nearing its end, Anders began what would become one of the most famous transmissions from space, a reading from Genesis in the Bible. It was the Christian account of the Creation, broadcast by those who were spending their Christmas further from home than anyone, across 386,160 kilometres (240,000 miles) of dark, forbidding space.

After Anders read the first section, Lovell picked up on cue. Borman then finished the passage, ending with "And from the crew of Apollo 8, we close with good night, good luck and a Merry Christmas to all of you, all of you on the good Earth".

APOLLO 8 CHRISTMAS EVE BROADCAST

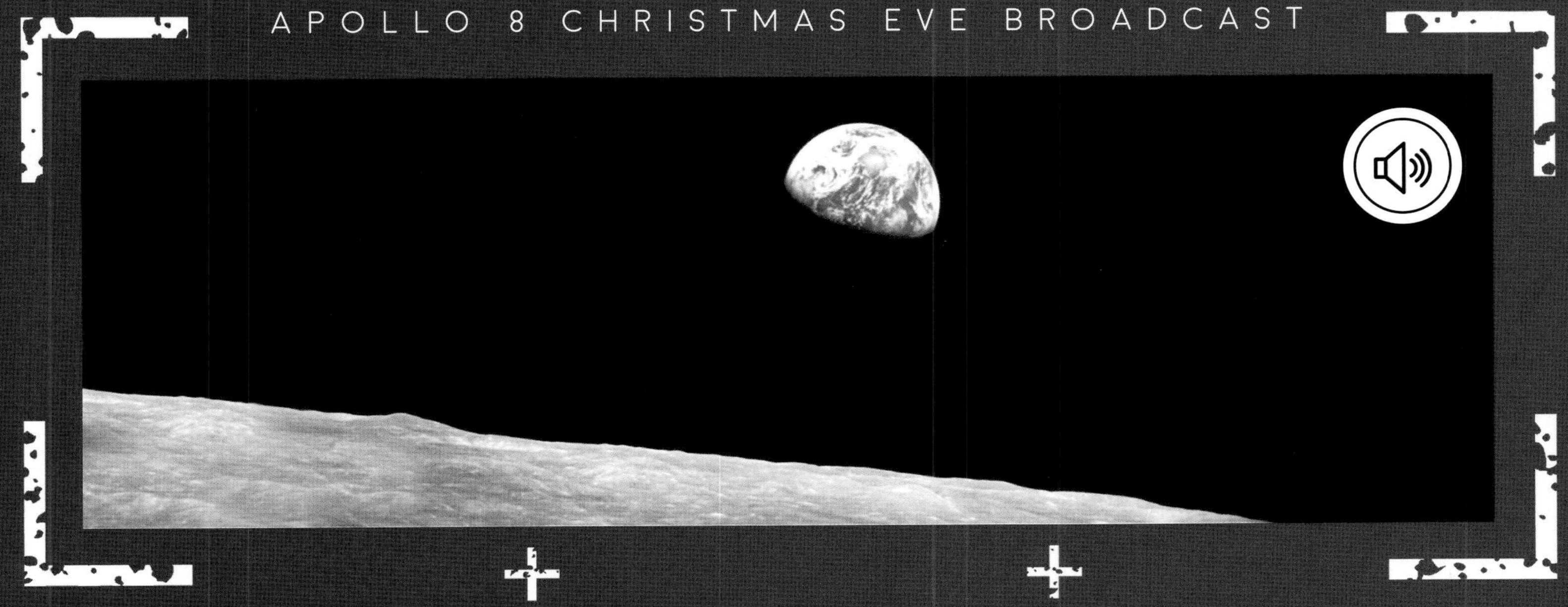

## TOO CLOSE FOR COMFORT

It was always a point of pride when an American space crew came back down to Earth close to the recovery forces. But Bill Tindal, a NASA expert in orbital mechanics felt that there were limits: "There are reports that the C Prime [Apollo 8] Command Module came down right over the aircraft carrier and drifted on its chutes to land only 4,572 meters [14,996 feet] away. This really strikes me as being too close... The consequence of the spacecraft hitting the carrier is truly catastrophic... I seriously recommend relocating the recovery force at least eight to 16 kilometers [five to 10 miles] from the target point." (NASA historical website, http://history.nasa.gov/SP-4205/ch11-6.html)

**Right** The Apollo 8 Command Module being prepared for hoisting onto the deck of the carrier after splashdown and crew recovery.

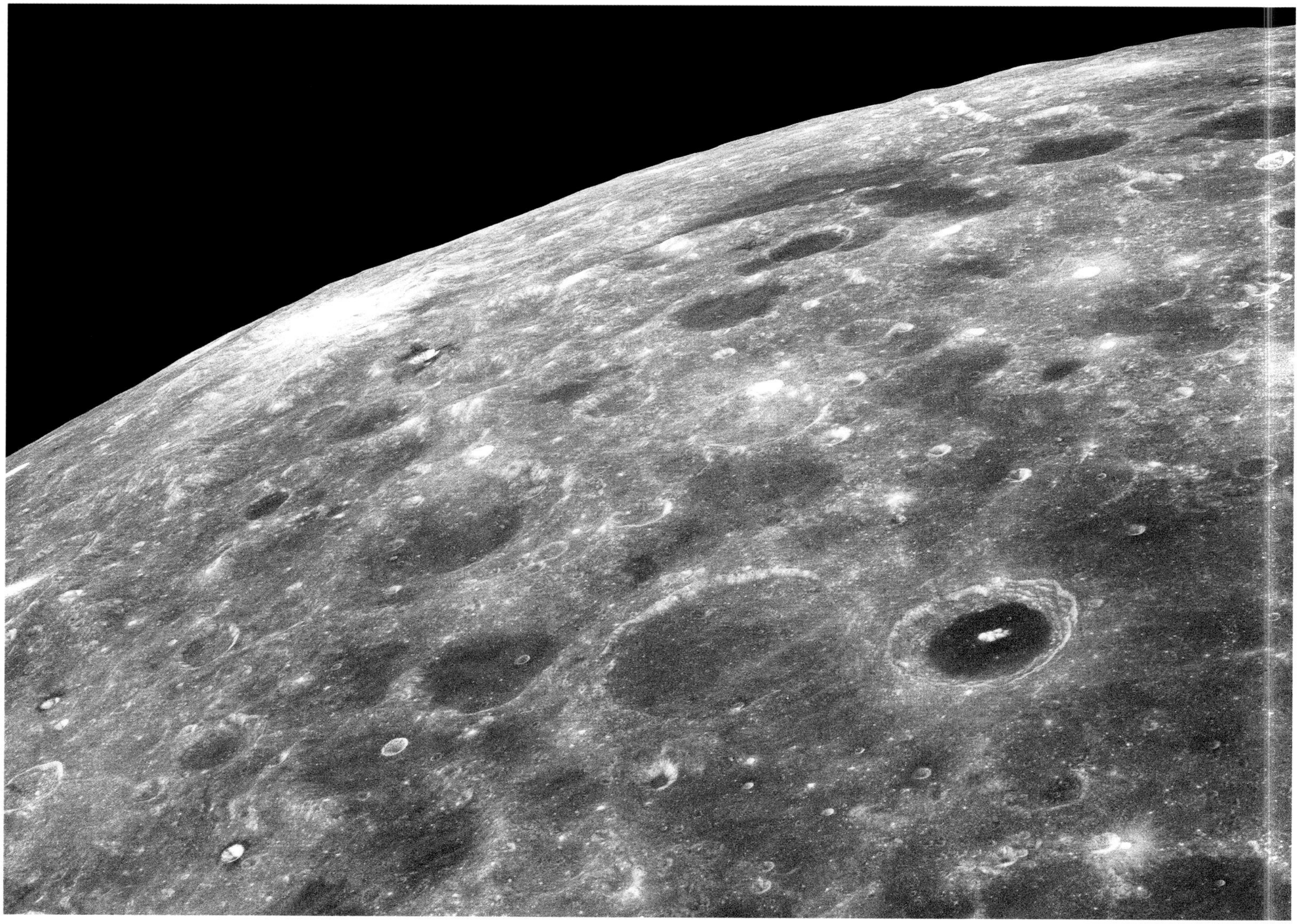

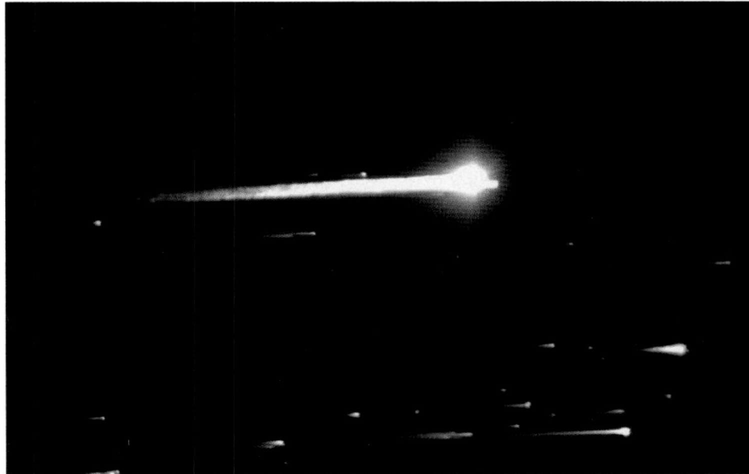

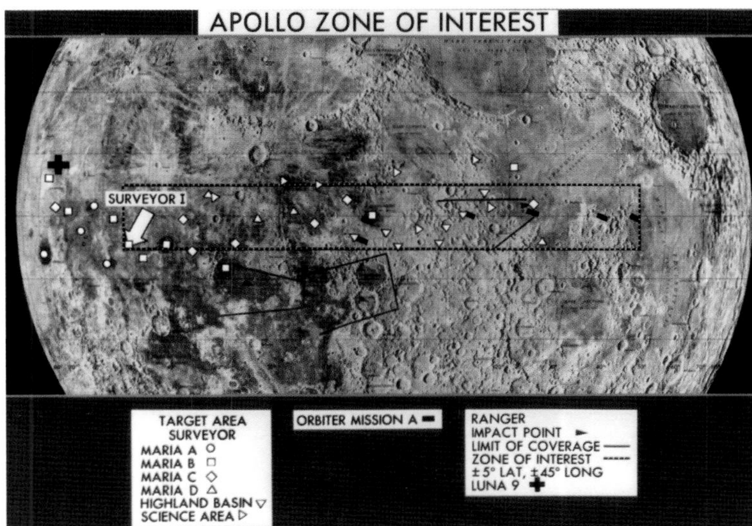


As orbit ten approached, Lovell had a difficult moment when he accidentally erased some of the data in the onboard computer. He had to perform a manual alignment of the navigation system using specific stars (which was how the Apollo moon voyages confirmed their position beyond Earth orbit). He succeeded, and all was ready for the trip home.

The Trans Earth Injection burn would also occur behind the moon, and for the second time in as many days, controllers sweated out the radio blackout. When the welcome telemetry from the spacecraft was received, it was followed by a transmission from the relieved Lovell, who said: "Please be informed, there is a Santa Claus!" Laughter rang out at Mission Control, and Apollo 8 was on its way home.

Two-and-a-half days later they re-entered the Earth's atmosphere. This was another critical point. No manned craft had ever returned from the moon, and none had re-entered at such a high speed – 40,225 kilometres (25,000 miles) per hour. Add to this the navigational trick of having to "skip" the Command Module off the atmosphere to shave off speed, and it was a hair-raising event. But minutes later, when the ionization caused by the friction-induced inferno around their craft had abated, controllers heard, for the last time, a welcome voice from Apollo 8. They were in the vast Pacific Ocean, bobbing in three-metre (ten-foot) swells, awaiting pickup.

## LEGAL TROUBLE

When Frank Borman approved the reading of scripture in orbit around the moon during the Apollo 8 flight, he probably never thought it would lead to trouble for NASA. But shortly after the victorious crew splashed down, NASA received a copy of a lawsuit filed by the Society of Separationists, who claimed that NASA's complicity in the religious reading from lunar orbit blurred the Constitutional line between church and state. The suit was unsuccessful, but NASA was more careful of such decisions in the future.

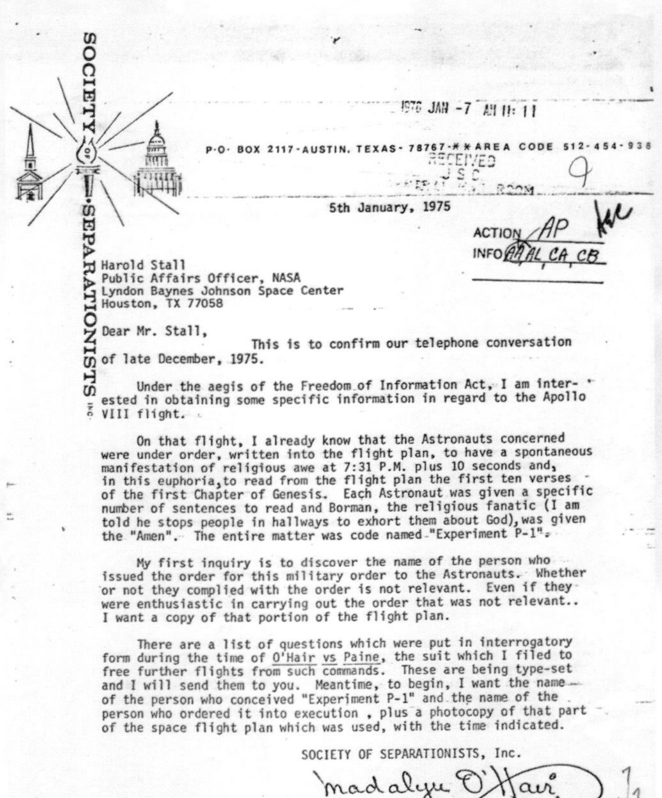

SOCIETY OF SEPARATIONISTS INC.

1975 JAN -7 AM 11: 11

P·O· BOX 2117·AUSTIN, TEXAS· 78767·★★AREA CODE 512·454·938

RECEIVED J S C ... ROOM

9

5th January, 1975

ACTION AP

INFO AA, AL, CA, CB

Harold Stall
Public Affairs Officer, NASA
Lyndon Baynes Johnson Space Center
Houston, TX 77058

Dear Mr. Stall,

This is to confirm our telephone conversation of late December, 1975.

Under the aegis of the Freedom of Information Act, I am interested in obtaining some specific information in regard to the Apollo VIII flight.

On that flight, I already know that the Astronauts concerned were under order, written into the flight plan, to have a spontaneous manifestation of religious awe at 7:31 P.M. plus 10 seconds and, in this euphoria, to read from the flight plan the first ten verses of the first Chapter of Genesis. Each Astronaut was given a specific number of sentences to read and Borman, the religious fanatic (I am told he stops people in hallways to exhort them about God), was given the "Amen". The entire matter was code named "Experiment P-1".

My first inquiry is to discover the name of the person who issued the order for this military order to the Astronauts. Whether or not they complied with the order is not relevant. Even if they were enthusiastic in carrying out the order that was not relevant.. I want a copy of that portion of the flight plan.

There are a list of questions which were put in interrogatory form during the time of O'Hair vs Paine, the suit which I filed to free further flights from such commands. These are being type-set and I will send them to you. Meantime, to begin, I want the name of the person who conceived "Experiment P-1" and the name of the person who ordered it into execution , plus a photocopy of that part of the space flight plan which was used, with the time indicated.

SOCIETY OF SEPARATIONISTS, Inc.

Madalyn O'Hair

Madalyn O'Hair,
AMERICAN ATHEIST

**Above** This letter was one of many in a continuing series of incidents that increased NASA's concern about what the astronauts were allowed to say from space.

**Opposite** A view of the rugged lunar surface from Apollo 8. As they orbited the moon, the crew was met with a constantly changing vista of dark greys and inky blacks. The variations on this theme were many depending on the angle of the sun.

**Top left** Apollo 8 Command Module creates its own welcome-home fireworks display as it streaks through the upper atmosphere. Frictional heating burns off the heat shield, resulting in a spectacular display.

**Above left** The early manned lunar orbital flights, such as Apollo 8, allowed NASA to develop a map of "Apollo Zone of Interest" for landing site decisions.

# FLYING TO THE MOON

## TOM KELLEY, CHIEF ENGINEER FOR THE LUNAR MODULE, HAD A PROBLEM. IT WAS A VERY BIG PROBLEM ABOUT SIX METRES (20 FEET) HIGH, NINE METRES (30 FEET) WIDE AND, WORST OF ALL, IT WAS HUNDREDS OF KILOGRAMS OVERWEIGHT.

It was the Grumman Aircraft Engineering Corporations Apollo Lunar Module, and it had become a grossly overweight nightmare. The craft would have to shed weight, or Grumman could be responsible for the failure of the entire Apollo project.

Grumman had clinched the Lunar Module contract, working from a very simple model the company had thrown together using balsa wood and paper clips, in 1962. But in the intervening five years, the design had changed and changed again. The current Lunar Modules were way over the 14,515 kilograms (32,000 pounds) finally specified by NASA.

The Grumman engineers were having nervous breakdowns over weight in the Lunar Module; for every kilogram added to the Lunar Module for in-flight operations, its launch weight increased by 1.8 kilograms (four pounds)!

It was a catch-22, times four. But they scraped, etched and machined their way into compliance. They switched from fuel cells to batteries for power, simplified the ascent engine, reduced the landing gear from five legs to four and changed a thousand other things. Slowly the Lunar Module became an odd-looking flyable reality. Never meant to fly in an atmosphere, it had always been bug-like, but now, with the tiny triangular windows and oddly-shaped fuel tanks, it looked truly extraterrestrial.

It was also delicate. In the ongoing programme to save weight, all metal components had been shaved thin. The most stubborn of these was the pressure hull, which was now about twice the thickness of a soft-drink can. It was covered with tiny ribs to enhance its strength, but the astronauts found that they could easily "pop" the hull with one finger. It was so thin that a dropped screwdriver could punch a hole through the floor. Some took to calling it the "aluminium balloon."

### G, H AND J

There were three different designs for the Lunar Modules that flew for Apollo. The "G" version, which landed with Apollo 11 was the only one of its kind to land on the moon. The "H" series used on Apollos 12, 13 and 14 had a lunar "stay time" of one-plus days and carried an experimental package in the descent stage. The later "J" version, flown on Apollos 15, 16 and 17 had a stay time of 3 days, improved cooling and internal systems and room for the Lunar Roving Vehicle in the descent stage.

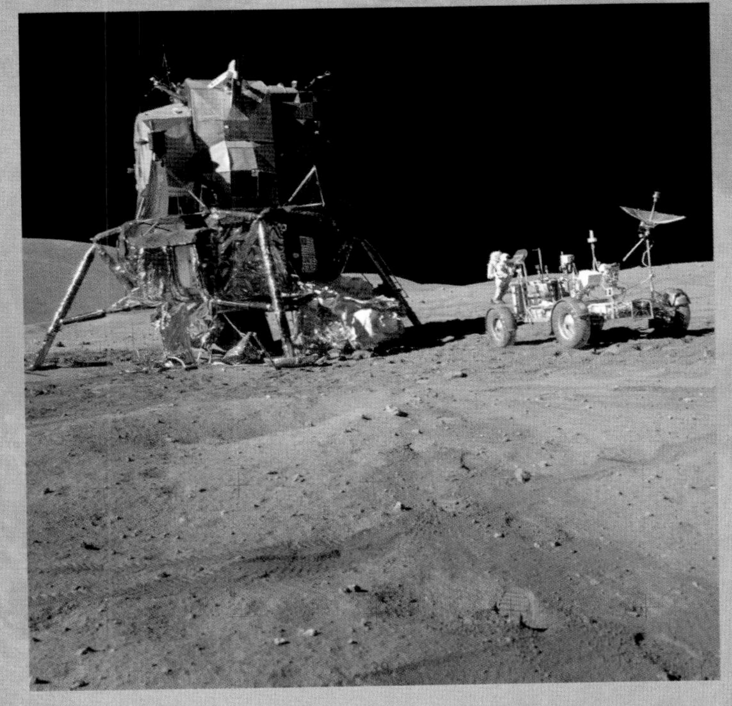

**Above** The original model that won the design and construction competition for Grumman. The rough wood model, with paperclips cleverly representing the landing gear, was the current mode of thought for designing a lunar lander in 1962. The eventual design for the Lunar Module lost a leg and gained a square front hatch, but was otherwise remarkably similar. Little did they know then the difficulties that lay ahead.

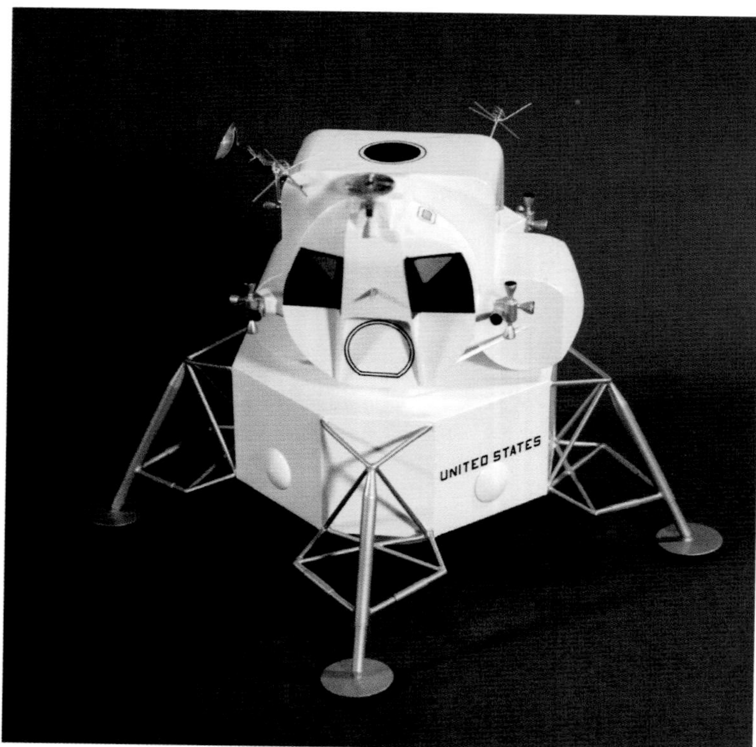

From the bottom up, the Lunar Module consisted of a landing stage and a crew/ascent stage. The landing stage carried a powerful descent engine and fuel enough to go from lunar orbit to the lunar surface. Tucked in its sides were a variety of instruments and experiments for deployment there; later Lunar Modules would also carry the Lunar Rover folded up inside this stage. Initially designed to have metal sides, it was eventually covered in gold-plated Mylar foil to save weight, increasing its fragile appearance.

Atop this was the Ascent Module. This housed the crew, all the flight control systems, the life support and the ascent engine. The ascent engine was a particular challenge, as if any system aboard failed they might never return from the lunar surface. It was light and simple, and designed for reliability above all.

As late as the first quarter of 1969, the Lunar Module was still overweight. In fact, the Lunar Module that flew on Apollo 10 was actually too heavy to land on the moon. The Grumman team persisted, refusing to let go of the problem, and within months, just in time for Apollo 11, Tom Kelley could relax. The Lunar Module was complete and underweight. It was Grumman's finest hour, and NASA could at last go to, and land on, the moon. But they still had to find their way there.

Obviously, heading across 386,160 kilometres (240,000 miles) of black space to another body is a challenge. But it is made all the harder by the fact that the moon is a constantly moving target. This means that while travelling at up to 40,225 kilometres (25,000 miles) per hour you have to aim at where it will be when you plan to arrive... and if, across the quarter-million miles you will traverse, you miscalculate by a degree or two, you will fly wide, missing the moon and flying off into deep space, or slam headlong into its Earth-facing side.

Coming home is no easier. It has been said that if the Earth was a basketball and the moon a softball, the re-entry corridor would be as thin as a sheet of paper. Missing that hair-breadth edge would end in death.

These metaphors were not encouraging. The Massachusetts Institute of Technology (MIT) had been tasked with designing the computer and software to navigate Apollo to the moon, to be built by defence contractor Raytheon. The result of their combined efforts was the Apollo Guidance Computer, or AGC. It was a first in many areas, including first use of integrated circuits, and one of the first truly compact computing systems (IBM mainframes still filled a large room in the 1960s). It ran at 1.024 megahertz, and had 32 kilobytes of memory, far less than the smallest digital watch today, and was remarkably reliable and robust.

The interface between the astronaut and the computer was called the Display Keyboard, or DSKY. It had a simple numerical display, a number of warning and status lights and a ten-digit keypad. Seemingly complex, it was actually fairly simple to operate and the astronauts mastered it in short order.

In the Lunar Module, things were more complex. The AGC in the Lunar Module was referred to as the Primary Guidance, Navigation and Control System, or PGNCS (pronounced "pings"). There was an additional, simpler backup computer called the Abort Guidance System, or AGS. This was for use in the ascent to the waiting Command Module only.

By the end of the Apollo 10 flight, the AGC was pronounced ready for the ultimate test – landing on the moon and rendezvousing in lunar orbit, on Apollo 11.

## THE FATHER OF THE AGC

Charles Stark Draper (1901–1987) helmed the MIT Instrumentation Laboratory during the development of the Apollo Guidance Computer. Draper pioneered the arcane art of flying by knowing only your point of departure, not unlike dead reckoning for sea navigation. Educated at Stanford University and MIT, he taught at the latter institution until he founded the Instrumentation Lab in the 1930s. His team was responsible for the hardware design of the AGC.

**Right** A rare picture of Charles Draper, the man often referred to as "the father of inertial guidance".

**Opposite left** Grumman's Lunar Module in 1964 which closely resembled to the final product.

**Opposite right** The Lunar Module Apollo Guidance Computer is seen here in a Lunar Module mock-up. This is the unit which flashed the 1202 and 1201 error messages during the descent of Apollo 11 (see page 93), and which ultimately rebooted and continued to guide them towards the surface of the moon.

**Above** A Lunar Module under construction, minus the outer skin. Note the hull bracing ribs, which were there to support the very thin metals used.

# DRESS REHEARSALS

## IT WAS EARLY 1969 AND NASA WAS PRIMED FOR SUCCESS FOLLOWING APOLLO 8' S IMPRESSIVE CIRCLING OF THE MOON JUST A FEW MONTHS EARLIER

However, there were still questions to be answered and systems to be tested before a manned landing could be attempted.

Of immediate concern were the cryptically named mascons. The acronym was shorthand for "mass concentrations", which were discovered in 1968 by scientists at the Jet Propulsion Laboratory from the data collected from an unmanned probe. Scientists at the laboratory had found that their Lunar Orbiter spacecraft was experiencing uneven orbits, and this caused concern at NASA as the Apollo spacecraft could be subject to the same irregularities.

Also of concern were the difficult rendezvous and dock/undock operations needed for a lunar landing mission. While Apollo 7 had orbited Earth and Apollo 8 the moon, the Lunar Module had not yet flown on a manned mission. It would probably work fine, but nobody wanted to test it on a live landing attempt.

Apollo 9 lifted off on 3 March 1969 with perhaps the most whimsical callsigns of the programme – the Command Module was called Gumdrop, and the Lunar Module Spider. The Mission Commander was Jim McDivitt, who would retire from active flight status after this flight, the Command Module Pilot was Dave Scott and the Lunar Module Pilot was Rusty Schweickart.

This mission represented the second manned flight of the Saturn V and the first of the Lunar Module. All manoeuvers for the lunar landing missions were tested: the Lunar Module ascent and descent engines and the rendezvous and docking operations of the Command Module and Lunar Module. In addition, the Portable Life Support System (PLSS) backpacks for use on the lunar surface were used for the first time in a vaccum.

**Above** The mission emblem for Apollo 9 depicts the Earth-orbital mission well. The Staurn V is to the left, with the Command/Service Module and Lunar Module in "station-keeping" positions (standing still relative to each other).

**Right** Rollout of the Apollo 10 "stack" from the Vehicle Assembly Building, bound for Launch Complex 39. Rollout of the Apollo 10 "stack" from the Vehicle Assembly Building, bound for Launch Complex 39.

## GIMBAL LOCK

As Apollo 10's Ascent Module of the Lunar Module (the silver part seen here) gyrated nearly out of control, Cernan and Stafford's eyes were glued to the Lunar Module control panel. At low centre would have been the "eight-ball", or artificial horizon indicator. If this swung too far, the guidance system would enter "gimbal lock", a condition in which the gyroscopes used for navigation would lock up and all guidance information would be lost. It was just this condition that Cernan feared when he made his alarmed (and eyebrow rising) call to Houston.

**Above** Apollo 10 was the final "dress rehearsal" before the landing attempt on Apollo 11. Here the Lunar Module pulls away from the Command/Service Module preparatory to descending to a simulated landing. Prior to touching down, though, the descent stage would be jettisoned and the ascent engine used to return to the CSM. It was a daring mission, with a few tense moments, but set the stage for Apollo 11 to succeed.

The Lunar Modules for Apollo 9 and 10 were still overweight for a lunar landing, but were perfectly suited for testing purposes. The Apollo 9 flight lasted for ten days and proved the equipment and procedures in Earth orbit.

Apollo was now running at full speed. On 18 May 1969 Apollo 10 departed from Florida in a mass of flame and smoke. The Saturn V pounded the crew with pogo oscillations, to the point that they found it difficult to focus their eyes on the instruments. It was a scary few minutes. Nevertheless, Apollo 10 was soon on its way to the moon with the shaken-but-healthy spacecraft. The crew were all Gemini veterans: the Mission Commander was Tom Stafford, with two Gemini flights under his belt; Gene Cernan, of Gemini 9 as Lunar Module Pilot and John Young, of Geminis 3 and 10, as Command Module Pilot.

Their arrival in lunar orbit allowed Houston to study the effects of the mascons, and, while still mysterious, it was clear that their presence would not endanger future missions.

On 22 May, Apollo 10 was cleared to rehearse the lunar landing approach for Apollo 11. Cernan and Stafford entered the Lunar Module and began their powered descent. Still too heavy to land and depart safely, the Lunar Module transported them to a tantalizing 16 kilometres (ten miles) above the lunar surface. At this point, they jettisoned the Lunar Module's descent stage and ignited the ascent engine to return to John Young, waiting overhead in the Command Module.

**Below** The crew of Apollo 10. From left, Eugene Cernan, Tom Stafford and John Young.

**Opposite** One of Apollo 10's high-resolution images of the moon's surface.

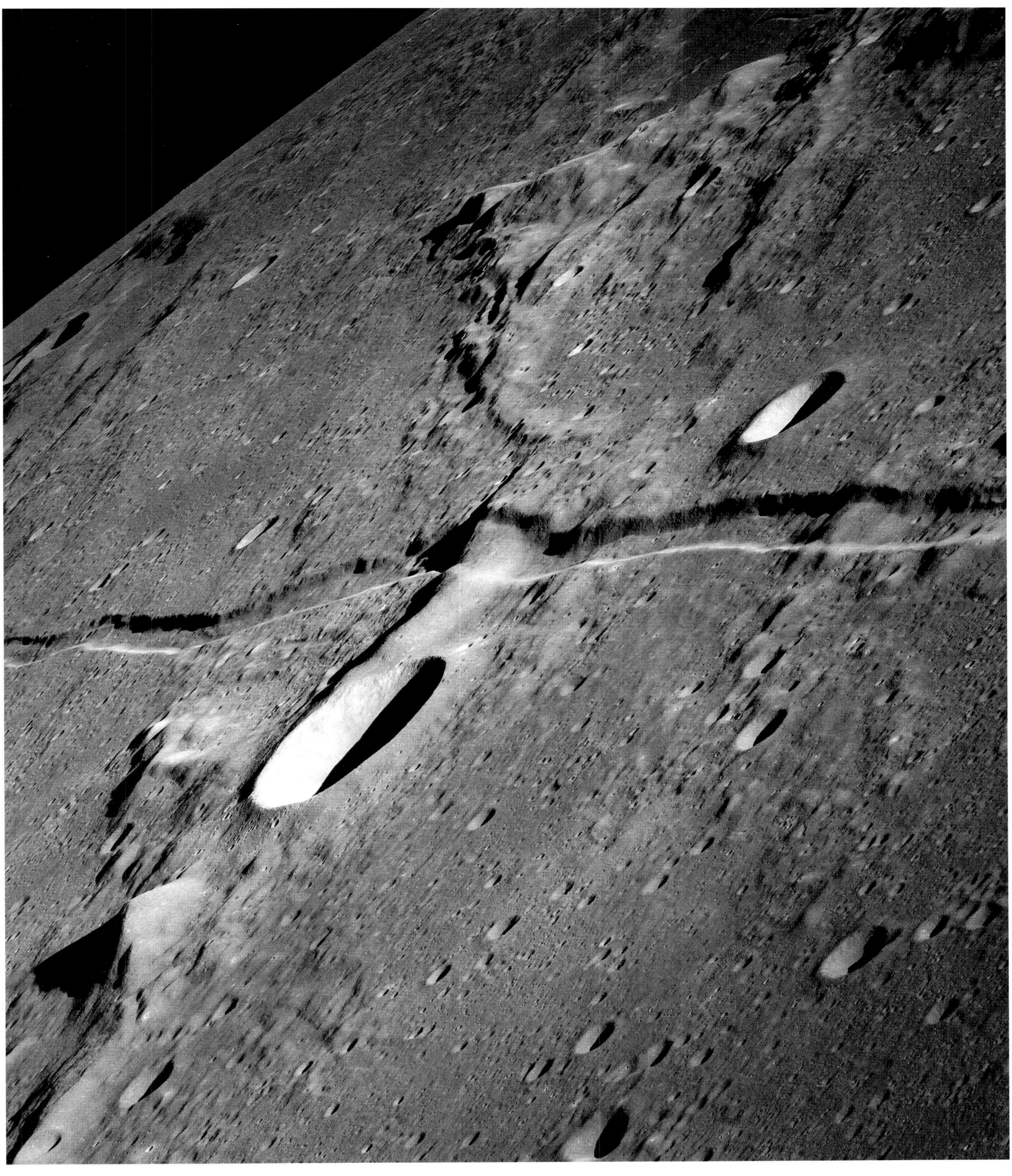

Almost immediately, Cernan expressed his alarm on the radio circuit. The ascent stage was gyrating wildly, and was almost out of control. The automatic guidance computer was firing thrusters seemingly at random and, for a few minutes, it seemed as if manoeuverability might be lost. By the time they regained control of the Lunar Module and headed back on course for the Command Module, they had come to within a few kilometres of crashing into the higher lunar mountains. The cause of the malfunction was a mistaken switch setting.

The rest of the mission went well, but trouble awaited Cernan when he arrived back on Earth. In the panic, he had uttered a single expletive and this was enough to cause NASA massive PR headaches when word got out, as outraged Americans wrote to the space agency signaling their displeasure. Crews of future flights were delicately counselled to use more polite language when their lives were in jeopardy.

As if to mock the absurdity of the situation, and NASA's timid response, the other astronauts strung up a banner to welcome the Apollo 10 crew back to Earth:

***"THE FLIGHT OF APOLLO 10 – FOR ADULT AUDIENCES ONLY"***

Next on NASA's fast track: landing on the moon.

**Above** Although just a "dress rehearsal" mission, Apollo 10 attracted plenty of viewers. Here, guests of NASA watch the launch from the viewing stands.

**Opposite** A NASA image of the moon showing various dark plains, including *Mare Tranquillitatis*, *Mare Crisium* and *Mare Smythii*.

## MASCONS

The mascons on the moon were initially a concern, but turned out to be merely an inconvenience. First noticed when they caused by orbital irregularities on unmanned lunar missions, they are caused by areas of increased mass in the lunar surface. They tend to emanate from the large basins, or mare, and are theorized to be caused by concentrations of the denser mantle material from within the moon.

**Above** Mare Smythii, a significant lunar mascon, was one of the areas studied for its effects on the orbits of the Apollo moonships.

# PREPARING FOR THE BIG ONE

THE COUNTDOWN CLOCK WAS TICKING IN HOUSTON IN JULY 1969. LAST MINUTE DETAILS WERE BEING HURRIEDLY ATTENDED TO, AND EVERYONE WAS CONCENTRATING ON THE UPCOMING APOLLO 11 MISSION.

This was the big one, the first lunar landing. Nobody wanted to be accused of causing the mission to fail.

The Apollo 11 crew had been burning up simulator time at a furious rate, seconded only by their backup crew. Every kind of problem, every malfunction in the books, had been thrown at them, and still they carried on, apparently supremely confident in their respective capabilities.

Neil Armstrong, the stoic, soft-spoken Mission Commander, had grown up in small-town Ohio. Neil did not make small talk or crack jokes – a rarity in the world of test pilots. When he did speak it was with self-assuredness and finality. Fascinated with aeroplanes ever since his youth, he had flown the fastest aeroplanes on the planet – including the X-15. He was one of the few pilots of the experimental X-15 rocketplane in NASA and the only man to have flown it as a civilian. It had been a dream come true. Now he could fulfil another dream – becoming the first man to step onto another celestial body.

Standing next to him in the Lunar Module simulator was Edwin "Buzz" Aldrin, who hailed from New Jersey. An enigma in the world of test pilots, Buzz rarely indulged in the fast life, preferring more intellectual pursuits. He earned a doctorate from MIT with a dissertation on the obscure discipline of orbital mechanics, which had come in handy during both his Gemini 12 flight and in the planning for the Apollo 11 mission. Buzz seemed to speak only when he had something that he felt was profound to say, especially about orbital mechanics, and then he would not stop. He was not terribly popular at parties.

In the Command Module simulator was Mike Collins. Born in Rome, Italy, Mike was the opposite in temperament to his colleagues.

**Above** A happy Apollo 11 crew during Command Module inspection. From left, Neil Armstrong, Michael Collins and Buzz Aldrin.

He was affable, friendly, philosophical and thoroughly puzzled by his fellow crewmembers. Later in life he would ponder aloud how the three of them ended up on the Apollo 11 flight together – there could not have been a more unusual team. That was typical of the way things worked at NASA, however – decisions were made by those in authority, and that was that. He would fly the Command Module with all the skills he possessed, and regardless of whether he was close to Neil and Buzz or not, he would do everything in his power to bring them home safely.

These three men worked as closely as they needed to in preparation for their epic flight. Rarely was a terse word spoken, though one night, when the three of them were bunking together in crew quarters, Buzz had engaged Mike Collins in an impassioned rant about a simulation that had gone sour that day. He and Neil had crashed into the moon and Buzz felt that Neil should have known better. Armstrong, who had retired early, wandered out of the sleeping quarters looking tense, and asked them to keep it down so he could sleep. Collins beat a hasty retreat to his own room, leaving the other two to work out their differences. It was one of the few instances of overt friction between the men that anyone could recall.

At the Cape, final equipment checks were in full swing. The components of the flight – the Command Module, Columbia, and the Lunar Module, Eagle, sat atop the Saturn V. Only recently had the Grumman engineers managed to trim enough weight off the Lunar Module to guarantee a safe landing and return – as much as that sort of thing could ever be guaranteed. Eagle, along with the rest of the rocket, was inspected and inspected again. There was no room for error.

The countdown marched on with nobody quite sure whether they were really ready, but with everyone anxious to go. It was time to fly.

## WHO'S ON FIRST?

The question of who would be the first man on the moon was fodder for much speculation, not least among the members of the Apollo 11 crew. There were two choices: Neil Amstrong, Mission Commander, or Buzz Aldrin, Lunar Module Pilot. In all previous spacewalks, per military tradition, the commander stayed with the ship while the second in command took the first outing. It was even indicated as such in some of the early Apollo documentation. In the end, it was about space, there was not enough room in the module for Aldrin to get past Armstrong, so Armstrong would go first.

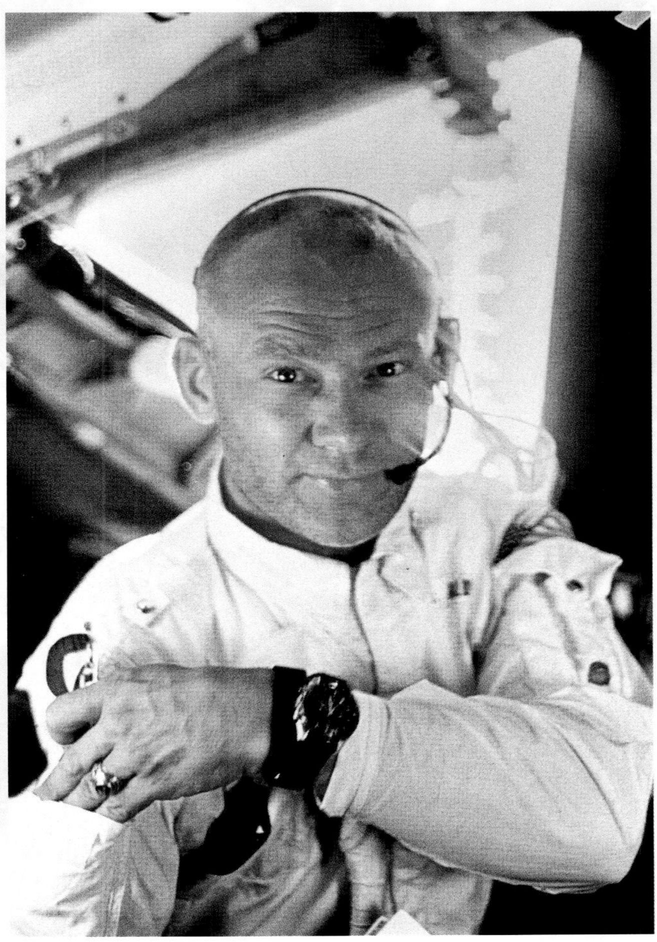

**Above** Buzz Aldrin is seen just prior to the landing attempt inside the Lunar Module. Soon they would make history by stepping onto the moon's surface.

**Opposite** Michael Collins, Command Module Pilot, in good cheer on launch morning for Apollo 11. Note the bulky headgear; large earphones and twin microphones were part ot the inside-helmet wear.

**Left** Wernher von Braun stands in front of his greatest legacy, the Saturn V. This one would carry Apollo 11 to the moon.

# CITIZEN/ ASTRONAUT

Neil Armstrong was not a military man when he came to NASA. Years after having received his wings as a naval aviator, he had begun his space career with the X-15 rocketplane at Edwards Air Force Base in the high desert of California, but flew as an employee of the National Advisory Committee for Aeronautics, NASA's predecessor. He flew the X-15 to 63,093 metres (207,000 feet), theoretically (and by Air Force standards) having been "in space". With this experience, and his calm reactions to emergencies both in his test flight career and the Gemini 8 incident (where his capsule had spun out of control until, against all odds, he was able to arrest the tumble), he was a natural choice to be the first man on the moon.

**Below** Neil Armstrong poses with the X-15. Alone among the moon-bound astronauts he had flown the rocketplane and, notably, was a civilian when recruited by NASA. Nine years after this photo was taken, he would be wearing a similar smile as he posed in the Lunar Module on the moon.

# INSURANCE FOR THE CREW

Just nine days before the flight of Apollo 11, a group of local businessmen were still trying to help NASA figure out life insurance policies for the Apollo crews. Many assume that the astronauts were well-paid for their efforts, but in truth, they were compensated just ike any other federal employee of their pay grade. Benefits like life insurance were comparable as well.

OPTIONAL FORM NO. 10
MAY 1962 EDITION
GSA FPMR (41 CFR) 101-11.6

AD/Hjornevik

UNITED STATES GOVERNMENT

*Memorandum*

TO : AA/Director

DATE: JUL 7 1969

FROM : AP/Public Affairs Officer

SUBJECT: Single-trip insurance for Apollo 11 crew

A group of local insurance men headed by Mr. John E. Smith of the Harlan Insurance Company have approached the Travelers Insurance Company of Hartford, Conneticut, to write a single-trip "travel" policy to cover the men who fly the Apollo 11 mission (prime crew or backup crew). The difficulty in getting insurance in the past apparently has been the inability of the companies to write rates. Travelers, working with the actuaries of several other companies, has settled on a rate of approximately 1 percent. According to representatives of the company, it is presumed that this rate or a lesser rate would be available to astronauts on subsequent flights. Travelers' representatives take the position that this is a first step toward writing rates for space flight.

Specifically, the proposal for the Apollo 11 crew is for Travelers to underwrite a $50,000 policy on each crew member which would cover him against all injuries incurred as the result of the flight from entry into the command module until release from quarantine. Coverage would extend for an additional 100 days for any disease which is "endemic to the lunar surface or its environs." It would not be necessary for the crew to sign policy applications in person. This could be done by Capt. Shepard.

A group of Houston businessmen who are associates of Mr. Smith would like to pay the premium on the policy although this, of course, is at the option of the crew.

The travelers insurance company would like permission, if the policies are accepted, to issue a single press release stating that the policy has been written and describing its conditions. The company states that it will not use the facts surrounding the policy in any form of paid advertising. The press release would be submitted to NASA for review.

Recommendation: In view of the obvious legitimacy of the offer and of the organizations and individuals involved and because of the fact that this offer may lead to the ability of future crews to secure insurance at

INDEXING DATA

| DATE | OPR | # | T | PGM | SUBJECT | SIGNATOR | LOC |
|---|---|---|---|---|---|---|---|
| 07-07-69 | MSC | | M | APO | (Above) | DUFF | 071-51 |

*Buy U.S. Savings Bonds Regularly on the Payroll Savings Plan*

10

2

reasonable rates, I would recommend that it be left to the crew's option whether or not to accept this offer.

Brian M. Duff

Enclosure
Proposed language for policy

cc:
NASA Hqs., Julian Scheer, F
AB/Mr. Trimble
AD/Mr. Hjornevik
AL/Mr. Ould
CA/Mr. Slayton
CB/Mr. Shepard

AP:BMDuff:cd 7/7/69

MOON.37.1181

HARLAN INSURANCE

The class of persons eligible to be insured under the policy includes and is limited to astronauts Neil Armstrong, Edwin Aldrin and Michael Collins, or any substitution for any thereof, comprising the flight crew of Lunar Command Module and its Lunar Landing Module of Lunar Flight Apollo 11.

The term "injuries" as used in this policy, or as used herein, means accidental bodily injuries of an insured person which are the direct and independent cause of the loss for which claim is made and occurred during the course of interplanetary flight or travel while this policy is in force as to such persons hereinafter called such injuries.

Such injuries shall be deemed to be inclusive of the contraction of disease which is endemic to the lunar surface or its environs.

The term "occurring during the course of interplanetary flight or travel" as used herein shall be inclusive of all acts or procedures necessarily performed during the continuance of the flight plan of Lunar Flight Apollo 11, including the entrance into the Command Module preliminary to ignition and takeoff of such Module, recovery therefrom, and the periods of required quarantine in the Lunar Receiving Laboratory.

# CHAPTER FOURTEEN

# THE VOYAGE OF APOLLO 11

IT WAS 16 JULY 1969. NEIL ARMSTRONG, MICHAEL COLLINS AND BUZZ ALDRIN HAD AWOKEN EARLY AND THE SUIT TECHNICIANS HAD SWARMED OVER THEM FOR WHAT SEEMED LIKE HOURS MAKING ENDLESS LAST-MINUTE CHECKS.

The trip from the crew quaters to Pad 39A in the NASA transfer van had been uneventful save for the reporters and well-wishers along the way. Now they were inside the Command Module Columbia, and had been strapped in for a couple of hours. The count was proceeding well, and was in its final moments.

At T-3 minutes before lift-off, the Saturn V was turned over to its internal automatic launch sequencer. At this point, it was under its own control, and would be stopped by the ground only if there was a problem.

"Firing command coming in now. We are on the automatic sequence", droned NASA PR man Jack King, the voice of Apollo Launch Control. If you didn't already know that a history-making voyage was about to begin, you certainly wouldn't have suspected it from King's tone of voice.

"Two-minutes, thirty-seven seconds... we are still go for Apollo 11 at this time", he said.

"T-minus-one minute, thirty-five seconds, for the Apollo mission, the flight to land the first man on the moon... all indications coming in, we are go..." an edge of excitement had crept into his voice.

At T-25 seconds Armstrong told the voice of Launch Control that it "feels good", which was immediately relayed to the listening world.

"T-minus ten, nine... ignition sequence start... six, five, four, three, two, one, zero... all engines running...". The roar began to wash over the crowd, and could be heard for miles.

"Liftoff, we have a liftoff at 32 minutes past the hour!" Apollo 11 thundered into orbit, leaving a dazed but jubilant crowd of onlookers.

**Above** The mission patch design for Apollo 11 proved to be a challenge. NASA knew this flight was one for the history books, and wanted to be sure that nobody would be offended. In the end they placed an olive branch in the eagle's talons.

**Right** Buzz Aldrin, Lunar Module Pilot, waits to be transported to the Saturn V which would carry Apollo 11 to the moon.

It was 9:32 am East Coast Time. King pushed back from his desk now that control and announcing had turned over to Houston. The excitement was now finally visible in his face.

The rocket picked up speed, leaving tremendous holes in the low-lying clouds that were haunting the Cape that morning. Soon, the S1C stage had burned through its 2,008,994 kilograms (4,429,000 pounds) of fuel and was dropped. The SII stage took over seamlessly.

By the time they reached the end of the S1VB stage, they were in Earth orbit and all had gone just as it had in the simulations. Two-and-a-half hours later, they programmed the Trans-Lunar Injection (TLI) burn into the computer, and punched "Proceed". The SIVB kicked into action, and they broke out of Earth orbit.

Half-an-hour later, Mike Collins took the controls of the Command Module. He separated from the now-inert SIVB and flew forwards, made a tidy 180 degree turn and then slowly, ever so slowly, edged closer to the

**Below** Apollo 11 departs amid flame and fury. The crew of three left Earth with the first Lunar Module, LM-5, that was light enough to accomplish a landing on the moon.

## THE VOICE OF LAUNCH CONTROL

When he arrived at the Kennedy Space Center firing room at 2:00 am on 16 July 1969, Jack King knew this was not just another flight. Although he had been the "Voice of Launch Control" for the Gemini flights, and for the few Apollos that had gone before, this was the most significant: a landing on the moon. It was a PR man's dream. Busy the weeks before with the 2,700 reporters, journalists and VIPs coming to the launch, he was running on adrenaline. But as he always did, he lent a voice to Apollo that was both authoritative and soothing, and when the narration switched to Houston it was always a disappointment for millions. As he put it, "Our policy was to report what was happening in real-time, without embellishment", (*Jack King, as quoted by Kay Grinter, in "Center employees saw Eagle crew launch to history" in Spaceport News, 16 July 2004*). This he did with expert proficiency.

**Above** Expectant controllers look out of the huge blast-proof windows (to right) of the launch control facility at the Kennedy Space Center during the launch of Apollo 11.

## APOLLO 11 LAUNCH

**Below** 16 July 1969: Apollo 11 blasts off from the Kennedy Space Centre in Florida, seen here in an appropriately patriotic photo. The ovoid plume at the centre of the rocket is from the liquefied fuels boiling off from the second stage.

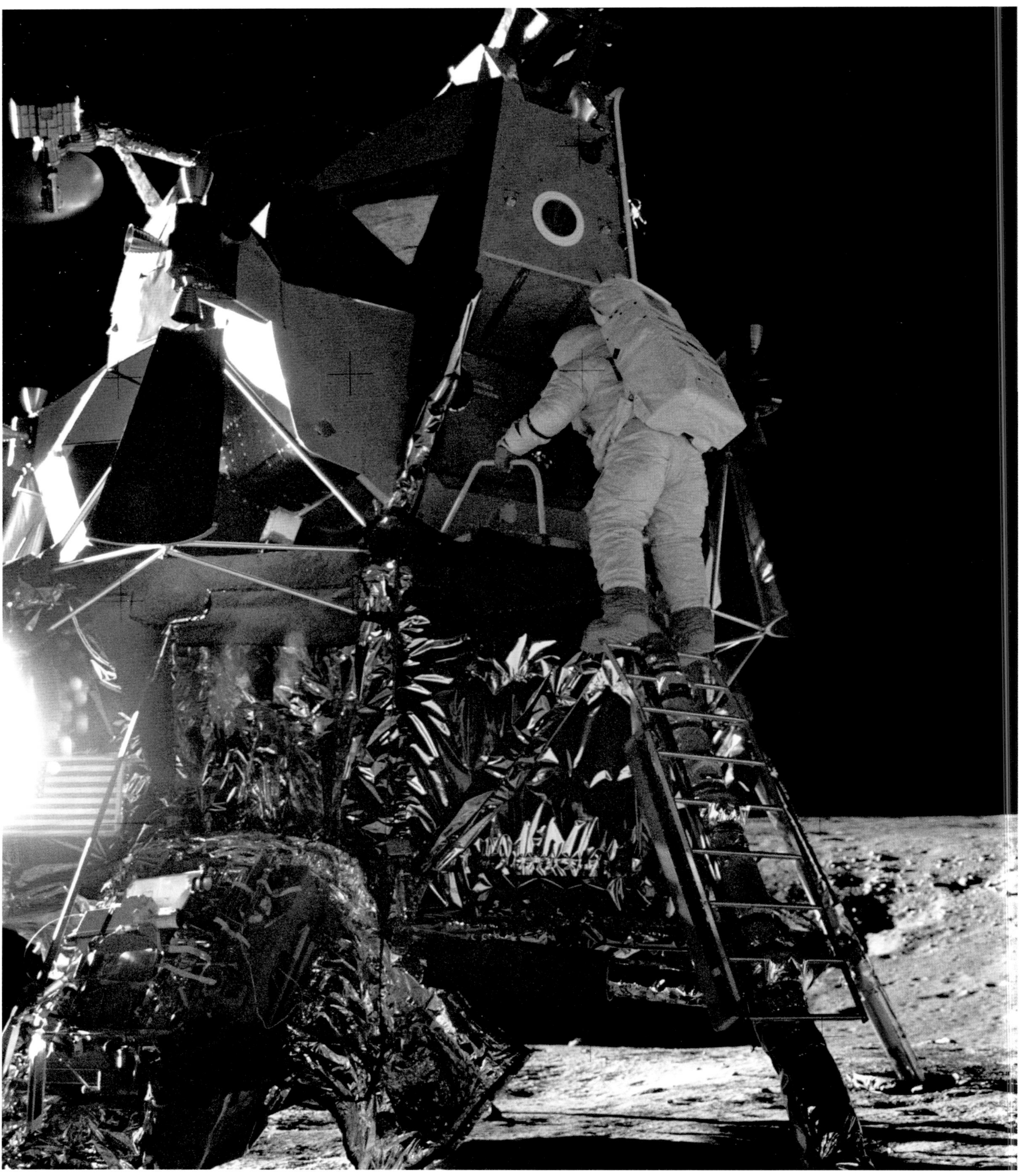

## A SINKING FEELING

For years the argument raged: what would the fate of the first craft and crew to land on the moon be? At least one scientist thought they would sink deep into moon dust and never be heard from again. Thomas Gold, a Vienna-born scientist who settled at Cornell University, first predicted that there would be a layer of dust on the lunar surface, which turned out to be correct. He later theorized that this layer could be up to four metres (12 feet) thick, or more and could pose dangers to the astronauts. In this case he was, fortunately, incorrect. Gold often bucked the system, but he claimed it brought him little joy. "I didn't enjoy my role as a heretic" (press release issued by Cornell University, 22 June 2004), he once said.

**Opposite** By the time Alan Bean climbed onto the lunar surface during Apollo 12, fears about sinking into moon dust had been laid to rest.

trailing booster. Inside the top of the SIVB was the Lunar Module Eagle, waiting to be picked up and pulled along. Collins nudged the thrusters deftly, making minute corrections to his trajectory.

Looking through a glass reticule, or eyepiece, he stared intently at the docking target on the top of the Lunar Module, which was marked with a small metal "X" over a white disk. It got larger and larger, seemed to be veering to one side for a moment, then there was a scraping sound.

The probe on the front of the Command Module slid into the guide on the Lunar Module. The welcome sound of docking latches clicking into place was heard, then Collins reversed the thrust of the vehicle to extract the Lunar Module.

Flying in tandem, the remaining elements of the Apollo 11 rocket sped off, with the Lunar Module in tow, into a hole in space where the moon would be, or at least ought to be, in about three days.

**Below** The view from the Command Module Pilot's seat: the Lunar Module nestled inside the SIVB stage, awaiting docking and extraction. Great care was required in docking so as not to damage the Lunar Module.

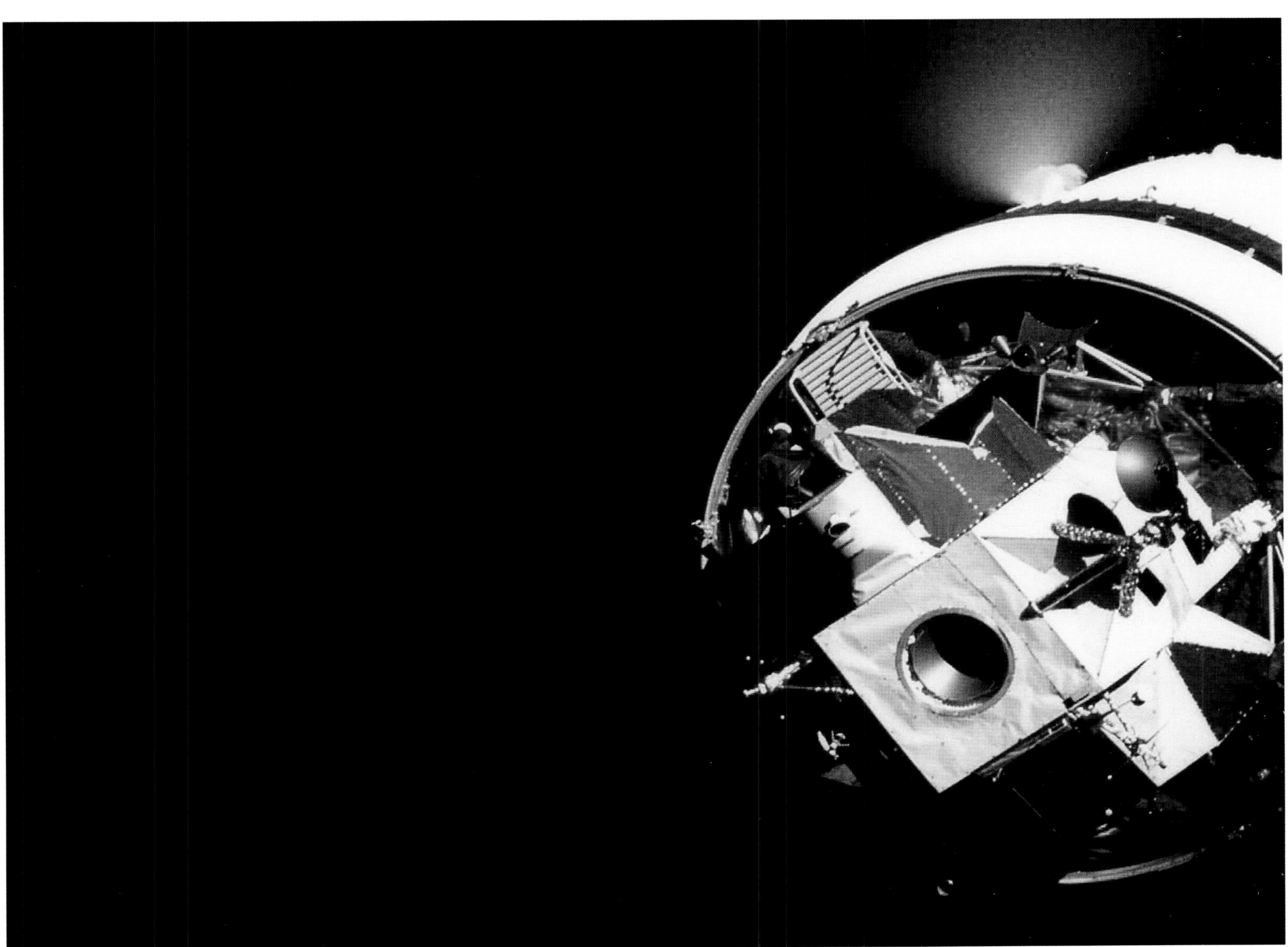

# CHAPTER FIFTEEN

## "CONTACT LIGHT!"

THEY HAD BEEN IN LUNAR ORBIT LONG ENOUGH TO CHECK OUT THE SYSTEMS OF BOTH CRAFT AND PRONOUNCE THEM HEALTHY FOR POWERED DESCENT INITIATION (PDI), WHICH WOULD SEND THE LUNAR MODULE TO THE SURFACE OF THE MOON.

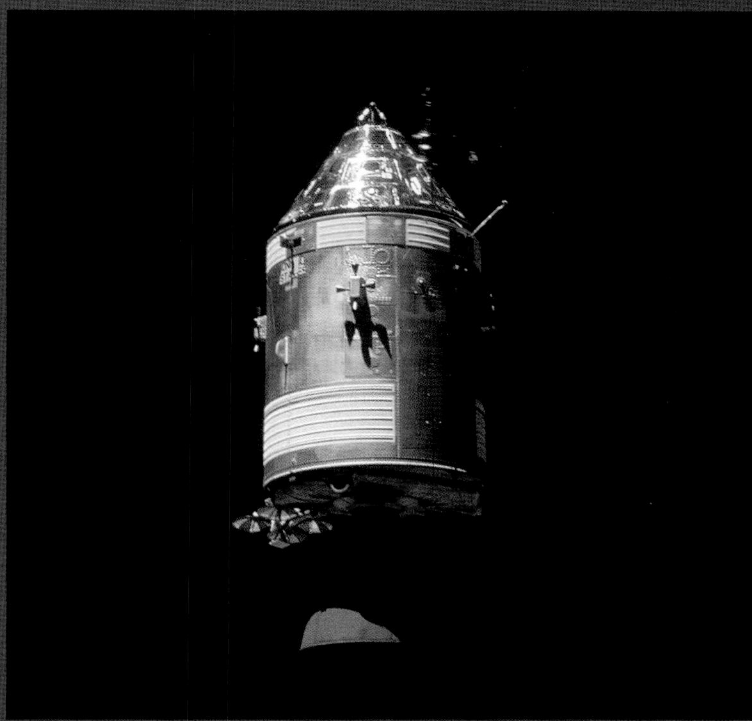

There was a "clunk" as the springs on the nose of Columbia pushed the Lunar Module away. They were now flying as two separate spacecraft. Collins fired the thrusters to adjust his position as Armstrong rotated Eagle in front of the Command Module windows to give his Command Module pilot Collins a good look at the landing craft. After Collins had confirmed that he was happy with the Lunar Module he bade them goodbye. "You guys take care..." he said, to which Armstrong replied, with economy, "See you later". (*Carrying the Fire: An Astronaut's Journey*, Michael Collins, 1983).

With the OK from Houston, Armstrong keyed the PDI sequence into the Lunar Module's computer and the engine fired, slowing them enough to allow them to fall out of lunar orbit. They were at 15,240 metres (50,000 feet); by the time they reached 14,021 metres (46,000 feet) their troubles began.

"Program alarm!" Armstrong called. This was followed by Aldrin relaying that it was a 1202 alarm. Blanched faces at Mission Control looked at each other – what was a 1202 alarm?

**Left** The Command/Service Module Columbia as seen from the Lunar Module Eagle, Apollo 11.

## THE LONELIEST MAN IN SPACE

It was probably the second most-asked question Mike Collins heard. The first was, "What's it like to go to the moon?" The second was, "Weren't you scared/lonely/nervous/worried/etc. when you were behind the moon and out of touch?" He answered this question in a journal-like fashion after the flight: "I am alone now, truly alone, and isolated from any known life. I am it. If a count were taken, it would be three-billion plus two on the other side of the moon and one plus god-only-knows-what on this side. I like the feeling". (*Carrying the Fire: An Astronaut's Journey*, Michael Collins, 1983).

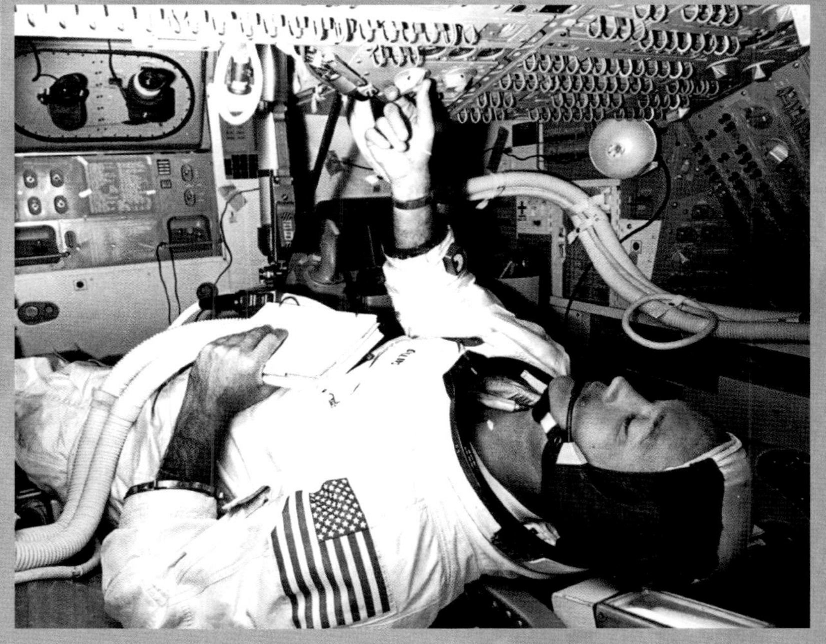

**Right** Mike Collins, seen here in the Command Module simulator. Note the small metal hoops near the hundreds of switches on the control panel; these were intended to avoid accidental switch-throws via bumping.

Within seconds, however, one of the controllers informed Flight Director Gene Kranz that they were still "Go" for landing. Kranz trusted his controllers enough not to ask why, and the descent continued.

Then, as Eagle descended past 1,524 metres (5,000 feet), the word came down again, this time a 1201 alarm. What were these computer error messages? Only one man, a controller named Steve Bales, seemed to understand what was happening. "We're still go… " he said.

The problem, he had realized, was that the computer was overloaded, it was receiving too much information. A mistake in the checklist had allowed the crew of Eagle to leave the rendezvous radar on, and since, at the same time, the landing radar was sending information to the computer, it simply had too much to do. The result was that it was abandoning some of the data and starting again.

Now another problem presented itself in a dramatic fashion to the crew of the Lunar Module. Below them, right where the computer was taking them, was a field of boulders, some of them the size of large cars. Armstrong took over control from the computer and began to hover horizontally, searching for a smooth place to set down. He was cool, as always, but both he and Aldrin knew that there was not much fuel to spare. If they could not land in the next few minutes, they would have to abandon the descent stage and light up the ascent engine, aborting the attempt. If they got too low, they would not even be able to do that, and they would simply crash, a crumpled ball of thin metal foil and two dead humans.

Meanwhile, Aldrin, whose eyes were glued to the computer and the attitude gauges, didn't have time to steal even a glance out of the windows. He was too busy providing a running narrative of data to Armstrong and the ground.

"Three-hundred feet, down three and a half, forty-seven forward…" Aldrin said. "How's our fuel?" responded Armstrong. "Eight per cent…" came the reply, displaying no emotion, just reporting the facts.

"Two-hundred twenty feet, thirteen forward… eleven forward, coming down nicely". It was silent in Mission Control as Aldrin's numbers came in.

"Sixty feet, down two and a half, two forward."

Soon the call came up from 386,160 kilometres (240,000 miles) away, "60 seconds…". It was Charlie Duke, Capsule Communicator (Capcom) and fellow Apollo astronaut, warning them that there was just one minute of fuel left before a mandatory abort. Armstrong scanned the surface, desperation gnawing at the corners of his consciousness.

Dust was starting to billow below the Lunar Module, as the descent engine's plume hit the surface. "Thirty seconds…" said Duke in a forced test-pilot drone.

**"You cats take it easy on the surface; if I hear you huffing and puffing I'm going to start bitching at you", Collins said as he prepared to undock Columbia from Eagle**

*Carrying the Fire: An Astronaut's Journey*, Michael Collins, 1983.

**Opposite** After separation and before PDI, Eagle rotates slowly in front of Columbia so that Collins can get a good look and pronounce it healthy. Of particular interest were the landing legs: they needed to be fully extended and locked, or the landing could be a disaster.

**Left** The view outside the Lunar Module Eagle, taken right after landing. Though a dull area with respect to geology, it was reletively flat and safe for a landing. For this first mission, that was good enough.

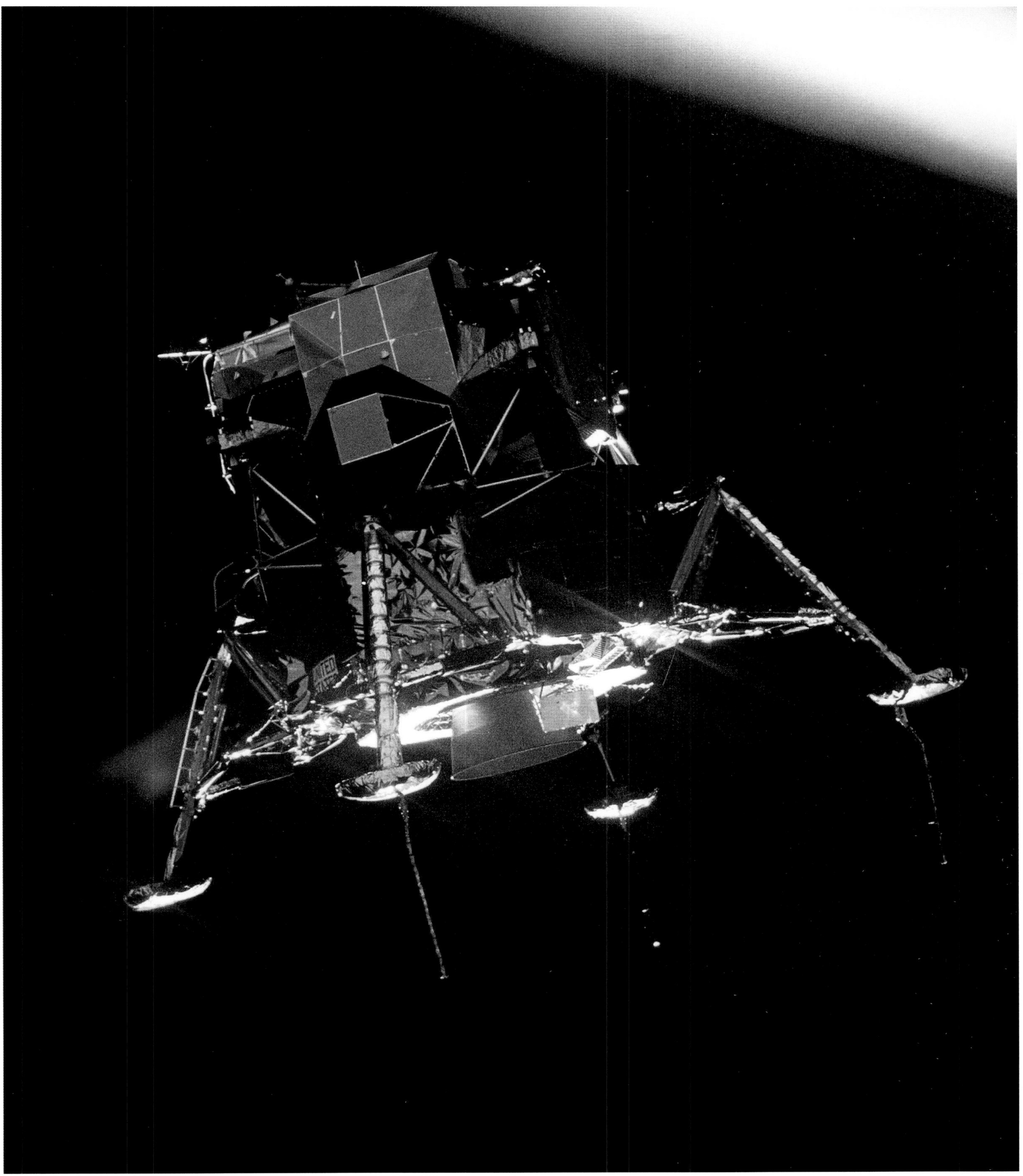

# THE APOLLO 11 DESCENT MAP

The Apollo 11 descent map was comprised of a mosaic of lunar orbital photos. It showed the best view NASA could generate of the landing zone for Armstrong's descent. The solid line represents an optimum trajectory. The map reads right to left, with the convergence near *Moltke* and *Sabine B* craters representing the intended landing site in Mare Tranquillitatis, or the Sea of Tranquility.

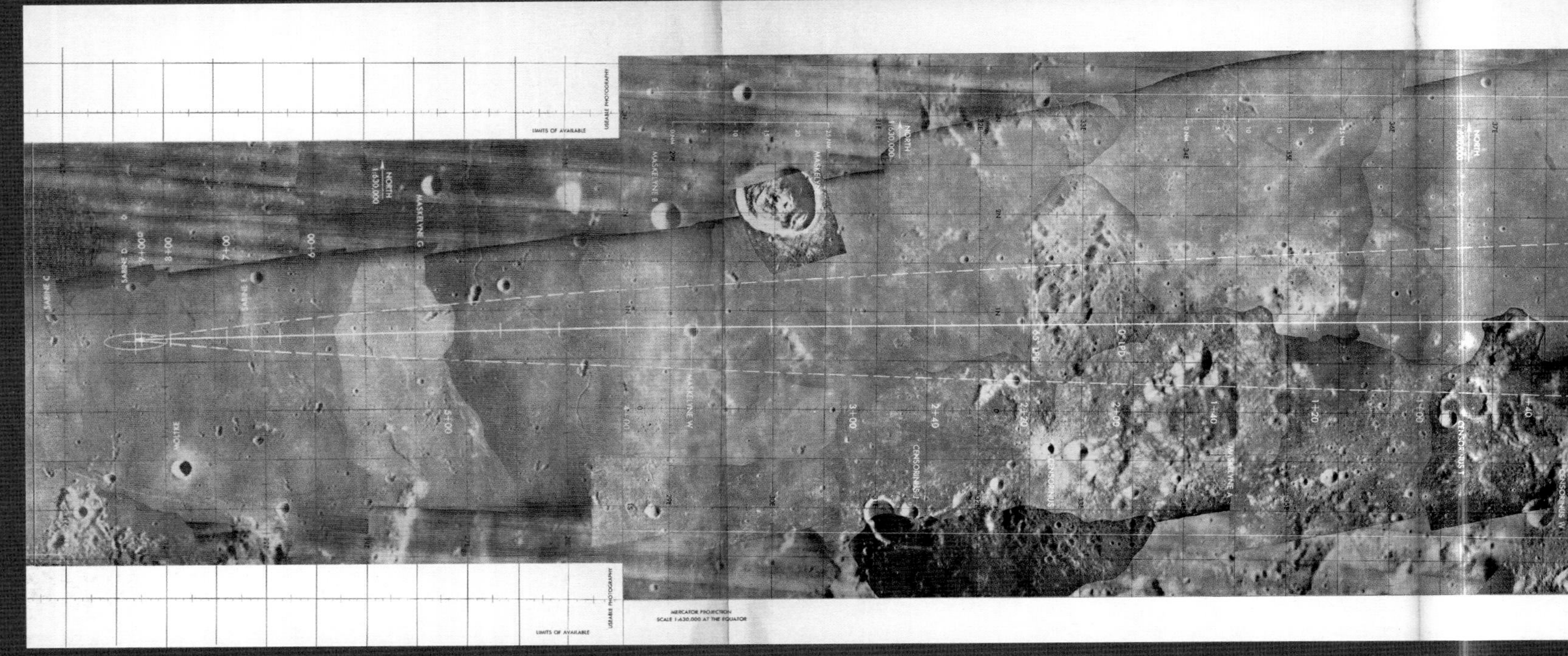

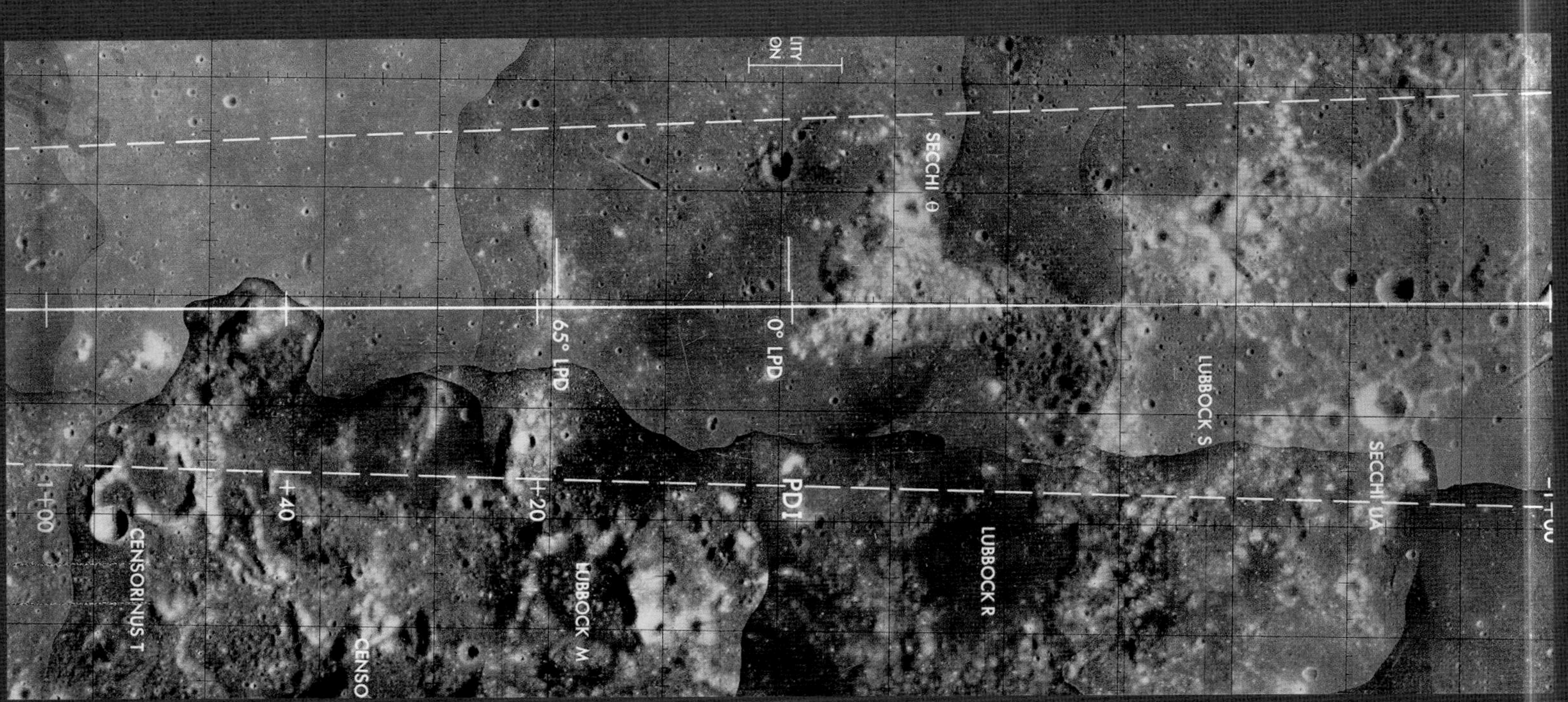

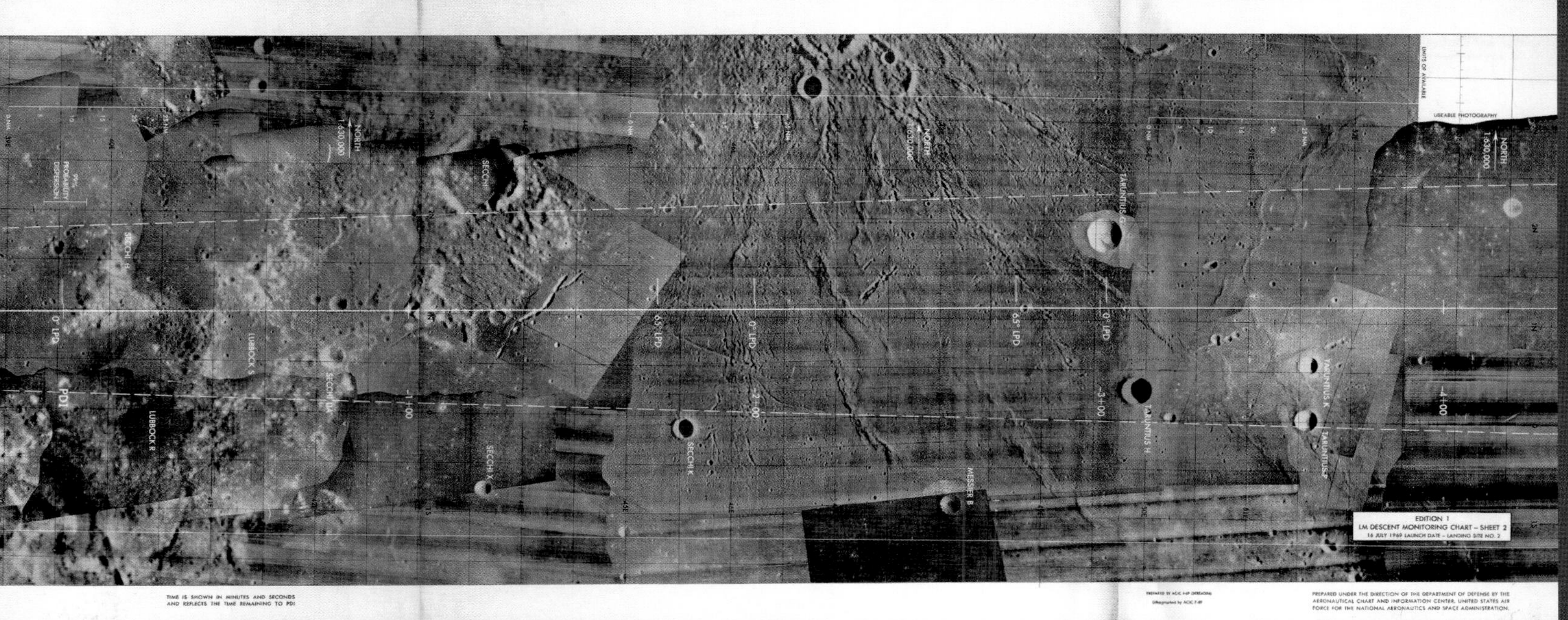
EDITION 1
LM DESCENT MONITORING CHART – SHEET 2
16 JULY 1969 LAUNCH DATE – LANDING SITE NO. 2
TIME IS SHOWN IN MINUTES AND SECONDS AND REFLECTS THE TIME REMAINING TO PDI
PREPARED UNDER THE DIRECTION OF THE DEPARTMENT OF DEFENSE BY THE AERONAUTICAL CHART AND INFORMATION CENTER, UNITED STATES AIR FORCE FOR THE NATIONAL AERONAUTICS AND SPACE ADMINISTRATION.

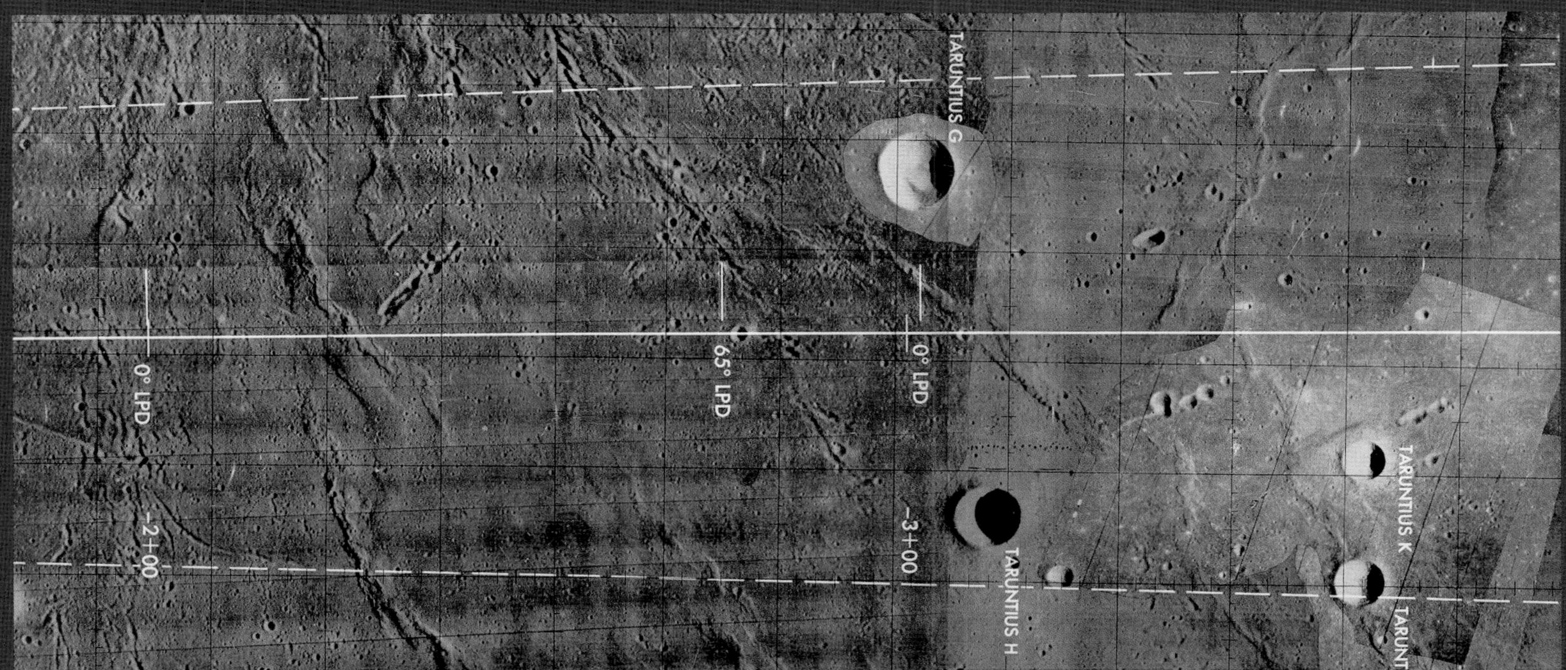
TARUNTIUS G
0° LPD
65° LPD
0° LPD
-2+00
-3+00
TARUNTIUS H
TARUNTIUS K

# LUNAR MODULE EAGLE

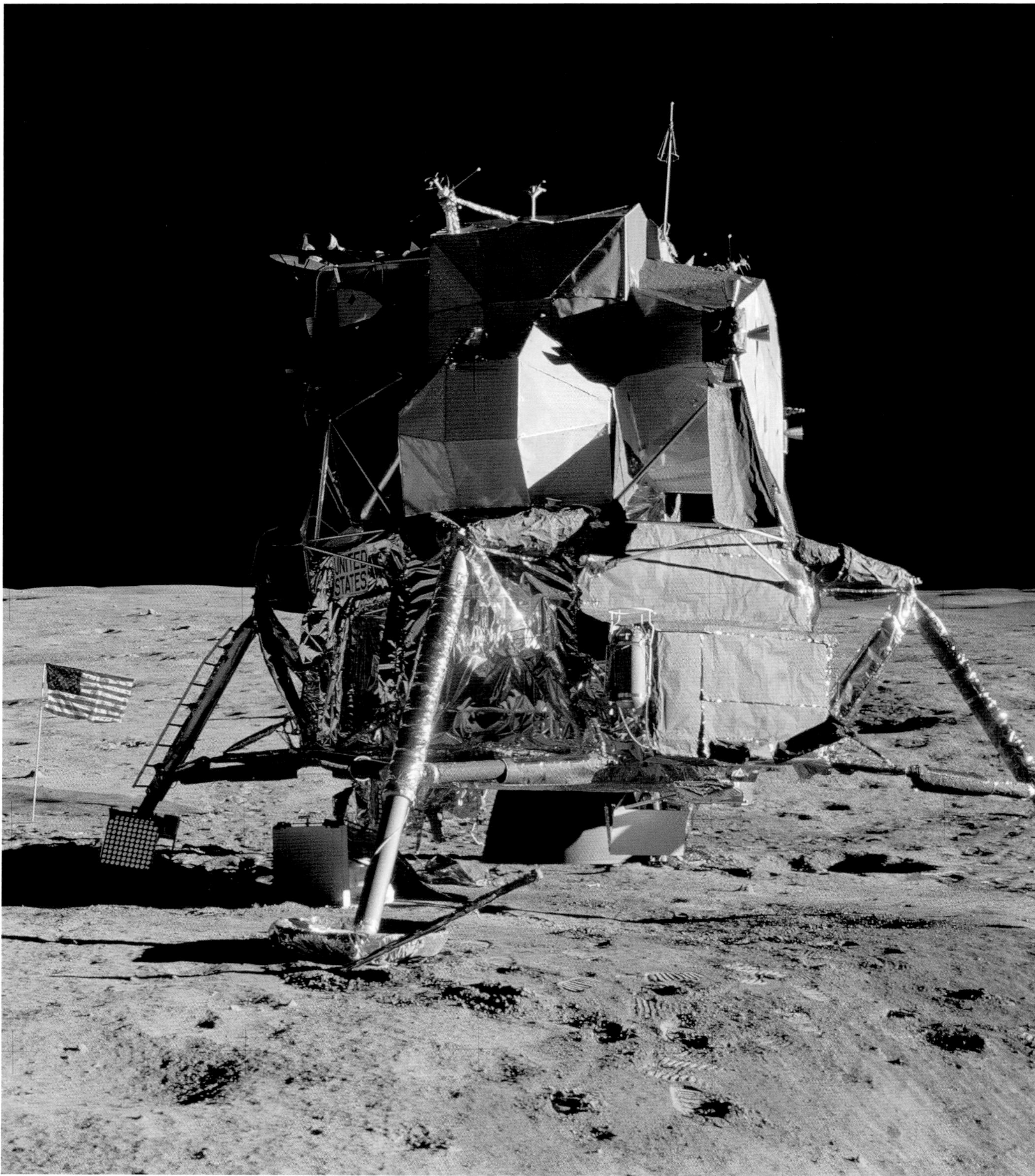

## FUEL PLUG

Shortly after landing, one of the consoles at Mission Control began to display an odd reading. Pressure was building up in one of the fuel lines in the Lunar Module's bottom, or descent stage. If this continued unabated the pipe could could rupture, and the descent stage could potentially even explode. Houston informed the crew, but before anyone could worry much, the latent heat in the descent engine melted the ice out of the fuel line, the pressure dropped and all was well. It was "GO" for the moonwalk.

**Opposite & Below** Seen here is the Apollo 14 descent stage of the Lunar Module, visually similar to Apollo 11's. which harboured the potentially dangerous fuel plug.

Then, before anyone had a chance truly to panic on the ground, welcome words tumbled out of the speakers. It was Aldrin... "Contact light", he said plainly. This meant that one of the Lunar Module's legs had touched luna firma. Armstrong cut the engine, and with a light "thump" Eagle settled onto the surface of the moon. The stillness of four billion years was broken.

After a stunned moment, Armstrong and Aldrin clasped hands, genuine warmth crossing the faces of both men. Armstrong keyed his mike.

"Houston, Tranquility Base here... the Eagle had landed."

Jubilation erupted in the normally stoic Mission Control. Gene Kranz later admitted that he looked down into his palm and realized that, unnoticed, he had snapped his pencil in two.

"We copy you down, Eagle", said Charlie Duke. "You got a bunch of guys down here about to turn blue... we're breathing again, thanks a lot!"

Around the world, 600 million people watching the landing on television or listening to it on the radio, cheered as one. Apollo 11 had achieved the impossible – man was on the moon.

## APOLLO 11 LANDING

**Below** The flags, cigars and cheers break the sanctity of Mission Control, Houston, when Apollo 11 lands. In the centre is Chris Kraft, Director of Flight Operations.

# MAGNIFICENT DESOLATION

ABOUT SIX-AND-A-HALF HOURS AFTER LANDING, NEIL ARMSTRONG WAS STEPS AWAY FROM BEING THE FIRST MAN TO SET FOOT ON ANOTHER WORLD. HE TOOK HIS TIME GOING DOWN THE LADDER, THEN STOOD IN THE LARGE BOWL OF THE FOOTPAD.

He turned to look out at the brightly lit moon beyond the shadow of the Lunar Module. "I'm going to step off the LM now..." he said simply. His boot made contact with the dusty surface. "That's one small step for man, one giant leap for mankind". It was one of the most debated quotes of the twentieth century, for Armstrong had intended to say, and thought he did, in fact, say, "One giant leap for *a* man..." but either he missed the word or the radio transmission dropped out at that moment. Nobody is sure, though close examination has led most to conclude that he fluffed his line.

Once on the moon, Armstrong confirmed the safety of their stay, checking the positioning of the Lunar Module's landing pads and his ability to climb back up the ladder for eventual departure. He hastily grabbed a handful of dirt and gravel with his scooper for the so-called "contingency sample", which was a random bit of soil to be pocketed for analysis just in case they had to depart right away following an emergency.

As it turned out, however, all was well. The mission and men were safe and, within half-an-hour, Aldrin joined Armstrong on the moon. Their conversation went like this:

**ALDRIN:** Beautiful view.
**ARMSTRONG:** Isn't that something? Magnificent sight out here.
*[Thoughtful pause]*
**ALDRIN:** Magnificent desolation.

**Below** Edwin "Buzz" Aldrin in one of the most famous photographs of the modern age of exploration.

ONE GIANT LEAP

## WHERE IS NEIL?

During the entire two-and-a-half hour moonwalk of the Apollo 11 mission, Buzz Aldrin didn't take a single picture of his partner, Neil Armstrong. It was the only moonwalk on which this occurred, and the reason has never been explained. Some have hypothesized that Aldrin may have been bitter over the decision for him to be second onto the moon's surface, but given his dedication and professionalism, this seems very unlikely.

**Right** Though there are no photographs of Armstrong on the surface of the moon during the EVA, Aldrin snapped this image of his partner once they returned, tired but elated, to the Lunar Module.

From a man who was far from a poet came the words that, more than any other, would define the nature of the moon post-Apollo.

Then the two moonwalkers, history's first, went to work. They had less than two hours left together on the lunar surface, and there was much to do. An American flag was erected, just barely standing in the thin soil. Next, with the clock urgently ticking, Houston informed them that President Richard Nixon was "on the line", waiting to congratulate them. Aldrin was taken by surprise, apparently Armstrong had forgotten to tell him about the call. There were some perfunctory remarks, congratulations all round and an invitation to dinner at the White House.

Then they got back to work. There was the EASEP to set up. This stood for Early Apollo Scientific Experiments Package, and would be the only one of its kind on the moon (later versions were called ALSEP, the "A" being for "advanced", with different instrumentation). The whole package had to be carefully sited on flat ground and set up with critical precision. Careful as they were, by the time they had finished the once-pristine equipment was a dark grey, as were their suits, from the fine dust that coated everything.

A detailed assessment of the condition of the Lunar Module was carried out, as was some documented rock and soil sampling, and then all too soon it was time to go back inside. Within the hour both men were back inside the Lunar Module, tired but elated, with the hatch closed and the cabin pressurized. It had been a long day – they had left orbit almost 11 hours ago and had been on the lunar surface for two-and-a-half hours.

After a short and very uncomfortable period of sleep – the Lunar Module was a noisy little place, with motors whirring and coolants gurgling – it was time to get ready to go. The two men went through the checklist carefully, then when Houston gave them the OK, they punched the ascent activation code into the guidance computer. It flashed a green symbol at them – "99" – which was the Apollo Guidance Computer's (AGC) way of asking "Are you sure you want to do this?" Armstrong hit the "PROCEED" button. After a short count, the explosive bolts connecting the ascent stage to the descent stage blew, the blade housed below them cut through the fat bundle of connecting wire and the two small valves in the ascent engine spun open, allowing the ascent stage to take off.

**Opposite** Buzz Aldrin carries components of the EASEP, the experimental package the Apollo 11 crew left on the moon's surface.

**Left** Buzz Aldrin's footprint. He was fascinated by the motion of the moon's dust particles as they sped away from his boot, and the cohesiveness of the bootprint.

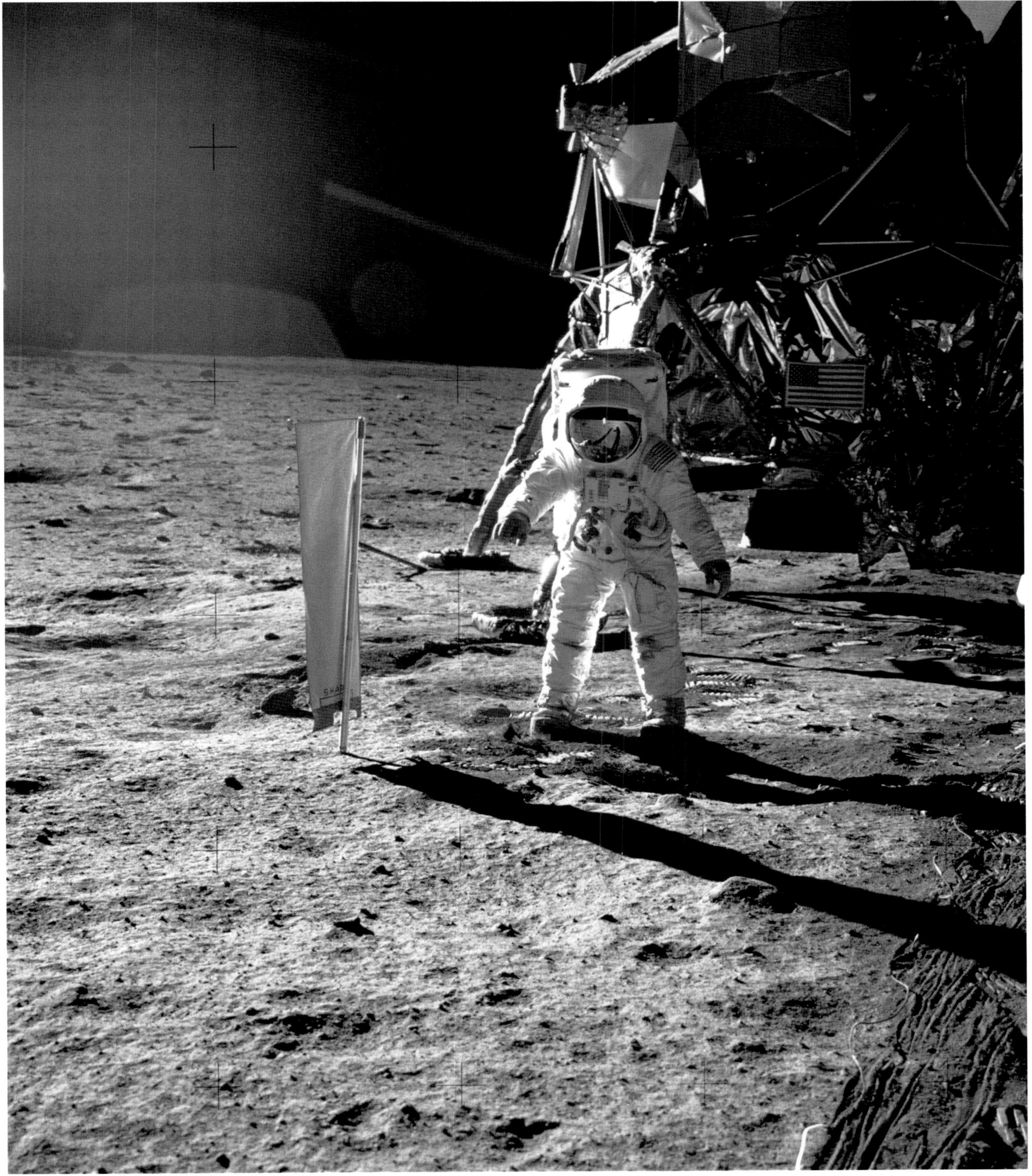

The Lunar Module upper stage ascended in a wobbly trajectory as the consumption of fuels, each of a different mass, continually changed the balance of the ship. Soon it smoothed out and they were in orbit. Within hours they had docked, transferred almost 23 kilograms (50 pounds) of moon rocks and surface core samples, camera magazines and other gear to the Command Module, cut Eagle loose, and Collins had fired the SPS engine to break them out of lunar orbit and speed them home.

At last Mike Collins, only the second man to be totally alone beyond Earth orbit (the first being John Young on Apollo 10) and the first to sweat out the question of whether or not the ascent engine would strand his crewmates on the moon forever, could relax. He hadn't told them, but he had placed the odds of their success at about 50–50. Now he knew that the story ended happily.

Before they knew it they were home. Ticker-tape parades and a world tour followed, and all three crewmen retired from active spaceflight. They had, however, accomplished their mission with distinction, and the world would be forever changed. Man had walked on the moon.

Above Mission Control, jubilant for a second time during the mission of Apollo 11. The crew had splashed down and were on their way back to Hawaii.

## CUSTOMS

In spite of their unusual journey, when the crew of Apollo 11 transited through Hawaii on their way back to the US they had to make a declaration at Customs. They had been out of the US after all, so they had to fill out the forms dutifully. It seemed odd, almost silly, but rules were rules and they complied gladly, happy simply to be going home. Their acquisitions? "MOON ROCK AND MOON DUST, SAMPLES", which were all duty-free.

**GENERAL DECLARATION**

**(Outward/Inward)**

AGRICULTURE, CUSTOMS, IMMIGRATION, AND PUBLIC HEALTH

Owner or Operator NATIONAL AERONAUTICS AND SPACE ADMINISTRATION

Marks of Nationality and Registration U.S.A. Flight No. APOLLO 11 Date JULY 24, 1969

Departure from MOON (Place and Country) Arrival at HONOLULU, HAWAII, U.S.A. (Place and Country)

**FLIGHT ROUTING**

("Place" Column always to list origin, every en-route stop and destination)

| PLACE | TOTAL NUMBER OF CREW | NUMBER OF PASSENGERS ON THIS STAGE | CARGO |
|---|---|---|---|
| CAPE KENNEDY | COMMANDER NEIL A. ARMSTRONG | | |
| MOON | | Departure Place: Embarking NIL; Through on same flight NIL | MOON ROCK AND MOON DUST SAMPLES Cargo Manifests Attached |
| JULY 24, 1969 HONOLULU | COLONEL EDWIN E. ALDRIN, JR. | Arrival Place: Disembarking NIL; Through on same flight NIL | |
| | LT. COLONEL MICHAEL COLLINS | | |

**Declaration of Health**

Persons on board known to be suffering from illness other than airsickness or the effects of accidents, as well as those cases of illness disembarked during the flight:

NONE

Any other condition on board which may lead to the spread of disease:

TO BE DETERMINED

Details of each disinsecting or sanitary treatment (place, date, time, method) during the flight. If no disinsecting has been carried out during the flight give details of most recent disinsecting:

Signed, if required ........ Crew Member Concerned

For official use only

HONOLULU AIRPORT
Honolulu, Hawaii
ENTERED

Customs Inspector

I declare that all statements and particulars contained in this General Declaration, and in any supplementary forms required to be presented with this General Declaration are complete, exact and true to the best of my knowledge and that all through passengers will continue/have continued on the flight.

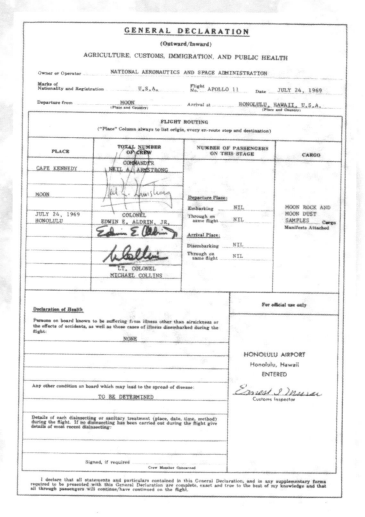

Above The customs declaration form filled out by the crew of Apollo 11.

# THE APOLLO 11 MISSION REPORT

The Apollo 11 Mission Report was released in November 1969, three months after the triumphant first landing. Overall, the flight was rated as "excellent."

NATIONAL AERONAUTICS AND SPACE ADMINISTRATION

APOLLO 11

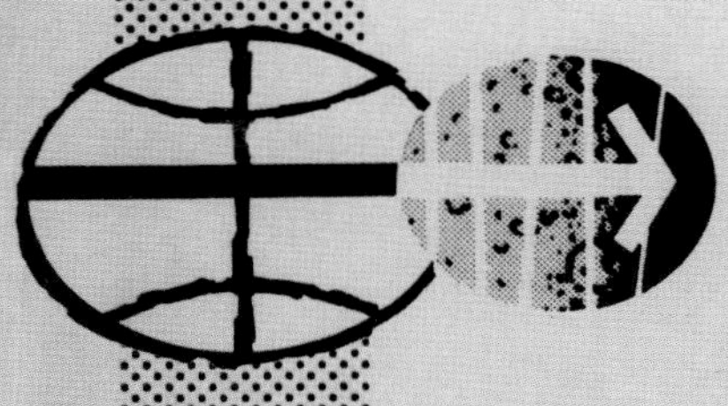

MANNED SPACECRAFT CENTER HOUSTON, TEXAS

# 3.0 MISSION DESCRIPTION

The Apollo 11 mission accomplished the basic mission of the Apollo Program; that is, to land two men on the lunar surface and return them safely to earth. As a part of this first lunar landing, three basic experiment packages were deployed, lunar material samples were collected, and surface photographs were taken. Two of the experiments were a part of the early Apollo scientific experiment package which was developed for deployment on the lunar surface. The sequence of events and the flight plan of the Apollo 11 mission are shown in table 3-I and figure 3-1, respectively.

The Apollo 11 space vehicle was launched on July 16, 1969, at 8:32 a.m. e.s.t., as planned. The spacecraft and S-IVB were inserted into a 100.7- by 99.2-mile earth parking orbit. After a 2-1/2-hour checkout period, the spacecraft/S-IVB combination was injected into the translunar phase of the mission. Trajectory parameters after the translunar injection firing were nearly perfect, with the velocity within 1.6 ft/sec of that planned. Only one of the four options for midcourse corrections during the translunar phase was exercised. This correction was made with the service propulsion system at approximately 26-1/2 hours and provided a 20.9 ft/sec velocity change. During the remaining periods of free-attitude flight, passive thermal control was used to maintain spacecraft temperatures within desired limits. The Commander and Lunar Module Pilot transferred to the lunar module during the translunar phase to make an initial inspection and preparations for systems checks shortly after lunar orbit insertion.

The spacecraft was inserted into a 60- by 169.7-mile lunar orbit at approximately 76 hours. Four hours later, the lunar orbit circularization maneuver was performed to place the spacecraft in a 65.7- by 53.8-mile orbit. The Lunar Module Pilot entered the lunar module at about 81 hours for initial power-up and systems checks. After the planned sleep period was completed at 93-1/2 hours, the crew donned their suits, transferred to the lunar module, and made final preparations for descent to the lunar surface. The lunar module was undocked on time at about 100 hours. After the exterior of the lunar module was inspected by the Command Module Pilot, a separation maneuver was performed with the service module reaction control system.

The descent orbit insertion maneuver was performed with the descent propulsion system at 101-1/2 hours. Trajectory parameters following this maneuver were as planned, and the powered descent initiation was on time at 102-1/2 hours. The maneuver lasted approximately 12 minutes, with engine shutdown occurring almost simultaneously with the lunar landing in the Sea of Tranquillity. The coordinates of the actual landing point

A-12

NASA-S-69-3797

Figure A-1.- Extravehicular mobility unit.

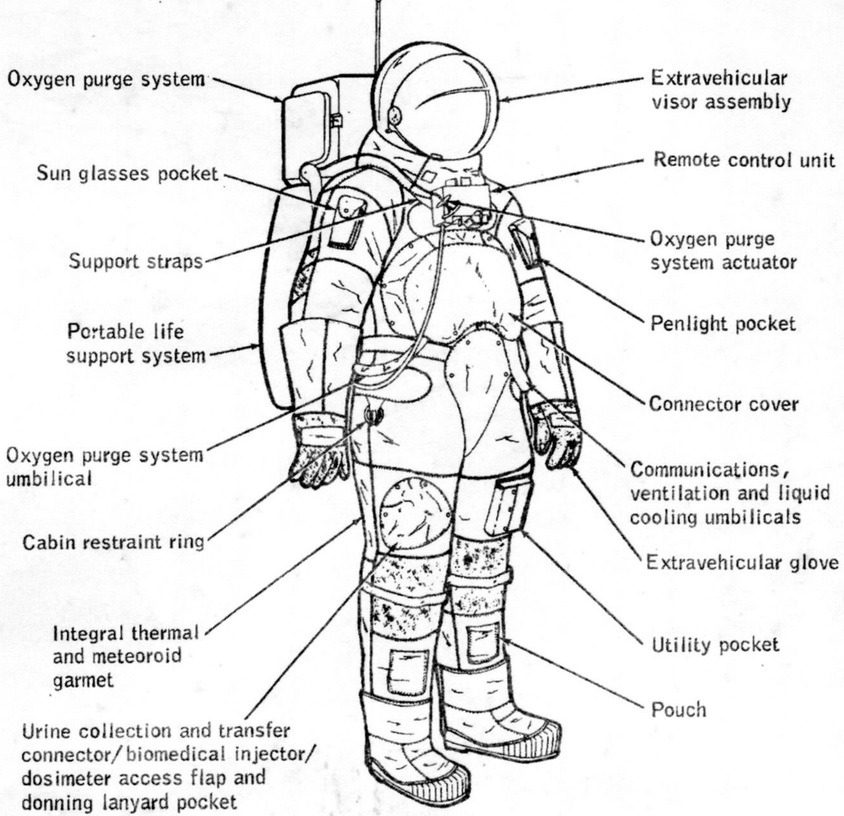


After reaching the Manned Spacecraft Center, the spacecraft, crew, and samples entered the Lunar Receiving Laboratory quarantine area for continuation of the postlanding observation and analyses. The crew and spacecraft were released from quarantine on August 10, 1969, after no evidence of abnormal medical reactions was observed.

# CHAPTER SEVENTEEN

# LAUGHS FROM LUNA: APOLLO 12

THE CREW OF APOLLO 12 WAS DIFFERENT FROM THE REST. CHARLES "PETE" CONRAD, MISSION COMMANDER; ALAN BEAN, LUNAR MODULE PILOT AND DICK GORDON, COMMAND MODULE PILOT, WERE THE BEST OF FRIENDS AND GENUINELY LOVED ONE ANOTHER.

It was Conrad who instinctively forged the bond. Together, these three men would thoroughly enjoy themselves throughout their entire mission.

During the launch on 14 November 1969 the only major emergency of the mission occurred. About 36 seconds after liftoff a muffled crash was heard inside the Command Module and suddenly dozens of warning lights came on. Nobody had seen this before, not even in the nastiest simulations. It was a technician on the ground named John Aaron who, with the help of Bean, recognized and solved the problem. They had been struck by lightning, twice, but the Command Module didn't seem to have suffered any damage and, true to form, the crew were chuckling about it within the hour.

After a leisurely cruise to the moon, Conrad and Bean climbed into the Lunar Module, and, following in the footsteps of Apollo 11, began their descent towards the lunar surface.

Conrad took over manual control of the Lunar Module during the last few hundred metres of the landing, just as Armstrong had done. But Armstrong had overflown his landing site, and Conrad was going to make a pinpoint landing if it killed him – and in space that sort of determination really could kill in the hands of a lesser man. As soon as they set down, however, he knew he had done it. For, just before they landed, he and Bean both saw it: Surveyor 3, launched some three years earlier, lay silently nearby. Part of their mission, if feasible, was to find Surveyor, then cut some pieces off and return them to Earth for study.

First, however, Conrad had to step out onto the moon, and he had something special planned.

Everyone wondered who wrote the scripts for the astronauts, and after Armstrong's immortal words on Apollo 11 there was an air of expectation about the first words of the second Mission Commander on the moon.

**Left** The Apollo 12 mission patch depicted a Yankee clipper, a nineteenth century American cargo vessel. Fast and agile, Mission Commander Pete Conrad felt that the image was a good representation of his Command/Service Module, also named "Yankee Clipper".

**Above** The "Three Amigos" of Apollo 12, from left: Charles "Pete" Conrad, Mission Commander; Dick Gordon, Command Module Pilot and Alan Bean, Lunar Module Pilot. They were the tightest crew in the Apollo programme, and would remain close friends for life.

## QUARANTINE!

While NASA privately scoffed at the idea, a percentage of the public was scared of moon germs causing some pandemic on Earth, so NASA quarantined the early lunar mission crews (Apollos 11, 12 and 14) for almost three weeks each. Upon leaving the capsule at splashdown, the crew were put in rubber bio-garments and sealed into an airtight trailer. After Apollo 14, with no reports of contamination, the practice was discontinued. They did, however, find germs on the Surveyor 3 camera they brought back during Apollo 12, but these were earthly organisms, Streptococcus mitis, which had survived the trip to the moon, a three-year stay and the return to Earth. They were lethal enough for a sore throat but little more.

**Above** President Richard Nixon visits the quarantined Apollo 11 astronauts.

**Above** Just after liftoff, lightning struck Apollo 12 – twice. The Command Module was lit up by warning lights, and an abort was a real option. But the crew stayed cool, fixed the problem and rode the rocket all the way to orbit.

**Right** Pete Conrad at the Surveyor spacecraft, a key objective of the mission. He would remove the TV camera and bring it back to Earth for study.

But Conrad was not Armstrong, this was not the historically significant first flight and, in the tradition of hotshot test pilots everywhere, Conrad had a bet to win, which he had made on the ground weeks before the launch. So when he descended from the ladder and set his foot onto the dusty soil of the Ocean of Storms, he surprised everyone.

"That may have been a small one for Neil, but it was sure a long one for me!" were Conrad's immortal first words. He was 167 centimetres (five foot six inches) to Armstrong's 183 centimetres (six feet). A number of the controllers in Houston shook their heads with a smile. It was classic.

Soon both he and Bean were on the surface, working hard. They would conduct two moonwalks, but as always with these missions the timeline was a full one with no room for any errors. As they were trying to unpack the power source for the ALSEP experimental package, stomachs tightened in Houston, when Bean laconically intoned his troubles.

**BEAN:** Hold it; you gotta be kidding.
**CONRAD:** Make sure it's screwed all the way down...
**BEAN:** That could make a guy mad, you know it?
**CONRAD:** Yup.
**BEAN:** Let me undo it for a minute, and try a different way...

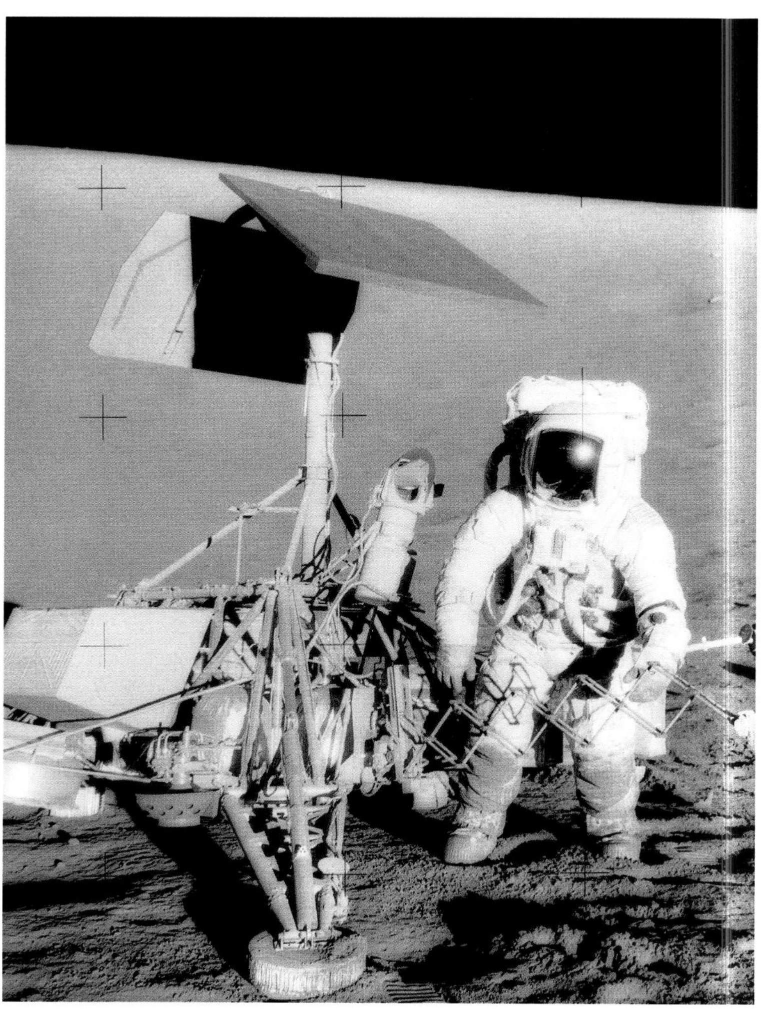

# IMPROVING LUNAR LANDING

After the long and harrowing final phases of the Apollo 11 lunar landing, it was decided that any additional "hover" time that could be given to Apollo 12, for Conrad's planned pinpoint landing, would be invaluable. This memo, dated just over a week after the Apollo 11 touchdown, describes a method to give Apollo 12's crew more fuel, hence more time, to land. As it turned out, Conrad did not need it.

OPTIONAL FORM NO. 10
MAY 1962 EDITION
GSA FPMR (41 CFR) 101-11.6

UNITED STATES GOVERNMENT

*Memorandum*

NASA - Manned Spacecraft Center
Mission Planning & Analysis Division

7-99

H-1 July

File 4

TO : FM/Assistant Chief, Mission Planning and Analysis Division

DATE: JUL 29 1969
69-FM8-71

FROM : FM8/Advanced Mission Design Branch

SUBJECT: Improving the lunar landing accuracy of Apollo 12

It is suggested that the flight plan for Apollo 12 be modified to permit a reduction in PDI navigated state uncertainties and to increase the hover and translation capability. This can be accomplished by performing the DOI maneuver with CSM propulsion three revolutions prior to PDI. The LM $\Delta V$ normally used for DOI is then available to extend the hover and translation capability by about 14 seconds. The PDI navigated state should be improved since the results of the actual DOI maneuver can be tracked for two front side posses and the LM state updated on the third pass prior to PDI.

The LM and CSM should remain docked during the first two passes in the 60 x 8 orbit with LM separation occurring just prior to the third apolune passage. The CSM will circularize at the third apolune passage. The abort and LM rescue situation remains the same as in Apollo 11.

The implementation of this technique should be started with MPAD obtaining answers to the following questions:

(a) Can the timeline be modified to accommodate this technique for Apollo 12?

(b) Is there sufficient SPS reserve to accommodate the additional 150 fps $\Delta V$ requirement? Are there any SM/RCS problems?

(c) What is the expected landed dispersion prior to manual take over?

(d) What is the expected translation distance capability?

James J. Taylor

James J. Taylor

APPROVED BY:

Jack Funk

Jack Funk
Chief, Advanced Mission
Design Branch

cc: (see attached list)

INDEXING DATA

| DATE | OPR | # | T | PGM | SUBJECT | SIGNATOR | LOC |
|---|---|---|---|---|---|---|---|
| 07-29-69 | MSC | 69-FM8-71 | M | LMP | (Above) | J. TAYLOR | 071-53 |

5010-108

*Buy U.S. Savings Bonds Regularly on the Payroll Savings Plan*

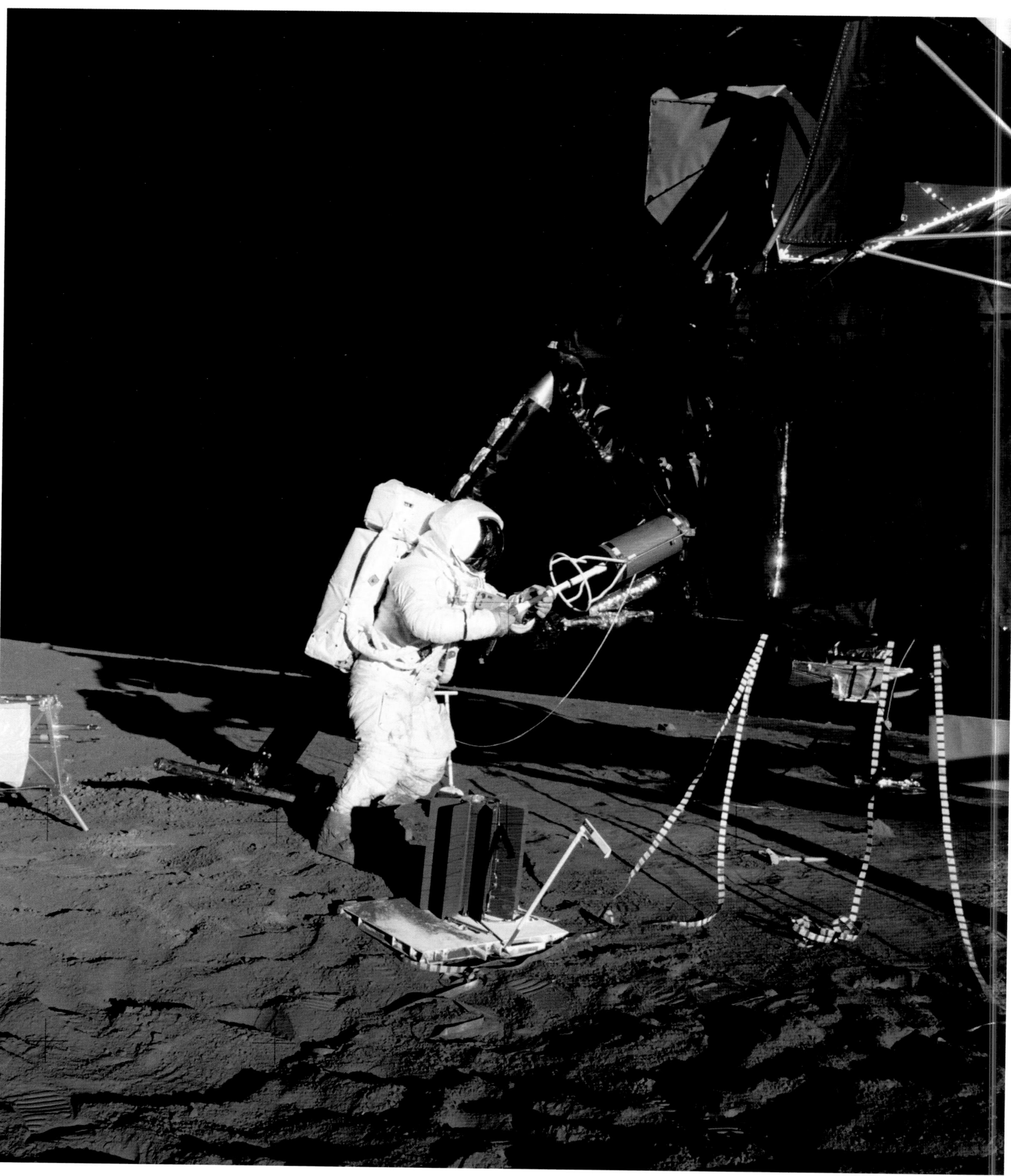

Bean had been trying to pull a radioactive fuel rod out of a sleeve, or "cask", on the side of the Lunar Module. This cask was supposed to prevent fallout from reaching the ground if for some reason the Apollo 12 blew up during launch. The rod was to power the ALSEP experimental devices but was stuck fast. Without it, a substantial percentage of the flight objectives wouldn't be met.

After a lot of finessing and mild cursing, Conrad got out what he termed "the universal tool" and approached the Lunar Module. Bean saw him approaching and was apprehensive. "Don't pound on anything…" he said. Conrad reassured him. "No, no. I'm not going to…".

Conrad had in his gloved hand a hammer, and he looked like he meant business.

For the next ten minutes or so he tapped gently, attempting to urge the problematic fuel rod out of its cocoon, but with no success. It wasn't long before they were ignoring their own warnings.

**BEAN:** Hey, that's doing it! Give it a few more pounds… gotta beat harder than that. Keep going, it's coming out… Pound harder!
**CONRAD:** Keep going.
**BEAN:** Come on, Conrad!! The hammer's a universal tool.
**CONRAD:** You better believe it.

Minutes later the dangerous isotopic fuel rod was nestled inside the ALSEP, providing power. Conrad had cracked the protective cask with his pounding, but nobody cared. The ALSEP was fuelled and ready to go, and would return data for years to come. It would be invaluable.

Their other major objective was to reach and investigate Surveyor 3. The robotic probe had come to rest on the inner slope of a crater three years before, and the scientists at NASA wanted a few pieces of it to see how baking, freezing and being exposed to micrometeorites on the lunar surface had affected it.

When they finally reached the craft down a slope in what Conrad called Surveyor Crater, Conrad cut off Surveyor's TV camera, held on three spindly arms. It was a struggle, but eventually, after more huffing and puffing, and opportunities to use the colourful language he was known for (but didn't stoop to this day), he had the prize. Into a bag it went, and back to the Lunar Module they went. Liftoff from the moon was just hours away.

When they docked with the Command Module, all three were relieved to be together again. They made the Trans Earth Injection burn, broke free of lunar orbit and laughed all the way home.

**Opposite** Al Bean begins his struggle to free the isotopic fuel rod from the Lunar Module safety cask. This cask was designed to keep the fuel (which was highly radioactive) from spreading in the event of a launch explosion. Once they landed on the moon, it was stuck fast. Only Conrad's hammer managed to free it.

## CONTRABAND

Pete Conrad was not shy. His practical jokes and wisecracking ways were legendary, but his luck ran out when he tried to pull a prank on the moon during Apollo 12. He smuggled a camera self-timer onboard in his personal effects and his plan was to take a shot of himself and Bean near the Lunar Module, a feat impossible with NASA cameras. When they went on one of their EVAs, he tossed the timer in a bag. Then, back at the Lunar Module, he and Bean tried to find the timer, but it had been swallowed up in moon dust and rocks in the same bag, and was nowhere to be found. So ended the chance for the first practical joke on the moon!

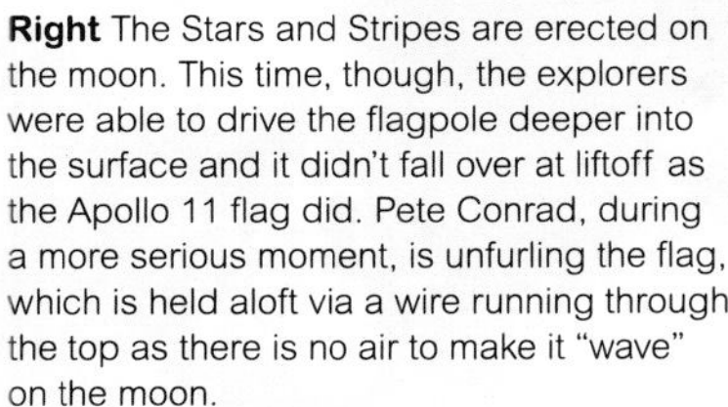

**Right** The Stars and Stripes are erected on the moon. This time, though, the explorers were able to drive the flagpole deeper into the surface and it didn't fall over at liftoff as the Apollo 11 flag did. Pete Conrad, during a more serious moment, is unfurling the flag, which is held aloft via a wire running through the top as there is no air to make it "wave" on the moon.

# A SUCCESSFUL FAILURE: APOLLO 13

GENE KRANZ HAD EXPERIENCED BETTER DAYS. HE STARED AT HIS LOGBOOK TRYING TO DECIDE HOW TO WRITE WHAT WAS GOING ON. SO WHAT IF THIS MISSION WAS NAMED 13 AND HAD LAUNCHED AT 13 MINUTES PAST THE THIRTEENTH HOUR ON 11 APRIL 1970?

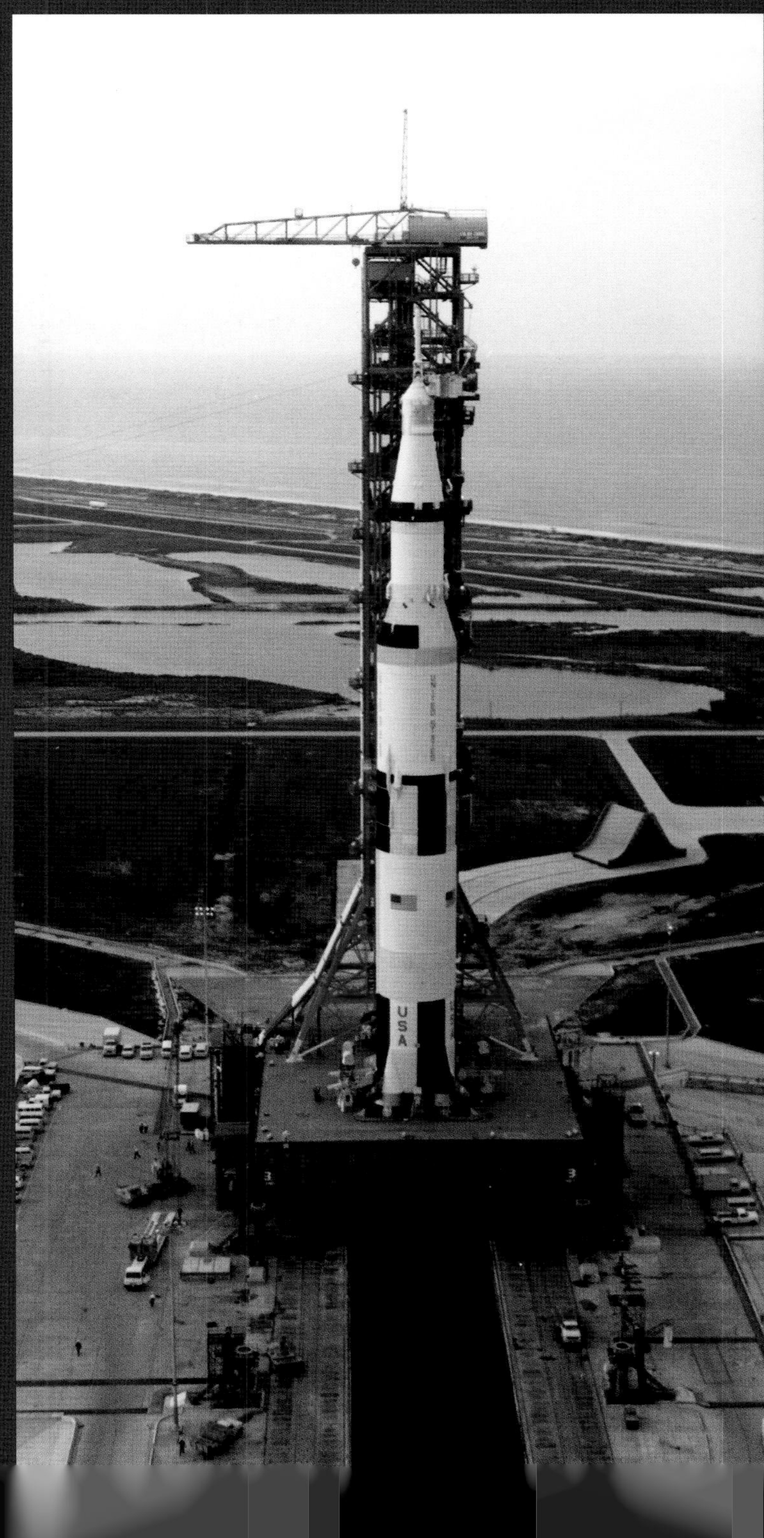


Kranz, the Apollo Flight Director, didn't believe in black cats or cracked mirrors, and neither, to his knowledge, did anyone else at NASA. There had been letters sent by concerned members of the public, giving advice on how to rename the mission, or how to bless the rocket before launch but they had been ignored. Still, he was unsure how to describe in his logbook that, on 13 April, at 55 hours into the otherwise routine mission, all hell had broken loose in space when something went "bang" in the Command Module.

The now well-known tale had its origins in Apollo 10. A large oxygen tank, located in the Service Module, the large cylinder behind the Command Module that held all the fuels and life support, had been removed for modification. It was reinstalled on Apollo 13 and deemed ready for flight without further testing. Waiting inside that tank was a time bomb.

The Apollo oxygen tanks were meant to hold liquefied oxygen, and were highly insulated. Cryogenic oxygen tends to become slushy, so a heater element and fan were installed to allow the Command Module pilot to "stir" the icy fuel from time to time in order to keep it flowing. When the system was originally constructed, it had been built at 28 volts, to NASA specifications. There had been a later upgrade to 65 volts, but somehow this particular tank was never retrofitted. Sometime months earlier, technicians had used the heater inside to "boil-off" some liquid oxygen, fusing the thermostat and melting the insulation off some wires.

**Above** The Apollo 13 mission insignia showed Apollo's chariot being pulled through space by three stallions. The Latin inscription reads: "From the moon, science."

**Left** Apollo 13, the evening before launch. What was not visible was the disaster waiting to happen in the oxygen tank, tucked in to the Service Module at the top of the rocket.

## THE SENATE SPACE COMMITTEE

When Jim Lovell testfied before the Senate Space Committee he was speaking to an audience representing a constituency of mixed emotions; some were anxious to get Apollo flying again with a minimum of delay, others felt that NASA had done enough and should discontinue the moon voyages. All were glad the astronauts had returned home safely. This meeting took place about a week after the crew, and all of the Mission Control team, had received the Presidential Medal of Freedom.

**Right** Apollo 13 Mission Commander Jim Lovell testifies to a special session of the Senate Space Committee about the trials of his mission. Behind him is Tom Paine, then NASA administrator.

So, at that fateful 55-hour mark, when Houston sent up the command to do a "cryo-stir" the wiring sparked and the entire tank exploded, taking one side of the Service Module with it. Three hours later, Apollo 13 had no oxygen left except for the supply in the attached Lunar Module. Had this happened on Apollo 8, with no Lunar Module, the crew would already have been dead.

So James Lovell, Mission Commander, Jack Swigert; Command Module Pilot and Fred Haise, Lunar Module pilot, hurriedly made their way to the Lunar Module, to use it as a lifeboat for the remainder of the voyage.

They rounded the moon after adjusting their course using the Lunar Module's descent engine (a task for which it was not designed), creating a "free-return" trajectory that would steer it to swing around the moon without entering an orbit, and then come home.

The remaining problems, however, were vexing.

The foremost problem was lack of water. All the systems on Apollo were cooled with water, and on the Lunar Module in particular, glycol

**Below** Inside Mission Control during the critical hours, with the big screen showing video of a feverish Fred Haise.

**Opposite** The Apollo 13 crew working with the Lunar Module in a test environment. This was as close to the surface of the moon as they got!

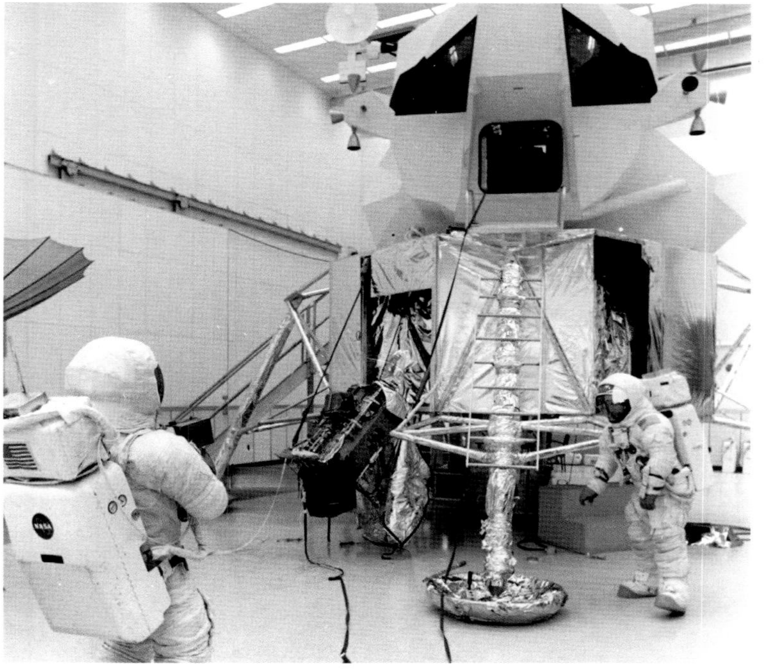

> ***Well, I'm afraid this is going to be the last lunar mission for a long time.***
>
> *– Jim Lovell, hours after the explosion*

## HOUSTON, WE'VE HAD A PROBLEM

**Below** Various members of the communications team in the Missions Control Room hours after crew members of Apollo 13 reported trouble with an oxygen cell on their spacecraft.

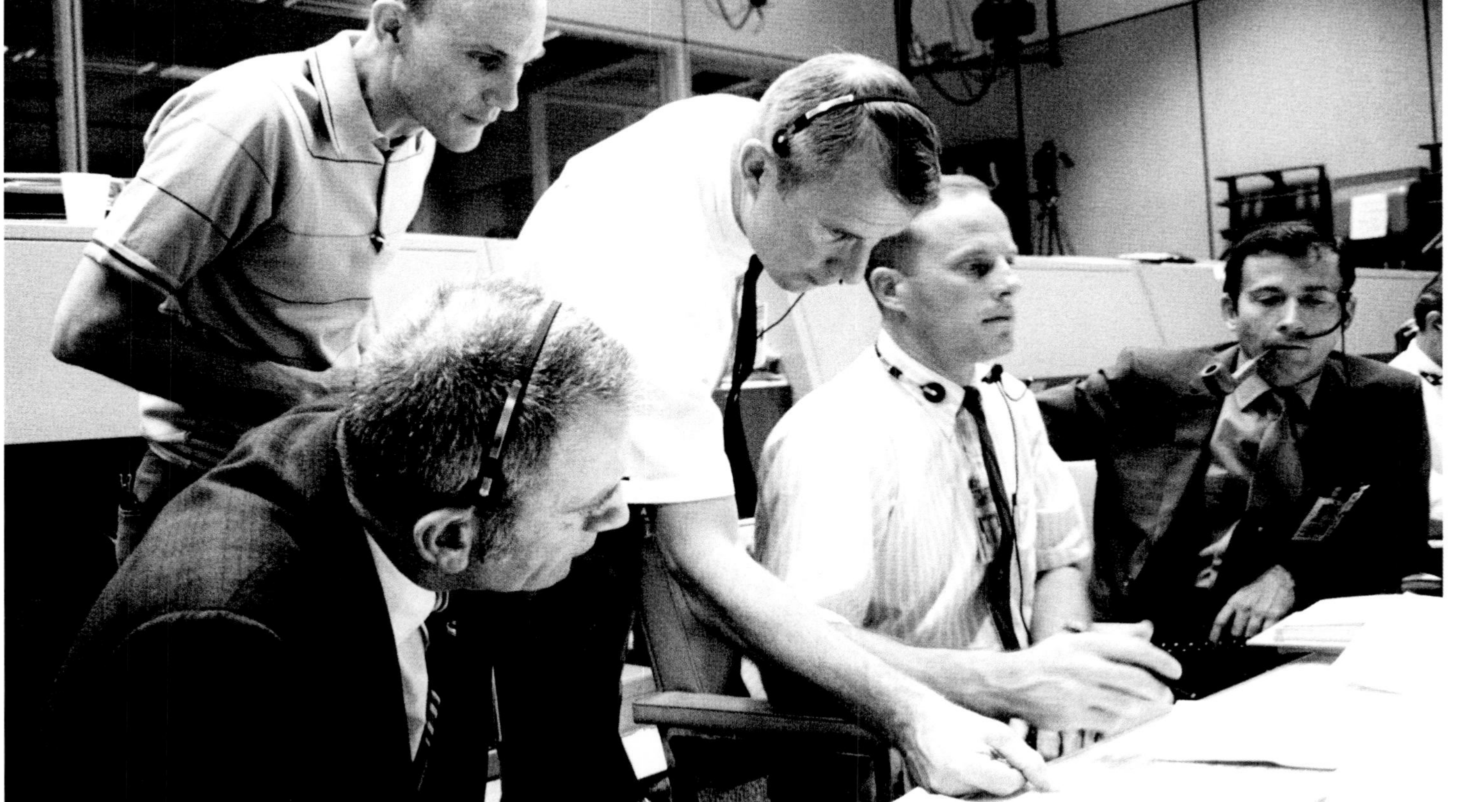

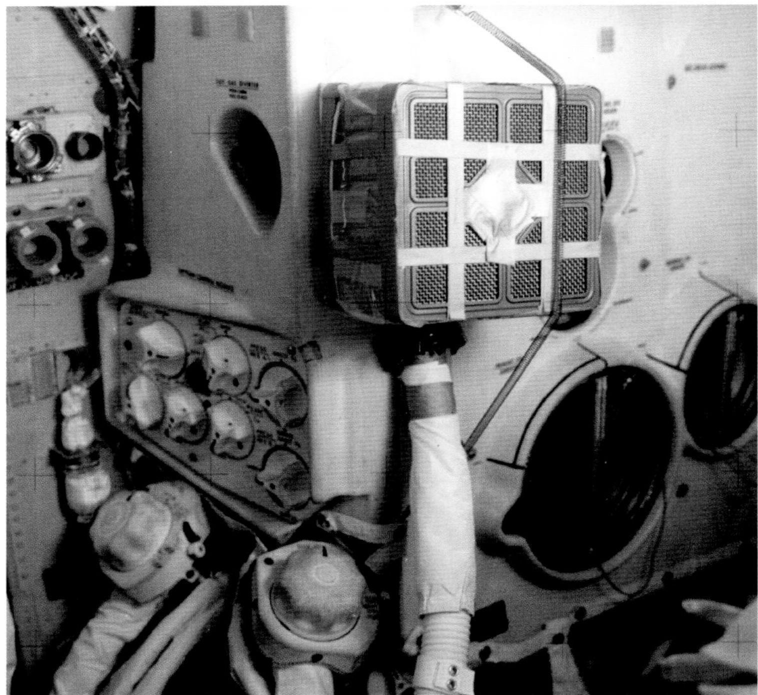

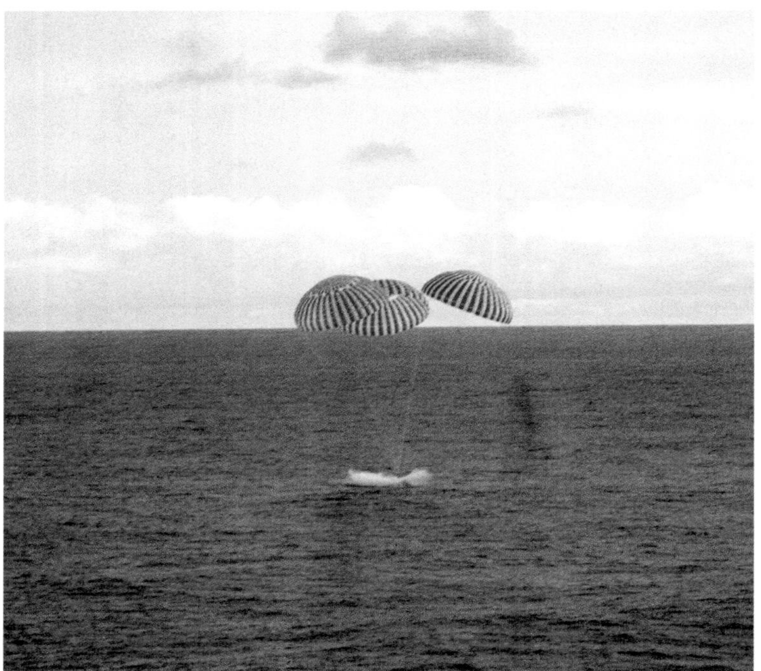

**Top** A view of "The Mailbox," made from two lithium hydroxide canisters, two LCG bags, two hoses from the red suits, a bungee cord and duct tape.

**Above** The Apollo 13 Command Module hits the water on 17 April 1970, after a harrowing brush with death in space. Their re-entry blackout period lasted a bit longer than usual, causing concern among the men at Mission Control. But soon the astronauts were in the rescue chopper and on their way to hot showers, clean clothes and a warm meal.

**Opposite top** The Service Module after being released just prior to reentry. The crew was aghast at the sight – a huge panel of the SM had been blown away by the explosion of the faulty oxygen tank.

coolant was fed past the hot electronics and then cooled by water which was vented into space to carry the heat with it as it vaporized. If they ran out of water, the craft would overheat and shut down, so water conservation reached extreme levels.

Then there was the air supply. The craft was pressurized with pure oxygen, and the Lunar Module had barely enough to last. Also, unless they could cope with the rising amounts of carbon dioxide in the cabin, they would be asphyxiated. The Lunar Module held a couple of CO2 "scrubbers", chemical packs that neutralized the gas, in the life-support system, but they would need the filter units in the Command Module as well. Unfortunately, the Command Module's CO2 scrubbers were designed for square housings, and the Lunar Module's scrubbers for more compact round housings. It was a design that worked, but in this unforeseen emergency, was life-threatening. Working quickly, the ground team suggested a makeshift solution, using the cover of the flight plan, two lithium hydroxide canisters, two LCG bags, two hoses from the red suits, a bungee cord and duct tape to rig the square filter over the round hole in the Lunar Module. They called it "The Mailbox", and, luckily, it worked.

But soon guidance problems reared their heads.Hitting the Earth's atmosphere at just the right angle at the incredible speeds at which the Apollo ships travelled required finesse and precise navigation. The Apollo Command Module had to enter the atmosphere briefly, "skip" off the dense air to reduce speed, then re-enter again. Apollo 13 was not currently on that course, so they would have to ignite the Lunar Module descent engine again to correct their trajectory.

Space navigation is a tricky business at the best of times, and now they had no computer to guide them. Again they improvised. After conferring with the ground, Lovell took a sighting of the Earth through the navigation telescope, placing the crosshairs on the edge of his home planet. It was inexact at best – they usually took their sightings on stars, but there was too much detritus from the explosion surrounding the craft to do that – but good enough, according to Mission Control.

Just before re-entry, they jettisoned the Service Module and got the shock of their lives:

**LOVELL:** There's one whole side of that spacecraft missing!
**CAPCOM:** Is that right?
**LOVELL:** Look out there, will you? Right by the high-gain antenna, the whole panel is blown out, almost from the base to the engine.

Fortunately, neither the explosion nor the cold of space had impaired either their heat shield or the pyrotechnic charges that activated their parachutes, and, within the hour, they were in the Pacific Ocean, awaiting pickup by the Navy.

It was the last space voyage for each of them. Lovell moved on to other ventures. Swigert was elected to Congress from the State of Colorado, but died of cancer before taking office. Only Haise remained with NASA, but after flying some of the landing tests in the Shuttle, left NASA before the spacecraft went into operational status.

Their landing zone was rolled over to the next flight, Apollo 14.

## *APOLLO 13*: THE MOVIE

The 1995 film *Apollo 13* is as good a telling of a NASA flight as ever was, but to compress days of spaceflight into a two-hour movie required some dramatic license. A couple of examples:

- Gene Kranz never said "Failure is not an option!", which was penned by the film's scriptwriters.
- During the re-entry phase the technicians did not celebrate when they heard from the crew but waited until they had confirmed a safe splashdown.

Nonetheless, the film is a magnificent tribute to the men and the mission and is mandatory viewing for anyone interested in Apollo.

**Below** In this still from the film, the Apollo 13 crew surveys the cold emptiness from the Lunar Module Aquarius, their lifeboat in space. From left: Bill Paxton as Fred Haise, Kevin Bacon as Jack Swigert and Tom Hanks as Jim Lovell.

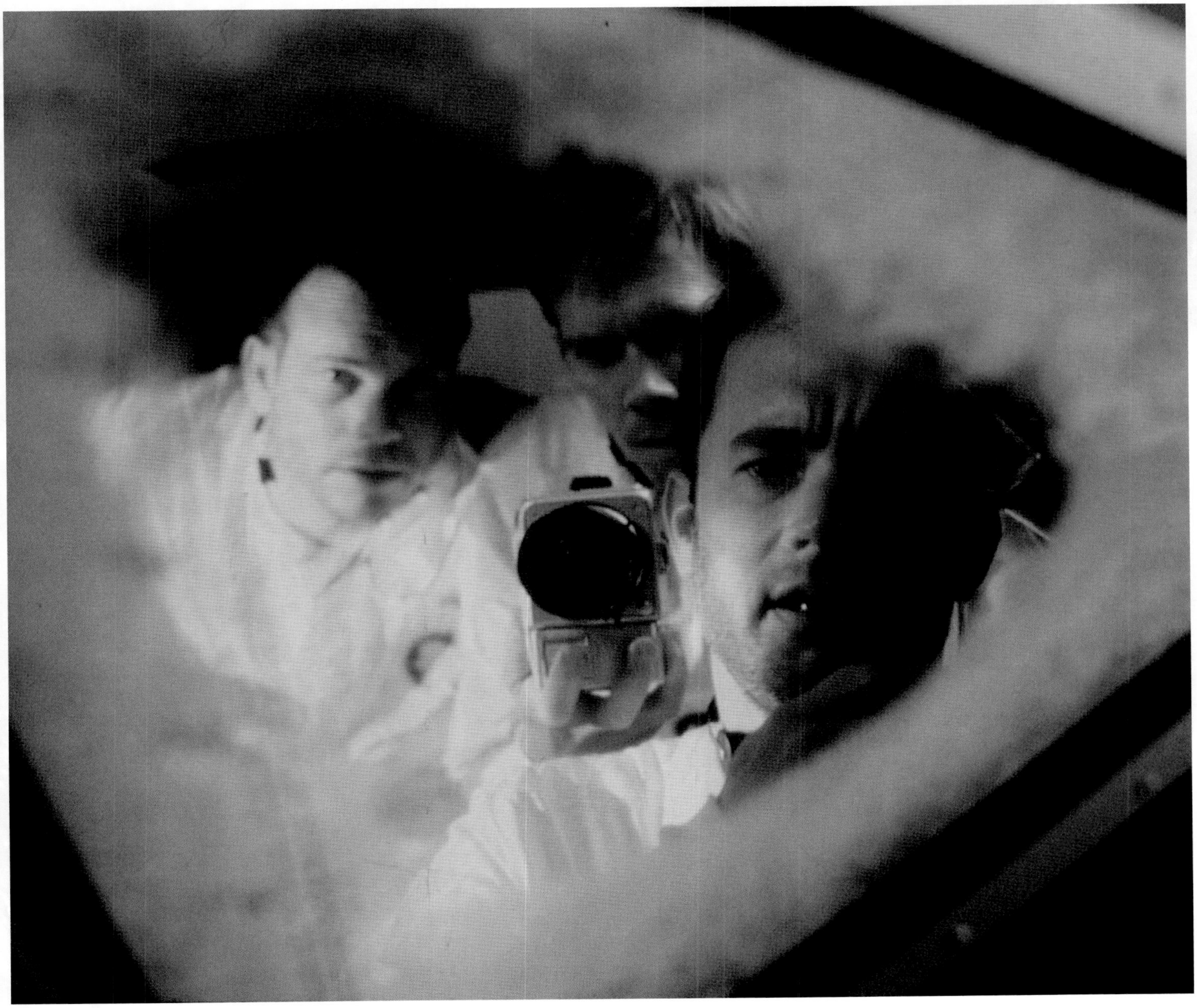

**Above** Mission Control celebrates Apollo 13's return to Earth. Second from left, clapping, is Gene Kranz in his trademark white vest.

**Left** The relieved crew of Apollo 13 on board the USS Iwo Jima, shortly after being lifted from the ocean. In a few moments, once they cleared the helicopter, they would be met by the ship's chaplain and join in thanks for their safe return.

# FLIGHT DIRECTOR'S LOG, APOLLO 13

Excerpts from the Flight Director's Log from Apollo 13. This journal contains an incredibly calm and matter-of-fact telling of key parts of a harrowing mission. Most of it is in the hand of Gene Kranz, while the other Flight Directors, Milton Windler, Gerry Griffin and Glynn Lunney also made entires during their respective shifts..

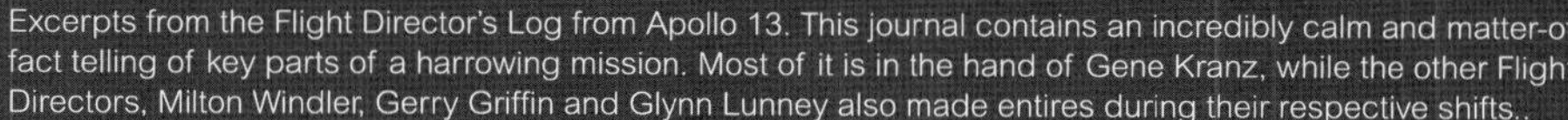

APOLLO 13

## A TELEGRAM TO APOLLO 13

A laudatory telegram sent during the Apollo 13 mission, at the conclusion of the flight, from former Vice President Hubert Humphrey.

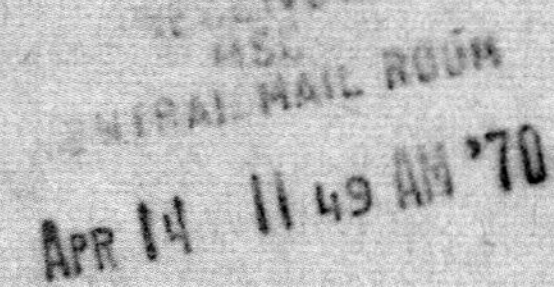


HOX163RDA089

PTTUZYUW RUWJEOA3032 QPRQUQTAUUUU--RUWTDRA.

ZNR UUUUU

P 141709Z APR 70

FM MARTIN MARIETTA CORP DENVER CO

TO OFFICE OF THE DIRECTOR NASA MSC HOUSTON TX

BT

UNCLAS ATTN DR. CHRISTOPHER C. KRAFT, JR. DEPUTY DIRECTOR

I UNDERSTAND AND SHARE YOUR IMMEDIATE CONCERN WITH APOLLO 13. IF OUR RESOURCES CAN BE OF ANY POSSIBLE USE TO YOU IN ANY MANNER WHATEVER, PLEASE DON T HESITATE TO LET ME KNOW. THEY WILL BE IMMEDIATELY AVAILABLE TO YOU.

SIGNED "K" HURTT VICE PRESIDENT MANNED SPACE SYSTEMS

BT

#3032

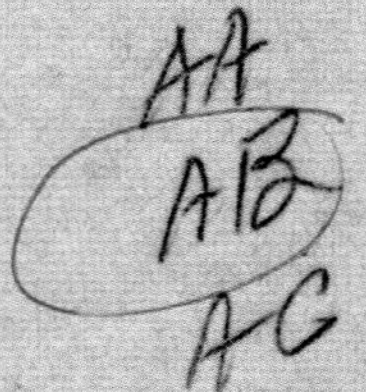

# A TELEGRAM TO CHRIS KRAFT

A telegram sent to Chris Kraft at Mission Control in Houston during the Apollo 13 mission, from a Vice President at Martin Marietta Corporation, offering any assistance possible. Dozens of such telegrams were received.

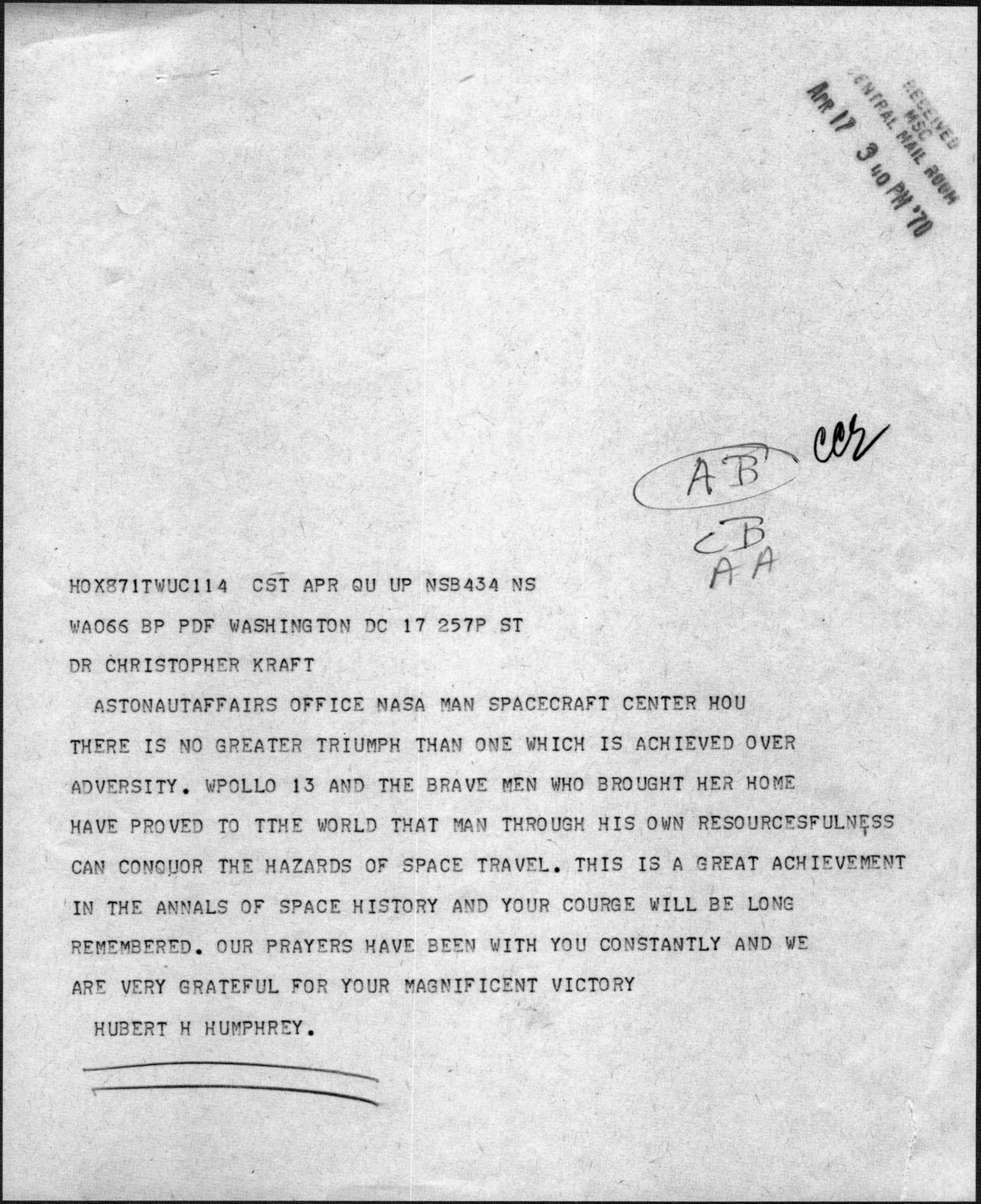

RECEIVED
MSC
CENTRAL MAIL ROOM
APR 17 3 40 PM '70

AB CCK

CB
AA

HOX871TWUC114 CST APR QU UP NSB434 NS

WA066 BP PDF WASHINGTON DC 17 257P ST

DR CHRISTOPHER KRAFT

ASTONAUTAFFAIRS OFFICE NASA MAN SPACECRAFT CENTER HOU

THERE IS NO GREATER TRIUMPH THAN ONE WHICH IS ACHIEVED OVER ADVERSITY. WPOLLO 13 AND THE BRAVE MEN WHO BROUGHT HER HOME HAVE PROVED TO TTHE WORLD THAT MAN THROUGH HIS OWN RESOURCESFULNESS CAN CONQUOR THE HAZARDS OF SPACE TRAVEL. THIS IS A GREAT ACHIEVEMENT IN THE ANNALS OF SPACE HISTORY AND YOUR COURGE WILL BE LONG REMEMBERED. OUR PRAYERS HAVE BEEN WITH YOU CONSTANTLY AND WE ARE VERY GRATEFUL FOR YOUR MAGNIFICENT VICTORY

HUBERT H HUMPHREY.

# SHEPARD RETURNS

ALAN SHEPARD, AMERICA'S FIRST MAN IN SPACE AND THE ORIGINAL MERCURY ASTRONAUT, HAD A TOTAL OF JUST 15 MINUTES OF SPACEFLIGHT TIME FROM HIS 1961 SUBORBITAL LOB.

After that he had been grounded by a rare inner-ear condition and become the curmudgeonly Chief Astronaut. Then, after a successful experimental operation, he was back on flight status, winning the assignment of commanding the third moon landing. He had jumped past such worthies as John Young and Gene Cernan. To many astronauts awaiting their turn for an Apollo mission in 1970 it didn't make sense. However, America needed a hero to captain the next moon flight after the perceived failure of Apollo 13, and they turned to their first and, arguably, finest.

So on 31 January 1971, Apollo 14 headed moonwards. Alan Shepard flew as the Mission Commander, Ed Mitchell was Command Module Pilot and Stuart Roosa was Lunar Module Pilot. Mitchell and Roosa were complete space novices and Shepard had his aforementioned 15 minutes of spaceflight time. It was the most inexperienced crew of all the Apollo flights, but Shepard understood the urgency; the programme was on the line.

**Above** The Apollo 14 mission insignia featured the astronaut pin logo headed off to the moon, looking much like the Saturn V.

**Below** The crew of Apollo 14. From Left, Stuart Roosa, Command Module Pilot; Alan Shepard, Mission Commander and Edgar Mitchell, Lunar Module Pilot. Between the three, only Shepard had spaceflight experience, and that had only been his 15-minute flight in 1961.

## WHERE IS CONE CRATER?

The search for Cone Crater was exasperating. Both Shepard and Mitchell badly wanted to find it. It would be humanity's first close look at a large moon crater. As they struggled to pull the Modularized Equipment Transporter (MET) over the rough, rocky surface, however, Cone remained out of reach. Shepard and Mitchell took turns pulling the MET, and whoever had free hands inspected the maps, but to no avail. The "back room" geologists at Houston tried to help, but could not. They never found the rim. Later, after their return, when the data had been triangulated, a sobering fact emerged: they had been within about 18–21 metres (60–70 feet) of Cone Crater's edge. It became clear at this moment that later missions would need better navigation methods, and with the Lunar Rover, they got them.

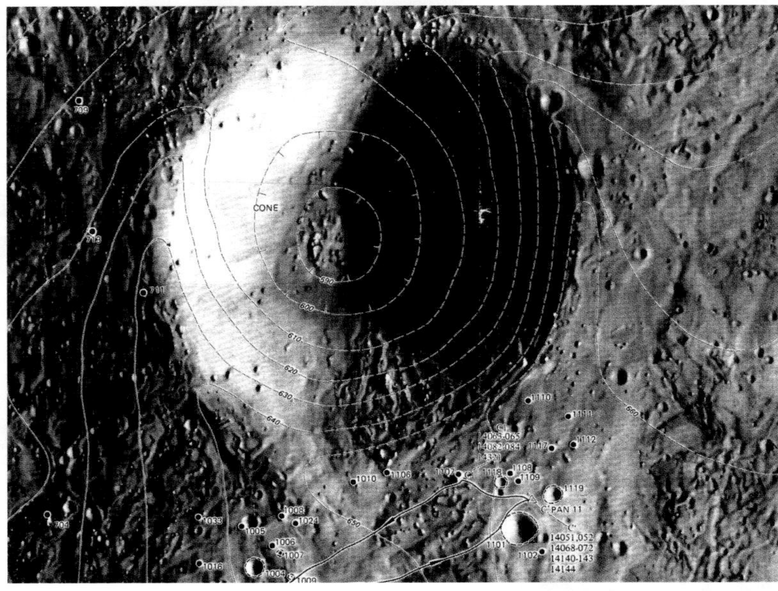


**Right** A traverse map of Cone Crater. One problem the astronauts had in locating it was that the maps, made from orbit, were almost useless from a ground level perspective.

The official inquiries after the Apollo 13 accident had raised questions regarding the validity of continuing the Apollo programme since Kennedy's challenge had been met. The flight of Apollo 14 had to be perfect to quell the dissent, and Alan Shepard was the right astronaut to achieve that goal.

By the time they landed on the proposed landing site of Apollo 13, the Fra Mauro formation, Shepard was as simulator-prepared as a man could be. This was the first mission to put geology ahead of safety. The Fra Mauro region included some ejected material from Copernicus Crater, a huge impact basin over 483 kilometres (300 miles) away, and desirable rocks from another basin, Mare Imbrium, for which geologists wanted to pinpoint a date of origin. That impact had also churned up older, deeper moonrocks and samples of those would be nearby.

The flight went smoothly – except for a difficult docking with the Lunar Module – until Shepard and Mitchell prepared for the powered landing. Just prior to starting the descent, the Lunar Module's computer began flashing an erroneous abort signal. If this occurred during the landing, the Lunar Module would automatically abort, dropping the descent stage and returning to orbit. It would be dangerous and could be deadly. The MIT engineers hurriedly wrote a substitute command sequence which Ed Mitchell keyed in to the guidance computer, forcing it to ignore the abort signal if it occurred.They were cleared to land.

Despite his brief flight time in space, Shepard made the second pinpoint landing of the programme, only 27 metres (90 feet) from the intended target, and the two men set out on their first EVA (extra-vehicular activity) shortly after. The first excursion concentrated on setting up the now-familiar ALSEP package and collecting samples. After a rest period, they embarked on their second exploration, heading for a feature called Cone Crater.

At 304 metres (1,000 feet) in width, Cone was the major geographical feature of the area, a preferred target for the earthbound geology team. Looking somewhat like polar explorers from the early twentieth century, they pulled their tools and samples behind them in a small metal rickshaw called the Modularized Equipment Transporter (MET). Under enormous pressure they struggled against the clock to find the crater. They had maps, but these were made from orbital photos and were of little use from the moonwalker's vantage point on the ground. They searched and they searched, but to no avail. Whenever they thought they were close, they would crest the next rise and be disappointed to see another ridge just beyond. They were also getting tired. Shepard, as Mission Commander, wanted to turn back but Mitchell was intent on pressing forward. Then Houston got involved.

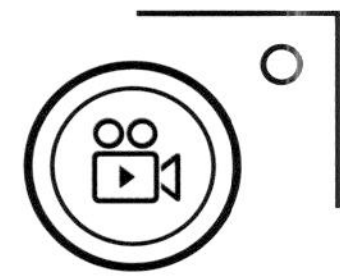

**Opposite** The launch of Apollo 14, 31 January 1971.

Shepard trusted his gut, which told him that continuing to search for the crater rim wasn't worth the risk of either missing sampling time on the nearby boulders, which certainly originated from inside Cone anyway, or overtiring himself and Mitchell. So, in the end, they took samples from where they were and trudged back to the Lunar Module with the MET, now full of rocks, in tow.

The last momentous event was typical of Al Shepard. With the world watching on TV, he fished a golf-club head out of his suit, attached it to a sampling arm and dropped a golf ball to the lunar surface. The Apollo suits were stiff, and his first two tries were more dust than ball. The third try, however, was the charm, and the ball sailed off in the loose one-sixth gravity. "Miles and miles and miles..." Shepard exclaimed, pleased with his prank. For the record keepers, though, he was off the mark, and later amended his range to about 183–366 metres (200–400 yards). Golf would never be the same for Al Shepard again.

UNITED
STATES

**Opposite** Apollo 14's Lunar Module Antares. Shepard landed on-target, but that target ended up being on a slope. It made sleep difficult for the two moonwalkers, who constantly felt like the Lunar Module was tipping over.

**Above** The tracks of the MET, compacted moon dust, shine in the low-level sun.

**Right** Cernan had this humorous mission patch made up for "the B-team".

## BACK-UP CREW JOKES

Apollo 14's back-up crew had a sense of humour. Gene Cernan, the back-up Mission Commander, had adopted the Warner Bros. cartoon characters Roadrunner and Wile E Coyote as mascots, and every reference to these annoyed Shepard, who was known for his ill temper. Cernan loved it. So Cernan had a batch of back-up crew patches made and hid them in dozens of locations on the Apollo 14 spacecraft before the flight. It seemed as if every time Shepard opened a box or locker, a "Beep, Beep!" patch would fall out. He eventually responded to the practical joke during an EVA by exclaiming "Beep, beep your ass!" Most were puzzled, but a satisfied Gene Cernan understood – and loved it.

# THE LUNAR ROVER

NASA VENTURED MANY IDEAS FOR LUNAR SURFACE TRANSPORT SINCE 1960. ONE RESULTED IN THE THE BENDIX CORPORATION PROTOTYPE, DESIGNED BEFORE WEIGHT AND SIZE CONSTRAINTS WERE DECIDED. THIS LOOKED MORE LIKE AN ASSAULT VEHICLE THAN A LUNAR CAR.

This concept was revised many times, but ultimately proved to be a dead end. There were also designs for a one-man lunar flyer, a lunar "jumper" and even an odd vehicle that looked and moved like a worm. Then there were the Grumman designs – utilizing parts of their Lunar Module – which made more sense but were beyond what NASA could afford to create for these early missions to the moon.

Ultimately, the challenge of building the first car for the moon, now dubbed the Lunar Roving Vehicle, or LRV, and usually referred to simply as the Lunar Rover, would fall to Boeing. This maker of civilian aircraft would have to design and build the Rover in less than 18 months. Contrary to most government contract fulfilments, they did it. Brilliantly.

The Lunar Rover was a masterpiece of engineering: a reliable transporter for two astronauts wearing bulky pressure suits and backpacks, carrying hundreds of kilograms of guidance and drive systems, as well as rocks and tools. It had to be light enough to fly within the Apollo system (remember the weight constraints of the Lunar Module), small enough to fit inside the descent stage of the Lunar Module and robust enough not to strand the moonwalkers who would drive it. Further, it must operate in the harsh environment of the moon, with its fine, highly abrasive and ubiquitous dust, and be able to fold up for transport.

**Below** The massive Bendix lunar vehicle. Built and tested as a prototype, it bore little resemblance to the final product. This original test vehicle resides today in a warehouse in Hutchinson, Kansas, in the US.

## MOON TRUCKS

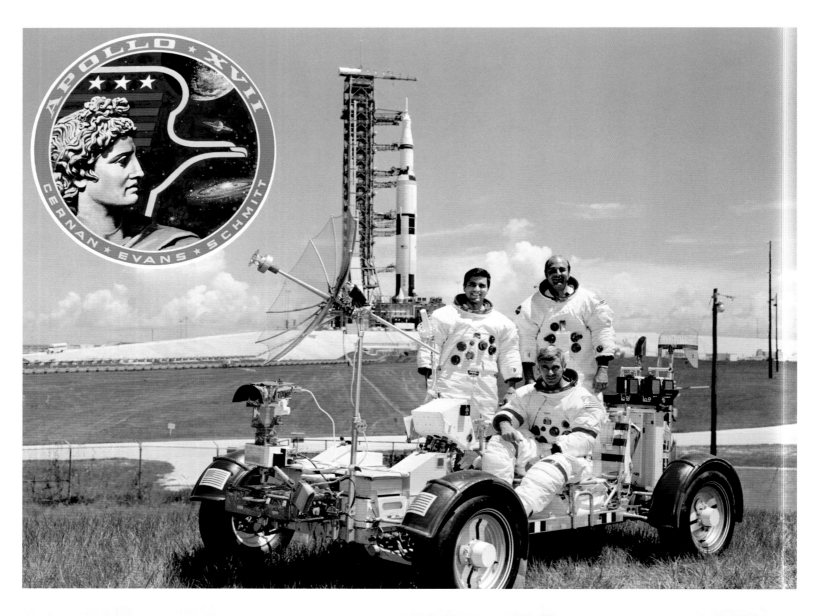

For future exploration of the moon, six wheels may turn out to be better than four. At least that's what the new crop of Lunar Roving Vehicles would seem to indicate. Most prototypes, now being studied for a 2020 return to the moon, have at least six wheels, some even more. The new all-terrain transports have increased range and more climbing ability. Some carry pressurized habitats. In this example, each wheel is independently steered and powered, making for maximum manoeuvrability and traction. Additionally, the driver's seat can turn 360 degrees for maximum visibility.

**Right** One of NASA's design studies for a new Lunar Rover, this machine has six sets of independently steered and powered wheels as well as the ability to move a large amount of cargo.

## TRAVERSE NAVIGATION

As previous moonwalkers had found, navigating on the surface was problematic. Without trees, houses or even atmospheric haze, it was almost impossible to guess distances on the moon. The small computer on the Lunar Rover would be started at the Lunar Module's landing zone, and then, using gyroscopes and acceleration measurements, would track distance and direction from the Lunar Module. It could tell the Lunar Rover Vehicle's driver which direction the Lunar Module was in and how far away they were from it. As the missions became more complex, and took place in rougher terrain, this became increasingly important. In many cases the crews were well out of visual range of the Lunar Module, but Boeing's Lunar Roving Vehicle always returned them home.

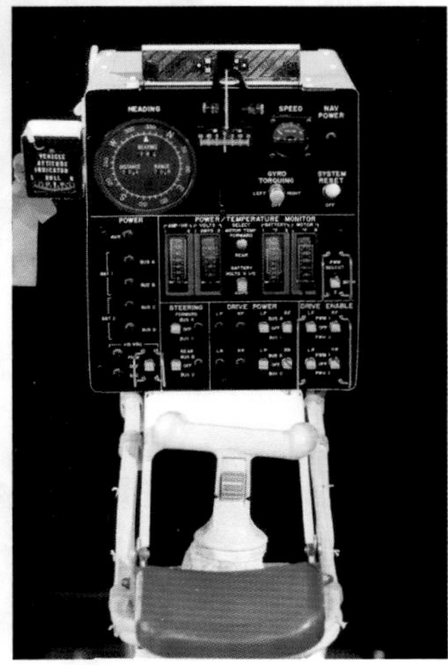

**Above** The controls of the Lunar Roving Vehicle. Designed around an inertial guidance system, the rover was capable of returning to its point of origin within a few dozen yards if needed. Controlled by a large "T" handle, seen lower centre, it was simplicity itself to drive.

**Opposite** The crew of Apollo 17 pose with a Lunar Rover mockup next to the Apollo 17 Saturn V. Standing, from left, Harrison "Jack" Schmitt, Lunar Module Pilot; Ron Evans, Command Module Pilot and seated, Gene Cernan, Mission Commander.

**Below** Upcoming moonwalkers pose near a rover mock-up in 1971. From left: John Young, Gene Cernan, Charlie Duke, Fred Haise and Anthony England. Haise and England would not reach the lunar surface but would later fly the Shuttle.

**Above right** Another design for advanced missions, this GM prototype would have allowed for long duration stays with multiple astronauts and a vastly extended range of operations, had it been commissioned.

The final design met the constraints with room to spare. Weighing only 1,225 kilograms (2,700 pounds) on earth – about 210 kilograms (463 pounds) on the moon – the rover could carry its own weight plus an additional 490 kilograms (1,080 pounds) of men and cargo – moon weight, 2,939 kilograms (6,480 pounds).

The Rover could top 30-centimetre- (one-foot-) high rocks, cross cracks and crevasses almost a metre wide and climb a slope of about 28 degrees. It had a battery-powered life of about 78 hours and a total range of about 100 kilometres (60 miles), dependent upon use. However, with NASA constraints demanding that the crew be able to walk back to the Lunar Module in the event of a Rover failure, it was never driven more than about ten kilometres (six miles) away from home base.

Given the difficulty of navigating by eye alone or with maps made from orbit, designers installed an onboard guidance system, which used dead reckoning from the point of departure. In practice, it was remarkably accurate.

Installed on the Rover were a TV camera with remote operation capability (so that it could be controlled from Mission Control), an adjustable antenna to maintain communication with Earth, a 16mm movie camera and all the tools and bags needed for geological exploration.

Each wire-mesh wheel was driven by a separate electric motor, controlled by a T-bar in the cockpit area. The astronauts found it very easy to drive and manoeuver. If it had a weakness it was the fenders. Made from fiberglass, they tended to be fragile, and cracked or broke free more than once, spraying the astronauts with sticky moon dust kicked up by the wheels – nobody ever said that exploring the moon would be easy, or clean!

Ultimately, it was the only piece of the advanced lunar mission planning that flew when the later Apollo missions were cancelled. But when it first made it to the moon on Apollo 15, the Lunar Rover accounted for a tenfold increase in scientific results.

# THE GENESIS ROCK

JAMES IRWIN AND DAVE SCOTT WERE ON A TRAVERSE BETWEEN SAMPLING STOPS ON THE SECOND EVA OF APOLLO 15. THE MISSION, LAUNCHED ON 26 JULY 1971, HAD BEEN SMOOTH AND DEVOID OF SURPRISES.

They rounded a boulder and there it was – a pristine, beautifully white rock, just crying out to be collected. So James Irwin, who would be so moved by his Apollo mission that he would leave NASA to found a Christian ministry upon his return to Earth, obliged.

Apollo 15 had already been one for the record books. With Dave Scott as Mission Commander, James Irwin as the Lunar Module Pilot and Al Worden as the Command Module Pilot, it was the first of the new "J" missions. The J flights were intended to be in-depth investigations. The Lunar Modules were improved, with more fuel for exotic trajectories and a longer staying ability. The astronauts had better spacesuits and more leisurely schedules (as if anything on a moon mission could be called leisurely), there were three EVAs instead of two and, most importantly, they would have the new Lunar Rover.

The upgraded Lunar Module and the Rover made all the difference. The Lunar Module was good for more than three days of operations, and the Rover could travel up to a sum total of about 100 kilometres (60 miles). With the Lunar Rover's help, the lunar EVAs had gone from strolls across a few acres to a grand driving tour of an entire geological formation. It changed everything.

Now, on their second EVA, James Irwin and Dave Scott were expanding their survey of the Hadley Delta region, in the Lunar Apennine Mountains. All told, they had 66 hours of surface time to collect more than 77 kilograms (170 pounds) of rocks and samples.

They were about 15 minutes into their work at a scheduled stop at Spur Crater. The two men were doing a quick visual survey of the area when Irwin spotted a rock, about the size of a large lemon, glistening on top of a pedestal of routine volcanic rock. He was transfixed, and said to Houston in a haunted tone, "I think we found what we came for".

It was a chunk of anorthosite, a bit of primaeval crust from the early moon. The previous landings had brought home hundreds of kilograms of great samples, but nothing from the moon's early history. This was the first ancient rock found on the moon, and it was "A beaut", as Scott described it. They photographed it, carefully documented its position and

**Above** After allegedly reviewing 544 designs, the crew of Apollo 15 settled upon this rendition of the lunar surface with three stylized birds overhead.

**Below** Preparing the Lunar Rover to leave "home base" for another EVA.

**Above** Another flag, another salute… America was laying claim, albeit for "all humanity", on the moon.

## THE PASTOR (1930–1991)

James Irwin joined NASA in 1966. He served as a mission back-up for Apollo 10 and 12, then flew his only flight on Apollos 15 as Lunar Module Pilot. Profoundly affected by the experience, he returned to Earth on an inner quest. He left NASA in 1972 and founded High Flight Ministry, a Christian church of which he was the head. Beginning in 1983, he began to search for Noah's Ark on Mount Ararat, leading a series of expeditions over the next ten years. Irwin died in 1991 of a heart condition.

## APOLLO 15 GALILEO EXPERIMENT

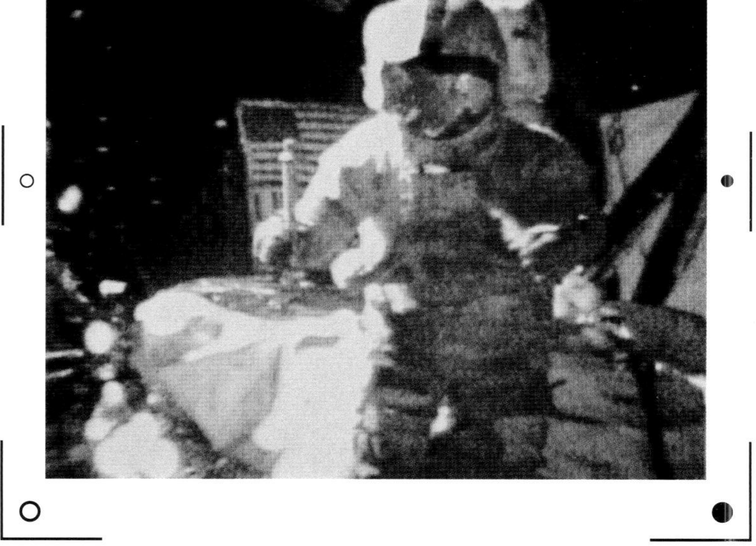

lovingly placed it in a special bag for the trip home where it was named the Genesis Rock.

But not everything on the mission came so easily. A new drill kit had been added to the inventory of geological sampling tools, and it proved to be the bane of Dave Scott's mission. He was possessed of great physical strength, yet every time he tried to drill a hole in the surface for an experiment, the core sample tube would go down a short distance and immediately bind up. It was immensely frustrating and time consuming.

Later in the same EVA Scott finally managed to get a drill-core sample down to about two metres (seven feet). Of course, when he tried to bring up the tubes it was like pulling the mythical sword from the stone. They called it a day.

Leaving the Lunar Module early the next day for their third and last EVA, he was determined to get that tube out. He tried jiggling it, banging it, even getting below the handles in an attempt to wrench it free, all with very minimal results. Finally, he and Irwin worked together, burning up valuable time, and with one Herculean last effort Scott was able to yank the tube out, spraining his shoulder in the process. While a dose of painkillers took care of the pain, having left the sample on the moon would have been much more painful.

They spent the remainder of the EVA exploring Hadley Rille, sampling fantastically large boulders made up of bits of lunar bedrock, and admiring the amazing view across the rille. It was a perfect end to a productive mission.

Upon their return to Earth, the scientists at the Lunar Receiving Laboratory raced to examine the deep drill-core sample, and to everyone's delight it showed over 50 distinct layers – a veritable timeline of lunar evolution. Between that and the Genesis Rock, Scott, Irwin and Worden had to agree that the mission had been well worth it, and (as any test pilot would decree), was the best yet.

**Above** James Irwin of Apollo 15 digs a trench in the lunar soil. Mount Hadley rises nearly 4,572 metres (15,000 feet) behind him. The device to the left is a "gnomon", used to determine level or slope and colour balance in their documenting photographs.

## THE STAMP AFFAIR

Over the years, all astronauts had taken personal items into space with them; it was an authorized and generally unregulated activity. On Apollo 15 the crew took along 398 commemorative stamp "covers" with them and, upon their return, sold them and put a portion of the proceeds into a college fund for their children. But the prices skyrocketed, and NASA received complaints. Congress got involved, and NASA was forced to take action. None of the three men ever flew again and from then on NASA scrutinized all personal effects taken on Apollo flights.

**Below** A NASA press release detailing the "stamp affair" from Apollo 15. The entire endeavour was blown open when brokers who supplied the stamps got greedy. The crew was eventually disciplined.

**NATIONAL AERONAUTICS AND SPACE ADMINISTRATION**
Manned Spacecraft Center
Houston, Texas 77058

John P. Donnelly
(202/755-3828)

FOR RELEASE:
July 11, 1972

RELEASE NO: 72-143

RELEASED AT NASA HEADQUARTERS

APOLLO 15 STAMPS

NASA has conducted an inquiry into the question of unauthorized postal covers reported to have been carried by the crew on the Apollo 15 mission last July.

Astronauts David Scott, Alfred Worden and James Irwin have acknowledged carrying approximately 400 unauthorized postal covers on this mission, 100 of which were given by the crew to an acquaintance who is now in Germany. These are the postal covers which apparently were later sold to stamp collectors for approximately $1500 apiece.

In the course of its inquiry, NASA learned that the Apollo 15 crew had at one time agreed to provide 100 of the covers to their acquaintance in return for a "trust fund" for their children. After the covers had been given to the acquaintance, however, they realized--on their own--that this was improper and they declined either to accept the "trust fund" or an alternative offer of stamps in exchange for the 100 postal covers.

NASA has authorized astronauts, within established procedures, to carry personal souvenir type items, including some postal covers, on Apollo 15 and other manned space flights, subject to the condition that these articles would be retained

- more -

**Below** A happy crew back on Earth. From left, Dave Scott, Mission Commander; Al Worden, Command Module Pilot and James Irwin, Lunar Module Pilot.

# LANDING IN THE LUNAR HIGHLANDS

THERE HAD BEEN NOTHING QUITE LIKE IT IN NASA'S HISTORY THUS FAR. FOR THE FIRST TIME EVER, THE TEXANS IN MISSION CONTROL AT LAST HEARD THEIR FAMILIAR SOUTHERN DRAWL FROM THE MOON DURING APOLLO 16'S APRIL 1972 MISSION.

This was not just an accent, but a voice littered with bad jokes and exclamations such as "Hot dog!" and "Whoopie!". It was Charlie Duke on his novice voyage as Lunar Module Pilot. John Young was the other voice from the moon, and spoke with more of a Kentucky slur than anything else (though he hailed from Northern California). He was the Mission Commander. Overhead, following their antics from lunar orbit, was Ken Mattingly, the Command Module Pilot, flying the mission that had been snatched from him on Apollo 13.

Apollo 16's landing site was the first in the lunar highlands, the old, mountainous regions that covered much more of the moon than the younger *maria* did (the other missions had all landed on, or near, mare areas). It was also another "J" mission, with a Rover and the extended-stay Lunar Module. Young and Duke made maximum use of both during their lunar visit.

They had an ambitious programme of three EVAs, each one averaging about seven hours. The ALSEP was first on the schedule, and was deployed according to plan – almost. Since Apollo 12 there had been efforts to set up an experiment to measure the flow of internal heat out of the moon, which would help to determine its origins. It required drilling holes and inserting probes, and had been one of the major problems on Apollo 15. The geophysicists in Houston were really looking forward to this experiment, especially because the drill had been redesigned and was working well. As Young was laying out another component, he felt a tug on his boot as he crossed the site and the following exchange was heard at Mission Control:

**YOUNG:** Charlie...
**DUKE:** What?
**YOUNG:** Something happened here.
**DUKE:** What happened?
**YOUNG:** I don't know. Here's a line that pulled loose.
**DUKE:** Uh-oh.
**YOUNG:** What is that? What line is it?
**DUKE:** That's the heat flow. You've pulled it off.
**YOUNG:**I don't know how it happened.
**YOUNG:** Pulled loose from there?
**DUKE:** Yeah.
**YOUNG:** God almighty.
**DUKE:** Well, I'm wasting my time.

Then, after a brief conference with Houston...

**YOUNG:** I'm sorry, Charlie. God Damn...

**Above** 16 April 1972: the last-but-one lunar mission, Apollo 16, lifts off from Florida. Once again it would out-do all previous missions.

## ORANGE JUICE

Owing to cardiac irregularities the moonwalkers on Apollo 15 had experienced, Young and Duke were instructed to drink lots of orange juice between EVAs to provide potassium. As Young so delicately pointed out, on an open mike for all the world to hear, it did not always agree with their stomachs…

**YOUNG:** I have the farts, again. I got them again, Charlie. I don't know what the hell gives them to me... I think it's acid stomach. I really do.
**DUKE:** It probably is.
**YOUNG:** I mean, I haven't eaten this much citrus fruit in 20 years! And I'll tell you one thing, in another 12 fucking days, I ain't never eating any more. And if they offer to supplement my potassium with my breakfast, I'm going to throw up! I like an occasional orange. Really do. But I'll be durned if I'm going to be buried in oranges.

And then, a call from Houston…

**CAPCOM:** Orion, Houston.

**YOUNG:** Yes, sir.
**CAPCOM:** Okay, John. We have a hot mike.
**YOUNG:** Uh… how long have we had that?
**CAPCOM:** … It's been on through the "debriefing"…

Young's attitude changed on a dime, and nothing more was mentioned on-air about the oranges for the rest of the flight.

**Below** The crew of Apollo 16: from left, Ken Mattingly, Command Module Pilot; John Young, Mission Commander and Charlie Duke, Lunar Module Pilot.

**Opposite** A view of the Command/Service Module Casper, with Mattingly alone at the helm, from the Lunar Module. Mattingly had been removed from Apollo 13 at the last moment, and Apollo 16 was his "makeup" flight.

## CHARLES DUKE DROPS THE HAMMER

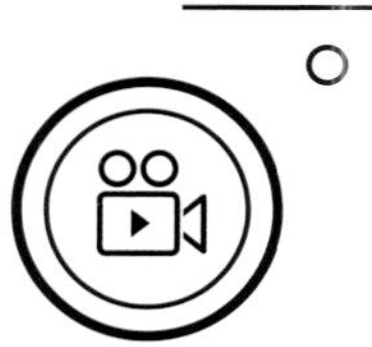

For Duke, the heat flow experiment had become a personal affair. Previous missions had tried to deploy it, but always, problems with the drill or some other component compromised the returns. For the only time in the flight he sounded dejected. Young, usually the dry-witted foil for Charlie's antics, was genuinely sorry, apologizing over and over again. They examined the torn wire; it was a poorly designed connector that had cut clean through the ribbon. It was irreparable.

They moved on, and completed the Rover trip out to nearby Flag Crater, hoping to find some rocks of volcanic origin. They never did.

Their second EVA went without a hitch, and the third finally rewarded the geologists with the find of the mission. They had hoped to discover one very large rock, a boulder, from which they could derive multiple samples. Duke had spotted a likely candidate on the way down from orbit, and sure enough, when they got to North Ray Crater, there it was. At first, because of the optics of the TV camera on the Rover and the odd perspective on the moon, the team back in Houston couldn't really tell just how big the rock was, but as the astronauts got smaller and smaller in the distance, it was clear that this was one massive rock. It was named, appropriately, House Rock, and was the largest sampled yet.

All too soon their time was up and the two tired but elated explorers had to make their final return to the Lunar Module. As other crews before them had, they tossed out unneeded gear – the backpacks, cameras and other heavy items, and readied themselves for their return to the orbiting Command Module and Ken Mattingly. It had been a rewarding mission, and although they had not found the volcanic rocks many were hoping for, they had gone further and explored more than any other Apollo crew. And then there was one. President Nixon had cancelled the remaining Apollo flights when Apollo 11 was taking place – Apollo 17 would be the end of the line.

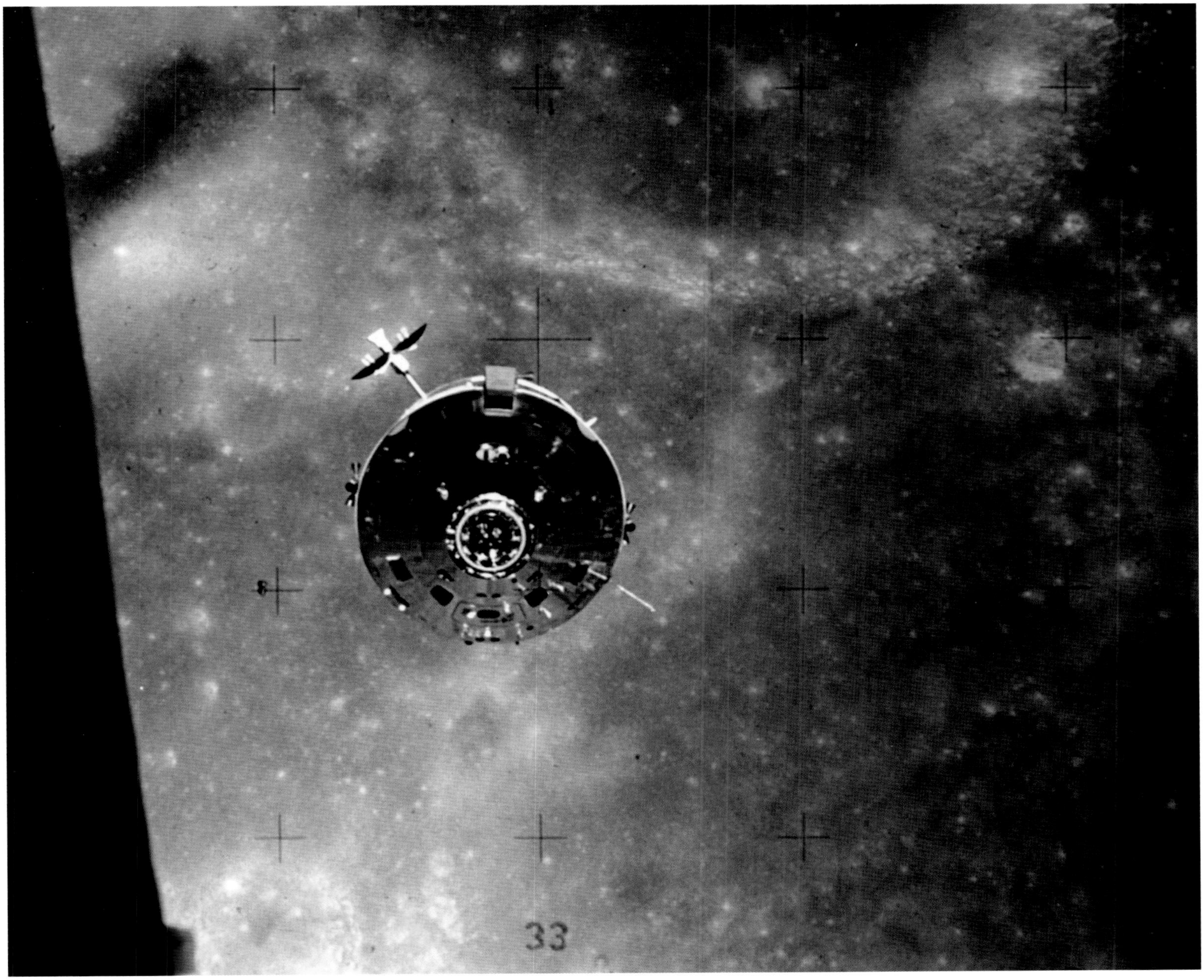

## THE LUNAR GRAND PRIX

A part of the planned activities for the Apollo 16 crew was to test the Lunar Roving Vehicle. Charlie Duke was to operate the movie camera while Young put the Rover through its paces. After a few passes, some swerves and a brake test, Young went for the lunar speed record for a wheeled vehicle: about 12 kilometres (8 miles) per hour. As usual, the Rover took the punishment with room to spare.

**Right** John Young "takes to the air" (or vacuum) as he puts the Lunar Roving Vehicle through its paces, testing its speed and handling capabilities.

# APOLLO 16 FLYER

An in-depth official NASA flyer about the Apollo 16 mission. Included are crew profiles, a mission timeline and key objectives.

# APOLLO 16 DATA SHEET

This Apollo 16 Data Sheet provides information on the projected schedule of key mission events, as well as a map of the expected traverses of the lunar surface. While mission timetables always slipped a bit, Apollo 16 remained fairly true to schedule. These sheets would have been given to the press, contractors and various staff not part of Mission Control.

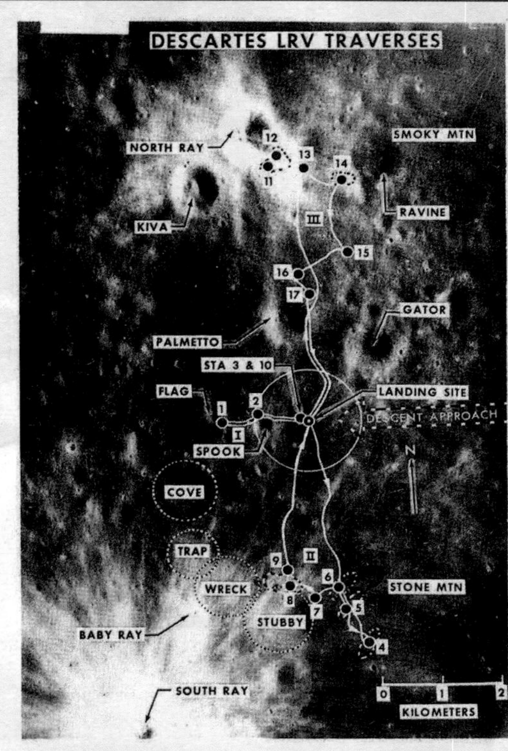

## APOLLO 16 MISSION EVENTS

| EVENT | G.E.T. HR:MIN | C.S.T. HR:MIN |
|---|---|---|
| ---SUN/APRIL 16--- | | |
| LIFT-OFF | 00:00 | 11:54 a.m. |
| EPO INSERTION | 00:12 | 12:06 p.m. |
| TRANSLUNAR INJECTION | | |
| BURN INITIATION ($t_B$ = 335 SEC) | 02:33 | 2:27 |
| CSM/S-IVB SEPARATION | 03:04 | 2:58 |
| TV COVERAGE (TRANS & DOCK, 19 MIN) | 03:09 | 3:03 |
| DOCKING | 03:14 | 3:08 |
| CSM/LM EJECTION | 03:59 | 3:53 |
| EVASIVE MANEUVER (PERFORMED BY S-IVB) | 04:22 | 4:16 |
| FIRST MIDCOURSE CORRECTION (MCC-1) | 11:39 | 11:33 |
| ---MON/APRIL 17--- | | |
| MCC-2 | 30:39 | 6:33 p.m. |
| ---TUE/APRIL 18--- | | |
| MCC-3 | 52:29 | 4:23 p.m. |
| ---WED/APRIL 19--- | | |
| MCC-4 | 69:29 | 9:23 a.m. |
| SIM DOOR JETTISON | 69:59 | 9:53 |
| LUNAR ORBIT INSERTION (LOI) | | |
| BURN INITIATION ($t_B$ = 375 SEC) | 74:29 | 2:23 p.m. |
| S-IVB PREDICTED LUNAR IMPACT | 74:30 | 2:24 |
| SELENOGRAPHIC LATITUDE = -2.3° | | |
| SELENOGRAPHIC LONGITUDE = -31.7° | | |
| DESCENT ORBIT INSERTION (DOI, REV 2) | | |
| BURN INITIATION ($t_B$ = 24 SEC) | 78:36 | 6:30 |
| ---THUR/APRIL 20--- | | |
| UNDOCKING & CSM SEPARATION (REV 12) | 96:14 | 12:08 p.m. |
| CSM CIRCULARIZATION (REV 12) ($t_B$ = 6 SEC) | 97:42 | 1:36 |
| POWERED DESCENT INITIATION (REV 13) | | |
| DPS IGNITION | 98:35 | 2:29 |
| HIGH GATE (P63 TO P64) | 98:44 | 2:38 |
| LOW GATE | 98:45 | 2:39 |
| VERTICAL DESCENT (P64 TO P65) | 98:46 | 2:40 |
| LM LANDING | 98:47 | 2:41 |
| SELENOGRAPHIC LATITUDE = -9.0° | | |
| SELENOGRAPHIC LONGITUDE = 15.5° | | |
| CSM FIRST PASS OVER LLS (REV 13) | 98:43 | 2:37 |
| FIRST EVA (7 HR) | 102:25 | 6:19 |
| TV COVERAGE (6 HR 47 MIN) | 102:25 | 6:19 |
| ---FRI/APRIL 21--- | | |
| SECOND EVA (7 HR) | 124:50 | 4:44 p.m. |
| TV COVERAGE (6 HR 35 MIN) | 125:10 | 5:04 |
| ---SAT/APRIL 22--- | | |
| THIRD EVA (7 HR) | 148:25 | 4:19 p.m. |
| TV COVERAGE (8 HR 04 MIN) | 148:45 | 4:39 |
| FIRST CSM PLANE CHANGE (REV 40) | | |
| BURN INITIATION ($t_B$ = 9 SEC) | 152:29 | 8:23 |

## APOLLO 16 MISSION EVENTS (CONCLUDED)

| EVENT | G.E.T. HR:MIN | C.S.T. HR:MIN |
|---|---|---|
| ---SUN/APRIL 23--- | | |
| TV COVERAGE (EQUIPMENT JETTISON, 12 MIN) | 170:08 | 2:02 p.m. |
| TV COVERAGE (LM LIFT-OFF, 25 MIN) | 171:30 | 3:24 |
| CSM SECOND PASS OVER LLS (REV 50) | 171:46 | 3:40 |
| LM ASCENT (REV 50) | | |
| LM LIFT-OFF | 171:45 | 3:39 |
| LM INSERTION ($t_B$ = 434 SEC) | 171:52 | 3:46 |
| TPI (APS) ($t_B$ = 3 SEC) | 172:39 | 4:33 |
| TV COVERAGE (RENDEZVOUS PHASE, 6 MIN) | 173:20 | 5:14 |
| RENDEZVOUS MANEUVERS | | |
| BRAKING | 173:20 | 5:14 |
| DOCKING | 173:40 | 5:34 |
| TV COVERAGE (5 MIN) | 173:46 | 5:40 |
| LM JETTISON (REV 53) | 177:31 | 9:25 |
| CSM SEPARATION | | |
| BURN INITIATION ($t_B$ = 13 SEC) | 177:36 | 9:30 |
| ASCENT STAGE DEORBIT | 179:16 | 11:10 |
| ASCENT STAGE LUNAR IMPACT (CSM REV 54) | 179:39 | 11:33 |
| SELENOGRAPHIC LATITUDE = -9.5° | | |
| SELENOGRAPHIC LONGITUDE = 15.0° | | |
| ---MON/APRIL 24--- | | |
| SECOND CSM PLANE CHANGE ($t_B$ = 16 SEC) | 193:14 | 1:08 p.m. |
| ---TUE/APRIL 25--- | | |
| SHAPING BURN | | |
| BURN INITIATION ($t_B$ = 2 SEC) | 216:49 | 12:43 p.m. |
| SUBSATELLITE JETTISON (CSM REV 73) | 218:02 | 1:56 |
| TRANSEARTH INJECTION (REV 76) | | |
| BURN INITIATION ($t_B$ = 150 SEC) | 222:21 | 6:15 |
| ---WED/APRIL 26--- | | |
| MCC-5 | 239:23 | 11:17 a.m. |
| TV COVERAGE (TRANSEARTH EVA, 1 HR 10 MIN) | 241:55 | 1:49 p.m. |
| ---THUR/APRIL 27--- | | |
| MCC-6 | 268:23 | 4:17 p.m. |
| ---FRI/APRIL 28--- | | |
| MCC-7 | 287:23 | 11:17 a.m. |
| CM/SM SEPARATION | 290:08 | 2:02 p.m. |
| ENTRY INTERFACE | 290:23 | 2:17 |
| CM LANDING | 290:36 | 2:30 |
| GEODETIC LATITUDE = 5.00° | | |
| LONGITUDE = -158.67° | | |

NASA-MSC-FOD
MISSION PLANNING & ANALYSIS DIVISION
MARCH 13, 1972

# CHAPTER TWENTY-THREE

# FINAL MOMENTS: APOLLO 17

PRESIDENT NIXON HAD CANCELLED APOLLOS 18, 19 AND 20, AND THE AMERICAN LUNAR PROGRAMME HAD REACHED THE END OF THE LINE: APOLLO 17. FORTUNATELY, THIS COINCIDED WITH THE MATURING OF THE MOON FLIGHTS.

Each of the "J" missions had pushed the boundaries further until Apollo 16, which fully utilized the potential of the improved Lunar Module and the Lunar Rover. Now it was up to Apollo 17 to compress the remaining questions and quest for answers into 75 hours on the lunar surface. And then, it would be all over.

Already, the assembly lines for the Saturns and the lunar flight hardware had been shut down. The contractors had either queued up to find work on the Shuttle programme, or moved onto other endeavours. Apollo 17 took flight on 7 December 1972, into the fading twilight of the space race.

Gene Cernan was the Mission Commander, returning to complete the ride he started in Apollo 10. The Command Module Pilot was Ron Evans, glad to have a seat on this last flight. The Lunar Module Pilot was supposed to have been Joe Engle, who had been working hard to keep his place in line. When the scientific community realized that Apollo 17 would be the final mission, there was a strong push to send a trained scientist to the moon. So Harrison Schmitt, with his PhD in Geology from Harvard, was given the slot. He had originally been scheduled to fly on Apollo 18. A few feathers were ruffled, but all concerned eventually saw the logic in the decision. This would be the last chance for a geological payoff from the moon.

And what a payoff it was. After navigating a landing in the topographically complex region, Cernan and Schmitt were eager to get a start on the first of their three seven-hour-plus EVAs. Their landing site, called the Taurus-Littrow region, was on the edge of Mare Serenitatis, the Sea of Serenity, which about four billion years ago was anything but. Something large and fast-moving had slammed into the moon here, and along the edges of the impact had churned up a huge volume of older material. And a part of that old rock was Taurus-Littrow. Setting up the ALSEP went well, and even the heat-flow experiment made it in one piece.

**Below** Schmitt sampling at Taurus-Littrow. Moon dust has covered the lower three quaters of his pressure suit; it was fine-grained, sticky and impossible to get off.

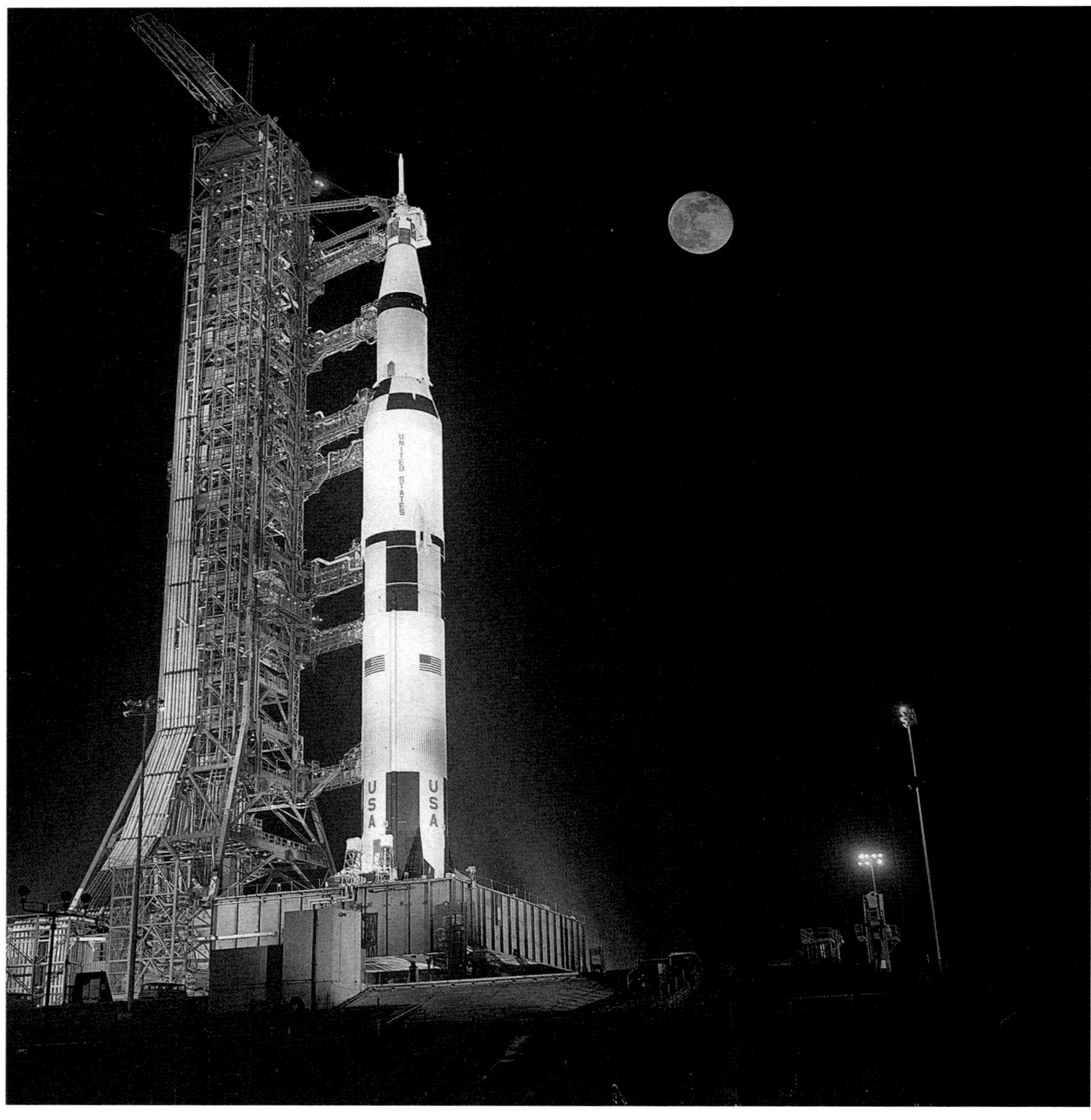


**Opposite** The last moon mission counts down for the first – and only – Apollo night launch.

Some of the earlier experiments had been dropped in favour of new ones, and the results from the nuclear-fuelled station came back for years (the radioisotopic generators on the ALSEPs could last for up to ten years).

On the second EVA the astronauts had a field day sampling rocks at a feature called the South Massif. With Schmitt acting as the expert on the ground, Cernan became his observer and trusted assistant. It was an odd role reversal for a Mission Commander, but Cernan took it in his stride and was enthusiastic and helpful.

The high point of the mission was yet to come, however. They drove to Shorty Crater, and once there made a sample stop. While Cernan took care of some housekeeping with the Rover, Schmitt walked over to look at a boulder, and then stopped short. What he saw made him gasp before Mission Control heard the following.

**SCHMITT:** There is orange soil!
**CERNAN:** Well, don't move it until I see it.
**SCHMITT:** It's all over! Orange.
**CERNAN:** Don't move it until I see it!
**SCHMITT:** I stirred it up with my feet
**CERNAN:** Hey, it is! I can see it from here.
**SCHMITT:** It's orange!
**CERNAN:** Wait a minute. Let me put my visor up... it's still orange!
**SCHMITT:** Sure it is! Crazy!
**CERNAN:** Orange! He's not going out of his wits. It really is.

It was the mission's most spectacular find. At the time, Schmitt thought it might be volcanic glass spewed out from a nearby fumarole, evidence of

## LEE SILVER

Once Harrison "Jack" Schmitt got involved with Apollo, he felt that the geology of the moon was getting short shrift from the astronauts. He got in touch with his old mentor, Lee Silver, then at Cal Tech in Pasadena, California. Silver took the astronauts on a field trip to the Orocopia Mountains in Southern California. By Apollo 15, this education had taken root, and it climaxed with Schmitt's brilliant investigations on Apollo 17. Silver can be seen here in the striped shirt, pointing, with Charlie Duke behind him and John Young in front.

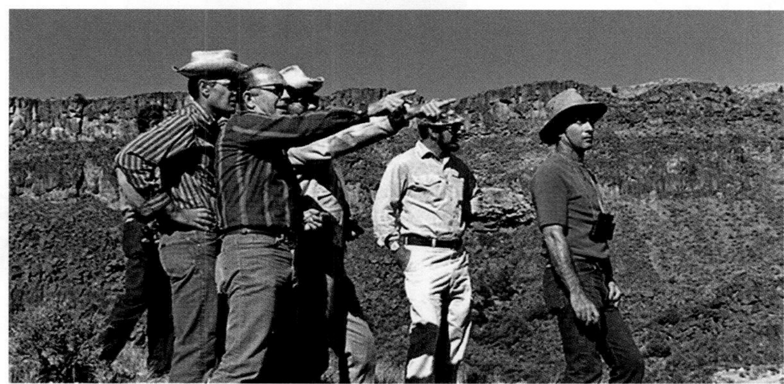

a hot moon (ie recent volcanic activity). It turned out the orange lava glass was old, but the crater was newer, and the two were unrelated. Still, it was a fascinating discovery and gave researchers a window to the past.

There was a third and final EVA, and when they returned to the Lunar Module, Cernan drove the Rover off to a distance so that the onboard TV camera could watch the Lunar Module liftoff. He trudged back to the Lunar Module and helped Schmitt load up the samples and experiments. Then, as they prepared to re-enter the Lunar Module, Cernan read aloud the contents of a plaque affixed to the Lunar Module leg strut, similar to those carried on all Lunar Modules.

**CERNAN:** We have a pictorial view of the moon, a pictorial view of where all the Apollo landings have been made; so that when this plaque is seen again by others who come, they will know where it all started. The words are, "Here man completed his first exploration of the Moon, December 1972 ad. May the spirit of peace in which we came be reflected in the lives of all mankind." It's signed, Eugene A Cernan, Ronald E Evans, Harrison H Schmitt and, most prominently, Richard M Nixon, President of the United States of America. This is our commemoration that will be here until someone like us, until some of you who are out there, who are the promise of the future, come back to read it again and to further the exploration and the meaning of Apollo.

Soon Schmitt climbed into the Lunar Module and Cernan paused at the footpad. From here he had taken his first step onto the moon, just as Neil Armstrong had, and from here he would take his last, anyone's last, for who knew how long? It was as good a place as any to radio home his final thoughts regarding this great adventure:

**CERNAN:**... as I take man's last step from the surface, back home for some time to come – but we believe not too long into the future – I'd like to just say what I believe history will record. That America's challenge of today has forged man's destiny of tomorrow. And, as we leave the Moon at Taurus-Littrow, we leave as we came and, God willing, as we shall return, with peace and hope for all mankind. Godspeed the crew of Apollo 17.

He climbed the ladder, closed the hatch and within hours they were back in orbit with Ron Evans. It had been the most productive mission yet, and provided scientists with fodder for many years of research.

After two more days cruising home and a splashdown, it was all over, just like that. What started with a challenge from a martyred president had come to fruition in just nine years. It would be the last time man left the orbit of his home planet for at least 40 years. The Golden Age of space exploration had come to a premature close.

But NASA had one more Saturn V being readied in the Vehicle Assembly Building, and the plans for it were truly epic in scale.

## APOLLO 17 LEAVES THE MOON

# APOLLO LUNAR ROVING VEHICLE

## THE BLUE MARBLE

**Opposite** Gene Cernan mounts the Rover. The moonwalkers had developed a boarding technique which combined a jump-and-drop while angling their legs inside the Rover at the same time. It was faster and easier than climbing in.

This photo, one of the most famous from the Apollo years, was taken about five hours after Apollo 17's launch and about two hours after Trans-Lunar Injection. It was the only clear, fully-lit photo from the programme. Used for years by environmentalists to demonstrate the fragility of the Earth, it is usually viewed inverted (as we are used to viewing globes) with the arctic at the top. It was only the particular orientation of Apollo 17's trajectory that allowed the photo to be taken.

# CHAPTER TWENTY-FOUR

# THE LEGACY OF APOLLO

DURING THE GLORY YEARS OF APOLLO, NASA HAD PLANS FOR MISSIONS AFTER APOLLO 17 AND THE APOLLO 18–20 MISSIONS WOULD HAVE BEEN THE MOST AMBITIOUS YET. BUT THERE WERE PROPOSALS TO MOVE BEYOND THE QUICK ADVENTURES ON THE MOON.

There were plans for a Mars voyage, using booster rockets fashioned from Apollo-derived hardware (clusters of eight or more F1 engines on a booster were envisioned), and dozens of proposals had been studied for extended lunar missions, with large manned bases, "moon-trucks" inspired by the Lunar Module and much more. The aerospace companies were scrambling to keep a hand in the space business, and had ambitious ideas of their own – some at NASA's request and others independent of official sanction.

In the end the Apollo programme went out with more of a whimper than a bang. Nevertheless, there were still great things ahead for the machines of Apollo.

First to fly was the spectacular Skylab programme. At over 90 tonnes (100 tons), it was the biggest manned facility in space until the current International Space Station. It had its origins in an early von Braun proposal called Project Horizon (which was more about an armed lunar base for military applications, than a research installation, but included an orbiting station) and in the Manned Orbiting Laboratory (MOL) of the Air Force – another military platform utilizing Gemini technology. In the end, however, Skylab was all Apollo.

Skylab was a Saturn SIVB stage that had been remodelled as a space station. Using a leftover Saturn V, the unmanned craft launched on 14 May 1973. It was soon followed by the launch of an older Saturn IB with a crewed Apollo Command/Service Module. Though there had been launch damage to the empty Skylab, the intrepid crew, led by Apollo 12's Pete Conrad, performed a dangerous repair EVA and saved the project. Two more crews followed, and then Skylab was shut down. Years later, as its orbit started to decay, NASA counted on the Shuttle to boost it to a higher orbit, but delays in that programme doomed Skylab to a fiery death via uncontrolled re-entry in July 1979.

Some remaining flight-worthy Apollo hardware was then redeployed for the Apollo–Soyuz Test Project (ASTP) in July 1975. Essentially a public-relations mission, the Apollo part of the two-spacecraft linkup would

## APOLLO / VENUS

As part of the Apollo Applications Program, a manned flyby of Venus was considered. As a manned landing is impractical, with surface temperatures approaching 482°C (900°F) and atmospheric pressures of 89.6 bar (1,300 psi), the spacecraft would loop past Venus and observe the planet instead. The mission would have taken about 14 months, and while fascinating to contemplate, it's difficult to imagine that it would have provided data more valuable than NASA's later Magellan and other unmanned Venus probes.

**Right** In the post-Apollo Venus flyby mission, Apollo hardware, along with a Skylab-like habitation and laboratory module, would have made a 14-month trip past Venus without landing.

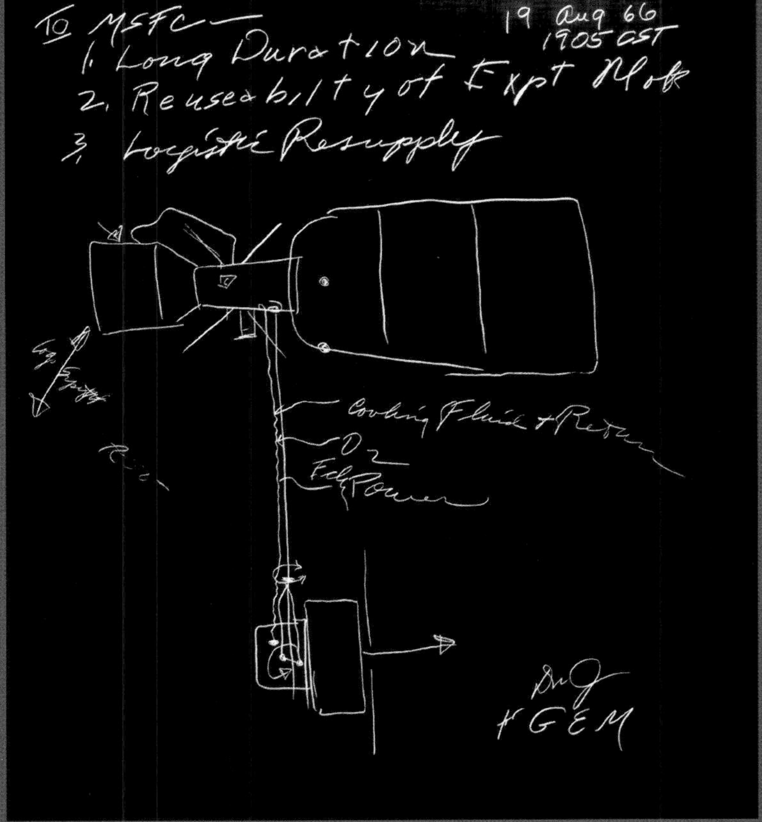


**Right** An 1966 Skylab concept sketch by George Mueller, NASA Deputy Director.

## THE X-20

As NASA was reaching for the moon, the US Air Force was following another German-pioneered path to space. Based on the Sänger skip-bomber, the X-20 was an orbital bomber and spy platform. Designed to be launched atop a Titan III, the X-20, also known as Dyna-Soar (short for dynamic soaring), resembled the later Space Shuttle (which it would have preceded by 15 years), but was smaller and designed for a crew of one or two. It never made it past the mock-up stage.

**Left** The X-20 would have placed an early variant of the Space Shuttle atop a modified Titan booster to achieve orbit in the late 1960s.

be commanded by Deke Slayton, one of the original seven Mercury astronauts who had been grounded by heart irregularities. Now certified to fly, Slayton plunged into the mission with passion, even travelling to the Soviet Union to train on Russian space hardware. The Soviet Soyuz was commanded by Alexi Leonov, the first man to walk in space. The two craft, Apollo and Soyuz, linked up in Earth orbit via a special docking adapter on 17 July. Handshakes and intercraft visits occupied the 44 hours that the craft were mated, and then they separated and came home. NASA would not fly people in space again until the Shuttle was inaugurated in 1981.

Then, there was Mars. Always the ultimate target for many NASA planners, the concepts for manned flights were studied hundreds of times between 1950 and the 1970s.

**Opposite** Skylab, as ultimately flown. The corrugated gold cover near the bottom of the photo is the heat shield deployed by Pete Conrad and his crew prior to inhabiting the station, and the solar panel on the right was supposed to have a matching twin on the other side.

**Left** The Apollo–Soyuz Test Project was a product of the Cold War, and occurred during perilous times for the US–Soviet relationship. The mission, billed as a "Handshake in space," was as much about PR as it was about technology.

Many of these mission plans utilized Apollo hardware in key roles, featuring, especially, a "stretched" Saturn V and augmented Command Modules. To view them shows what could have been.

Ultimately, however, after Skylab and the ASTP, humanity would have to learn to settle for ground-based spin-offs from Apollo. Examples of the influence of Apollo on life on Earth can be seen in the following:

- The Apollo Guidance Computer was the first compact computer utilizing integrated circuits, and was the precursor of the highly miniaturized computers we enjoy today.
- Waste-water purification technology was advanced during the Apollo years for use onboard and during extended missions.
- Famously, Teflon was developed for various Apollo applications and Teflon and its derivatives are still very much in use.
- Kidney dialysis machines were advanced through the need, during the Apollo era, to remove toxins from liquids.
- Medical commuted tomography (CT) scans and magnetic resonance imaging (MRI) are a development from Apollo demands for imaging and quality-control technologies.

There are hundreds more. While far more prosaic than spaceflight itself, these are valued additions to our daily lives.

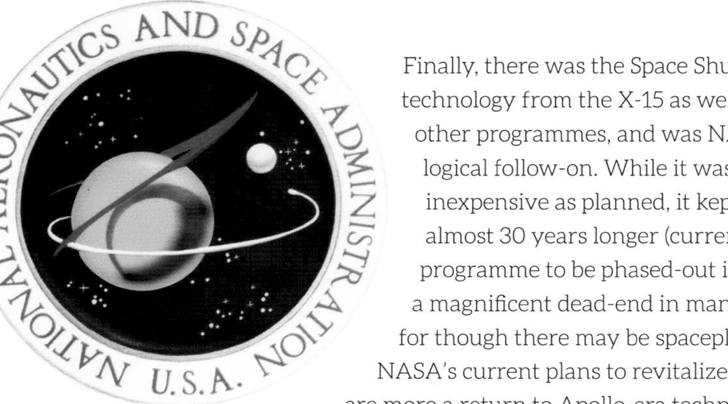


Finally, there was the Space Shuttle which applied technology from the X-15 as well as Apollo and other programmes, and was NASA's choice for a logical follow-on. While it was never as reliable or inexpensive as planned, it kept the US in space for almost 30 years longer (current plans call for the programme to be phased-out in 2010). It was a magnificent dead-end in many ways, however, for though there may be spaceplanes in our future, NASA's current plans to revitalize the space programme are more a return to Apollo-era technology for the new Constellation launch system.

It is worth remembering that a certain amount of luck travelled with those early pioneers to the moon. Apollo 13 was the exception, but even that potential disaster resulted in a safe return of the crew. In a long-duration Mars mission, or on a lunar station far from home, further such emergencies could have life-threatening implications.

The question before us, then, is not what could have been, but what can we achieve in the future with the lessons learned from Apollo and its follow-on programmes? What are we willing to dream, to reach for, and to risk?

**Above** The original NASA logo dates back to 1959. The orange ball represents a planet, and the red delta shape represents aeronautical research. The bright white object circling the planet is a spacecraft.

**Below** NASA's Space Shuttle. This project has been a broad mix of success and failure; success that the world's first (and so far only) manned spaceplane has been flown for over 25 years, and failure in that it has proved to be both expensive and dangerous. The Shuttle will be retired in 2010.

# FUTURE PLANS FOR APOLLO

A 1969 memo concerning future plans for Apollo. Just weeks before the Nixon administration would begin to implement cuts to this series of flights, NASA was still planning through to Apollo 20.

From NASA Hdq.

NATIONAL AERONAUTICS AND SPACE ADMINISTRATION
WASHINGTON, D.C. 20546

AUG 4 2 12 PM '69

REPLY TO
ATTN OF:

July 29, 1969

TO: A/Administrator

FROM: M/Associate Administrator for Manned Space Flight

SUBJECT: Manned Space Flight Weekly Report - July 28, 1969

1. APOLLO 11: First manned lunar landing accomplished: July 16-24, 1969. First footstep on the moon at 10:56:25 p.m. EDT, July 20.

2. APOLLO 12: On July 24, Apollo 11 splashdown day, all centers and supporting elements were instructed to transfer to the alternate lunar exploration phase of the program. Our second landing mission, moving into the initial phase of a comprehensive lunar exploration program, will head for Site 7 in the western mare area -- Oceanus Procellarum -- several hundred feet from the Surveyor III landing point; Site 5 will be the backup site. Apollo 12 launch readiness is now targeted for November 14, with November 16 as the alternate date.

3. APOLLO 13: Apollo elements were also directed to proceed toward an earliest launch readiness date of March 9, 1970, aiming toward a touchdown in the Fra Mauro Highlands area of the moon.

4. CURRENT APOLLO PLANNING SUMMARY: Through Apollo 20, the fifteenth Saturn V flight, the tentative planning schedule stands as follows:

PA-MGR ✓
PA-M.CSM ✓
PA-M.LM ✓
PA-M.LLO
PA-A.MgFLS ✓
PA-TecAst ✓
PA2
PD
PE
PF
PP
PT
FILES ✓
NA

| FLIGHT | LAUNCH PLANS | | TENTATIVE LANDING AREA |
|---|---|---|---|
| Apollo 12 | November | 1969 | Oceanus Procellarum lunar lowlands |
| Apollo 13 | March | 1970 | Fra Mauro Highlands |
| Apollo 14 | July | 1970 | Crater Censorinus Highlands |
| Apollo 15 | November | 1970 | Littrow volcanic area |
| Apollo 16 | April | 1971 | Crater Tycho (Surveyor VII impact area) |
| Apollo 17 | September | 1971 | Marius Hills volcanic domes |
| Apollo 18 | February | 1972 | Schroter's Valley - river-like channelways |
| Apollo 19 | July | 1972 | Hyginus Rille region - Linear Rille-crater area |
| Apollo 20 | December | 1972 | Crater Copernicus - large crater impact area |

5. MSFC/LRV: The pre-proposal bidder's conference was held on July 23 at Michoud. Eight firms were represented: Allis-Chalmers, Bendix, Boeing, Chrysler, General Motors, Grumman, TRW, and Westinghouse. The next major milestone is August 22, when the proposals are due to Marshall.

INDEXING DATA

| DATE | OPR | # | T | PGM | SUBJECT | SIGNATOR | LOC |
|---|---|---|---|---|---|---|---|
| 07-29-69 | HQS | | M | APO | (Above) | MUELLER | 071-53 |

# EUROPE RETURNS TO SPACE

WHEN THE EUROPEAN SPACE AGENCY (ESA) WAS FORMED IN 1975 IT RAISED A FEW SCEPTICAL EYEBROWS AT THE TIME ACROSS THE ATLANTIC. THE HOME OF MOST SUCCESSFUL SPACE EXPLORATION TO DATE.

In the glare of Apollo's dazzling successes, it was easy to forget that an important precursor of space exploration had started in Germany not so many years before. Although 17 nations have been involved in ESA missions, Germany and France have been the two largest contributors.

Headquartered in Paris, ESA has control centres in Germany and throughout Europe. Their primary launch facilities are in Kourou, French Guiana, which borders the North of Brazil in South America. They share this with the Centre National d'Etudes Spatiales (CNES), the French space agency. This launch site is unusual in that it has access to a near-equatorial launch profile, so more weight can be launched by a given booster than by major US or Russian launch complexes.

## SWEDES IN SPACE

The ESA is a consortium of European nations, and a broad range of talent is available for their space exploration ventures. An example is Swedish scientist Christer Fuglesang (below) who flew on NASA's STS-116 mission in 2006. A physicist by trade, Fuglesang performed multiple spacewalks for construction of the International Space Station. Performing a total of 18 hours, 15 minutes of EVA, he worked on a truss segment (a primary element of the station), helped to rewire the power system and repaired an ailing solar panel. He was the first Nordic citizen in space.

**Above** An ESA/CNES Ariane 5 rocket departs from Kourou, French Guiana. The Ariane has become one of the world's most popular commercial launchers.

**Above** An artist's conception of the Huygens probe on the surface of Titan. The machine transmitted for 90 minutes after impact.

**Right** The Columbus Laboratory Module for the International Space Station. Delivered in 2008, it houses up to 10 major experiments at a time.

Early ESA launches were exclusively aboard the Ariane rocket, but the Europeans subsequently made a deal with Russia for the use of their Soyuz rocket at their launch complex in French Guiana. This deal is said to be nearing its end, however. While ESA still uses the Ariane 5, its new Ariane 6 should be flying by 2020, replacing other boosters.

The ESA has flown a number of important unmanned exploration programmes. Missions such as Giotto and Rosetta have explored comets, with Rosetta dispatcing a small lander, Philae, to explore the surface of its target. Mars Express has been in continuous operation at the Red Planet since 2003, returning terabytes of valuable data about water on Mars. The ExoMars Trace Gas Orbiter (which was designed in coordination with a Russian lander, which failed during its landing attempt), has also been in orbit around the Red Planet since 2016, searching for water and trace gases such as methane, a possible indicator of microbial life, in the Martian atmosphere. An ExoMars rover is scheduled to land on Mars in 2020 with astrobiology instruments to seek life in the Martian soil. Other projects include orbiting X-ray, gamma ray and solar telescopes, which operate best when above the Earth's atmosphere, unveiling the secrets of distant galaxies and the sun. ESA also operates a variety of Earth science satellites studying climatic and geophysical processes on Earth.

A recent mission, the Smart-1 lunar probe, was a small craft that utilized advanced ion-propulsion technology. It launched in 2003 and gathered valuable new data about potential water on the moon, as well as identifying peaks near the lunar poles, which are bathed in perpetual sunlight, valuable for potential energy generation.

ESA's BepiColumbo probe launches in 2018, and is a joint mission with the Japanese Space Agency to explore Mercury. In 2022, the JUpiter

esa
esa

ICy Moons Explorer (JUICE) mission will head towards the outer solar system to explore Jupiter and three of its moons, Ganymede, Callisto and Europa. This builds on ESA's prior efforts in the outer solar system, the most important being the Huygens Titan lander that traveled to Saturn's moon aboard NASA's Cassini probe. Huygens landed on Titan in 2005, returning the first data and imagery from the surface of another planet's moon and confirming the presence of large bodies of liquid hydrocarbons on its surface, as well as sweeping dunes composed of organic molecules scattered across Titan's equatorial regions.

Arguably the closest ties with NASA have been with the creation of the International Space Station. ESA built the Columbus laboratory module, five by seven metres (15 by 23 feet) in size. It can house ten active experiment modules, which can range from biosciences to solar astronomy to fluid mechanics, and was delivered in early 2008.

**Opposite** ESA's Jules Verne ATV, or Automated Transfer Vehicle, nears the International Space Station in the artist's rendering. The ATV is unmanned, so its entire payload can be used for extra fuel, consumables or parts for the station.

The future of ESA includes plans for manned missions, including lunar exploration and flights to Mars. In many ways, their plans have taken up where NASA's ended in the 1970s, with the shift to Shuttle operations.

The Aurora Programme was created in 2001 as an overall framework for both unmanned and manned exploration of the moon and Mars. A Mars Rover and sample return mission are in development in conjunction with NASA. Manned lunar missions are slated for about 2024, with a Mars mission split between NASA and ESA in the 2030 timeframe. Cooperation with their Russian counterparts is also being explored.

ESA has also been active in cooperation with NASA on the International Space Station, as well as preparing astronauts for Space Shuttle missions over the last 20 years. One of their premiere contributions has been the Jules Verne Automated Transfer Vehicle (ATV), which, like the Russian Progress module, delivers freight and consumables to the International Space Station. The ATV has also been used to refuel the station, and boost the structure to higher orbits.

ESA's contributions to space exploration are varied and broad and, along with the Russian space programme, promise a bright future for international cooperation in the cosmos.

## AHEAD OF ITS TIME: HOTOL

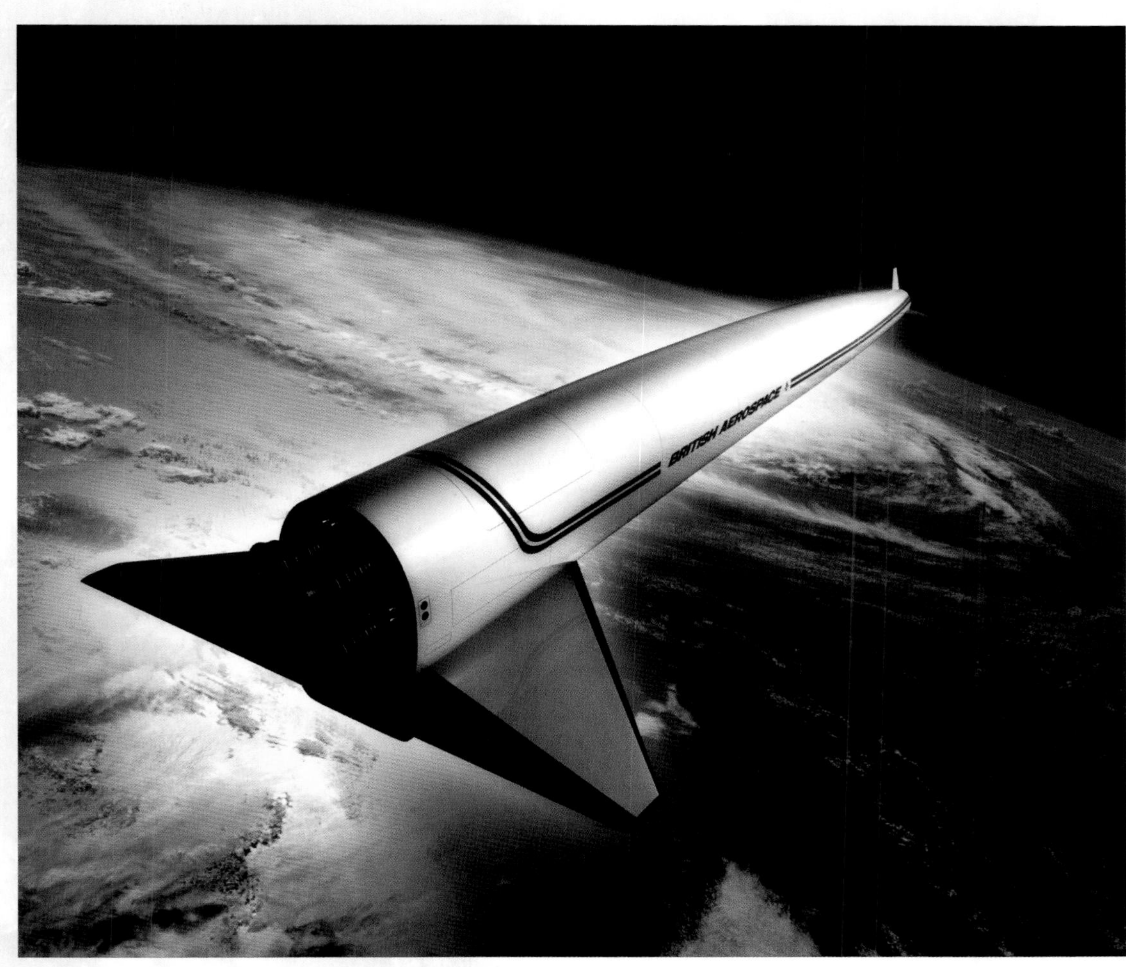


Great Britain sat out much of the space race, with one exception being the short-lived Horizontal Take-Off and Landing (HOTOL) unmanned spaceplane. Begun in 1982, the small orbiter was unique in that it would extract its oxidizer from the atmosphere rather than carrying liquid oxygen. A joint venture between British Aerospace and Rolls Royce, HOTOL's designers encountered a number of technical challenges that simply could not be solved with the limited budget allocated. In 1986 the project was cancelled, but a similar project, Skylon, continues privately funded development today.

**Left** An artist's rendering of the British Aerospace HOTOL. This single-stage-to-orbit (SSTO) spaceplane would have carried very little cargo, but would be only a fraction of the cost of the Shuttle to fly, had it been successful. Sadly, it never left the drawing board.

# CHAPTER TWENTY-SIX

# ASIA ASCENDANT

WHERE EXACTLY DID THE SPACE AGE BEGIN? WAS IT AMERICA, WITH ITS MERCURY ROCKETS? OR WAS IT THE USSR WITH SPUTNIK? OR PERHAPS IN GERMANY, AS THEY LAUNCHED THEIR V2 ROCKETS TOWARDS LONDON DURING THE SECOND WORLD WAR?

These are all good candidates, but it really began in China, well over a millennium ago. After the discovery of gunpowder, the Chinese took one of the most powerful agents of change ever invented, packed it into paper tubes and made objects of adornment, amusement and even war. That was the birth of the rocket. While the scientists of the modern Western world were the first to fly rockets into space and to the moon, China has once again looked to the stars. This time, they will go, as may Japan.

China's modern space programme dates back to 1955, when Mao Zedong first announced the need for his nation to equip itself with modern missile technology as well as nuclear weapons. Chinese missiles flew as early as 1958, using clones of Soviet rockets. Despite a cooling of relations between China and the Soviet Union in the early 1960s, China continued to develop missiles to carry conventional and nuclear warheads.

**Below** The end of the Shenzhou 5 flight, the first to fly with a crew onboard. The press was on hand to meet them as they disembarked.

In the late 1960s China declared the initiation of a manned space programme. However, while designs were drawn up and experimented with, politics and economic realities hindered progress until the death of Chairman Mao in 1976, when Deng Xiaoping called an end to the programme, citing other urgent national needs.

In 1993, the Chinese national space programme was reinvigorated and a manned mission was at last on its way to fruition. In 1999, Shenzhou 1 flew unmanned, followed by three more flights with various animals and sensors on board. Finally, on 15 October 2003, Shenzhou 5 flew with taikonaut (Chinese astronaut) Yáng Lìwei into Earth orbit and returned successfully.

Outside observers were not surprised to see that the spacecraft was a dead-ringer for the Russian Soyuz craft. But although much of the technology was indeed borrowed from the 1962 Soviet design, Shenzhou is an updated, larger and more capable design. It is, perhaps, the spacecraft Soyuz would have become if the Soviets had made it to the moon.

Another Shenzhou flight, Shenzhou 6, flew into orbit in 2005 with two taikonauts, Fèi Jùnlóng and Niè Haishèng aboard. This mission lasted almost five days and was very successful.

For the future, the Chinese have already landed robotic rovers on the moon and announced plans for manned missions by the mid 2030s. When they will actually arrive is uncertain, as spaceflight, especially a lunar voyage, is remarkably difficult even today. What is certain, however, is that, barring any major national upheavals, they will get there. To the East, Japan is plotting its own course into the cosmos. Smaller in scope, Japan's programme has been more incremental and collaborative. The Japanese Space Agency, originally launched in 1969 as the National Space Development Agency (NASDA), was consolidated with other agencies into the Japan Aerospace Exploration Agency (JAXA) in 2003.

Since 1992, Japan has flown astronauts on the US Space Shuttle with Mamoru Mohri being the first. Others have followed, and Japan has also contributed hugely to the International Space Station with the Japanese Experimental Module (JEM), known as Kibo ("Hope"). It is an orbiting laboratory and the largest single module in the space station. Kibo allows astronauts to conduct research hitherto impractical in space.

Japan has flown a fleet of its own rockets for decades. Its first satellite, Osumi, orbited in 1970. In 1994, the much larger H-II rocket allowed the Japanese space program to expand its operations. A solid-fuelled rocket called the M-V has followed. These boosters lifted a variety of increasingly ambitious robotic space missions, ranging from lunar orbiters and orbiting observatories to comet and asteroid exploration.

In 1985, Japan launched two spacecraft to investigate Comet Halley. In 2003, the Hayabusa probe flew to rendezvous with comet Itokawa, returning samples to Earth in 2010. A lunar orbiter called Kaguya took striking high-definition imagery and gathered scientific data from the moon for almost two years. Finally, in mid-2018, Japan's Hayabusa 2 probe rendezvoused with an asteroid called Ryugu, dispatching multiple landers, and in planned to return samples of Ryugu to Earth in 2020.

Like China, Japan has aspirations for manned missions to the moon. One plan calls for lunar flights by 2020, and a base by 2030. Following the success of the ISS, Japan is committed to international collaboration for lunar missions. The scope of the country's own exploration will be determined, in a large part, by the commitment of its international partners. If international funding dries up, they may, like China, decide to go it alone.

**Opposite** A Long-March II-F booster launched on 25 September 2008, sending Shenzhou 7 into orbit. This mission made China the third nation to achieve a spacewalk in Earth orbit.

## MAMORU MOHRI (1948– )

With a doctorate in chemistry, Mamoru Mohri was a logical choice as Japan's first astronaut to fly on the US Space Shuttle. Born in 1948, Mohri has flown on the Shuttle twice – on STS-47 in 1992, and STS-98 in 2000. During the former flight, he participated in 43 experiments in the Spacelab-J programme, a cooperative venture between NASA and the Japanese government. Mohri is currently the Executive Director of the Miraikan, Tokyo's National Museum of Emerging Science and Innovations.

中国航天
CZ-2F

**Above** Japanese astronaut Soichi Noguchi, performing an EVA during Shuttle mission STS–114.

## CHINA AND INDIA INTO SPACE

China is the first nation other than Russia and America to orbit human crews and perform orbital EVA's. On 25 September 2008, China launched Shenzhou 7, one of a series of flights patterned after the Russian Soyuz spacecraft (the most recent is Shenzhou 11, launched in 2016). Following on the success of previous Shenzhou missions, this included a spacewalk by taikonaut Zhai Zhigang. India is also aiming for space. The Indian Space Research Organization (ISRO) works extensively with NASA on space research. India's first large rocket flew in 1979, and by 1994 they had flown their current workhorse, the Polar Satellite Launch Vehicle (PSLV). India is active in the International satellite launching market and cooperates with NASA in many unmanned missions. They launched their own lunar probe on an Indian booster On 22 October 2008.

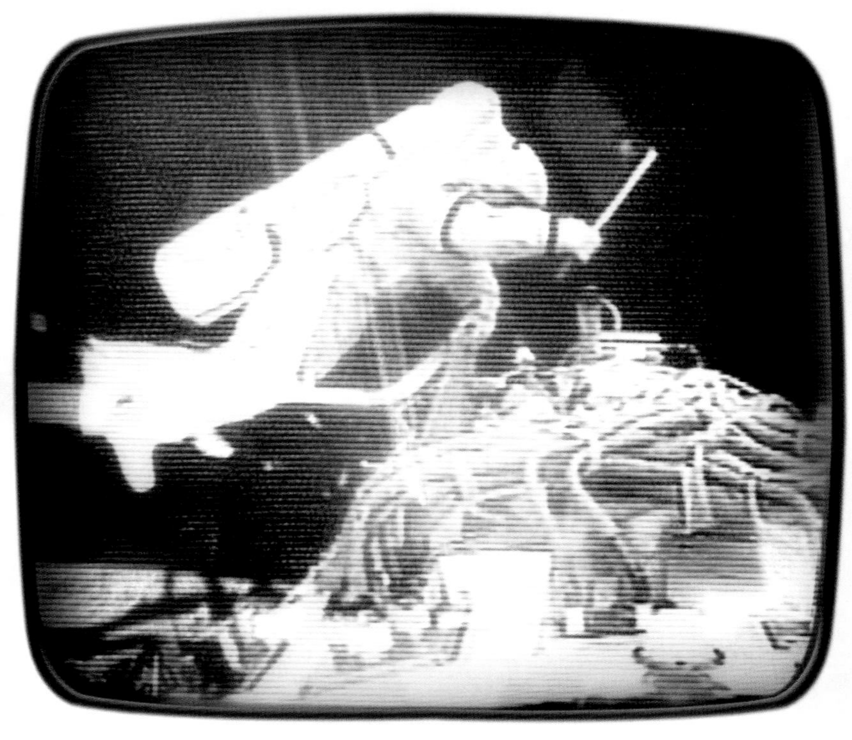

**Right** In this video image, Chinese taikonaut Zhai Zhigang is seen during his spacewalk on the flight of Shenzhou 7, carrying a Chinese flag.

# JAPAN'S LUNAR PROBE

A bilingual brochure about Japan's successful lunar probe Selene/Kaguya. It was launched in September of 2007 and has returned spectacular views and mountains of data from the moon. JAXA is the current Japanese space agency, having replaced the previous NASDA.

空へ挑み、宇宙を拓く

JAXA

## 月周回衛星「かぐや」

SELENE : SELenological and ENgineering Explorer "KAGUYA"

2007年9月14日、日本初の大型月探査機がH-IIAロケットによって打ち上げられました。この探査機は「かぐや(SELENE:SELenological and ENgineering Explorer)」と呼ばれ、アポロ計画以来最大規模の本格的な月の探査計画として、各国からも注目されています。

これまでの探査計画でも月に関する多くの知識が得られましたが、月の起源・進化に関しては、依然として多くの謎が残されています。「かぐや」は搭載された観測機器で、月表面の元素分布、鉱物組成、地形、表面付近の地下構造、磁気異常、重力場の観測を全域にわたって行います。これらの観測によって、月の起源・進化の謎を総合的に解明できると期待されています。また、プラズマ、電磁場、高エネルギー粒子など月周辺の環境計測も行います。これらの計測データは、科学的に高い価値を持つと同時に、将来月の利用の可能性を調査するためにも重要な情報となります。

Japan's first large lunar explorer was launched by the H-IIA rocket on September 14, 2007 (JST). This explorer named "KAGUYA (SELENE: SELenological and ENgineering Explorer)" has been keenly anticipated by many countries as it represents the largest lunar exploration project since the Apollo program.

The lunar missions that have been conducted so far have gathered a large amount of information on the Moon, but the mystery surrounding its origin and evolution remains unsolved. KAGUYA will investigate the entire moon in order to obtain information on its elemental and mineralogical distribution, its geography, its surface and subsurface structure, the remnants of its magnetic field and its gravity field using the observation equipment installed. The results are expected to lead to a better overall understanding of the Moon's origin and evolution. Further, the environment around the Moon including plasma, the electromagnetic field and high-energy particles will also be observed. The data obtained in this way will be of great scientific value and also be important information in exploring the possibility of utilizing the Moon in the future.

# CHAPTER TWENTY-SEVEN

# MOONBASE

## IS THE MOON THE WORLD' S ULTIMATE MILITARY "HIGH GROUND" ? OR IN THE FUTURE WILL IT BECOME A PLACE OF INTERNATIONAL COOPERATION AND COLLABORATIVE RESEARCH ON A SCALE NEVER BEFORE SEEN?

"There is a requirement for a manned military outpost on the moon. The lunar outpost is required to develop and protect potential United States interests on the moon; to develop techniques in moon-based surveillance of the earth and space, in communications relay, and in operations on the surface of the moon; to serve as a base for exploration of the moon, for further exploration into space and for military operations on the moon if required; and to support scientific investigations on the moon."

*Reference letter dated 20 March 1959 to Chief of Ordnance from Chief of Research and Development, CRD/1 (S) Proposal to Establish a Lunar Outpost (C)*

The above memo excerpt, recently declassified, was circulated in 1959, for the US Army's Project Horizon. This was a plan to build a military base on the moon, beginning in 1964 with a total of more than 100 Saturn I and Saturn II launches. Two men would conduct primary assembly, and 12 "soldiernauts" would eventually man the station. Its primary purpose was Earth surveillance and nuclear-counterstrike capability, and it was to be armed with nuclear missiles, low-yield battlefield nuclear rockets and anti-personnel mines. Apparently, even close-quarters lunar-surface combat was foreseen between Soviet and US forces on the moon.

Fortunately, this plan never left the drawing board and, for better or worse, nuclear missiles moved inside submarines instead. But the idea of a lunar base has always intrigued the spacefaring powers, and continues to do so. In modern scenarios, however, the new explorers will be scientists and not warriors.

NASA, still the premiere space research organization of our time, has plans to return to the moon. In the first decade of the new millennium, the Constellation project became NASA's marquee space exploration programme. Constellation included a much-improved, Apollo-style crew capsule: The Orion Crew Exploration Vehicle (CEV). It also explored a modern launcher system for the Orion capsule called Ares – the Constellation's version of the famous Saturn V.

**Below** The Orion Multi-Purpose Crew Vehicle could carry a crew of four and embodied NASA's current focus on technologies suited to a variety of mission types – anything from low-earth orbit to landing on Mars.

**There is a requirement for a manned military outpost on the moon. The lunar outpost is required to develop and protect potential United States interests on the moon; to develop techniques in moon-based surveillance of the earth and space, in communications relay, and in operations on the surface of the moon; to serve as a base for exploration of the moon, for further exploration into space and for military operations on the moon if required; and to support scientific investigations on the moon.**

*Reference letter dated 20 March 1959 to Chief of Ordnance from Chief of Research and Development, CRD/1 (S) Proposal to Establish a Lunar Outpost (C)*

Sadly, the economic crisis of the late 2000s brought renewed scrutiny to government spending. In 2010, President Barack Obama cancelled the Constellation programme, citing cost overruns and a lack of innovation. The President faced substantial criticism for the decision and by 2011 the best parts of Constellation were reconstituted and remain the core of NASA's current plans for moon exploration.

Announced in 2011, the Orion Multi-Purpose Crew Vehicle (Orion MCPV) is the successor to the Orion Crew Exploration Vehicle (CEV) of Constellation. The Orion MCPV is designed to fit many roles in space exploration: from ferrying supplies to the International Space Station to landing on an asteroid, the Moon or even Mars.

Drawing from both the cancelled Ares launcher system as well as the Space Shuttle programme, the Space Launch System (SLS) is the current heavy launch vehicle for deep space exploration. Like Orion, it is a flexible launch system suited to a variety of missions.

Based on the progress of both the Orion capsule and Space Launch System programs, President Donald Trump signed the Space Policy Directive 1 on December 11, 2017. In it, he formally directed NASA to refocus its efforts on human space exploration and, specifically, landing astronauts on the moon for the first time since 1972.

NASA now plans to return to the moon in 2019. The mission will use the Space Launch System to send an unmanned Orion crew capsule to the moon and back. The test will establish the safety of Orion prior to any manned flights. If the unmanned tests are successful, work can proceed in earnest.

The first, permanent, foothold on the moon may come in the form of the Lunar Orbital Platform-Gateway (originally named the Deep Space Gateway and abbreviated as LOP-G). Like the International Space Station, LOP-G is a collaboration between NASA, Roscosmos, the European Space Agency, Japan Aerospace Exploration Agency, and the Canadian Space Agency. LOP-G will be constructed in lunar orbit and will include a habitat for astronauts, docks for other spacecraft, logistics modules, and air locks. When constructed, it will be a key staging ground for manned and unmanned missions to the lunar surface and perhaps, missions to Mars or other destinations in the solar system. The first module of the LOP-G is scheduled to launch in June of 2022.

One unique feature of the modern space programme is the pioneering role private enterprise has taken. In particular, SpaceX has demonstrated an uncanny ability to push technology and capture headlines in the process.

In February 2017 they announced plans to send two space tourists on an Apollo 8 style trip around the moon. In September 2018, they named Yusaku Maezawa as the first of these space tourists –he plans to take 6–8 artists with him. In February 2018, SpaceX launched CEO Elon Musk's Tesla Roadster as payload for their Falcon Heavy rocket launch test. In the driver seat of the Tesla was "Starman", a mannequin dressed in a space suit. The Falcon Heavy is a partially-reusable launch system which, if perfected, will greatly reduce the cost of space travel.

Images of Starman filled newsfeeds and social media pages. Alongside Starman were videos of two of the Falcon Heavy's three boosters landing successfully at Cape Canaveral. The collective outpouring of interest and excitement are a testament to humankind's enduring love of exploration. Funding may fluctuate, and systems change but one day humans will return to the moon and venture beyond.

**Opposite** A rendering of NASA's Space Launch System (SLS) that will drive exploration beyond Earth's orbit.

**Right** The mission logo for NASA's first test of the Orion capsule on December 5, 2014.

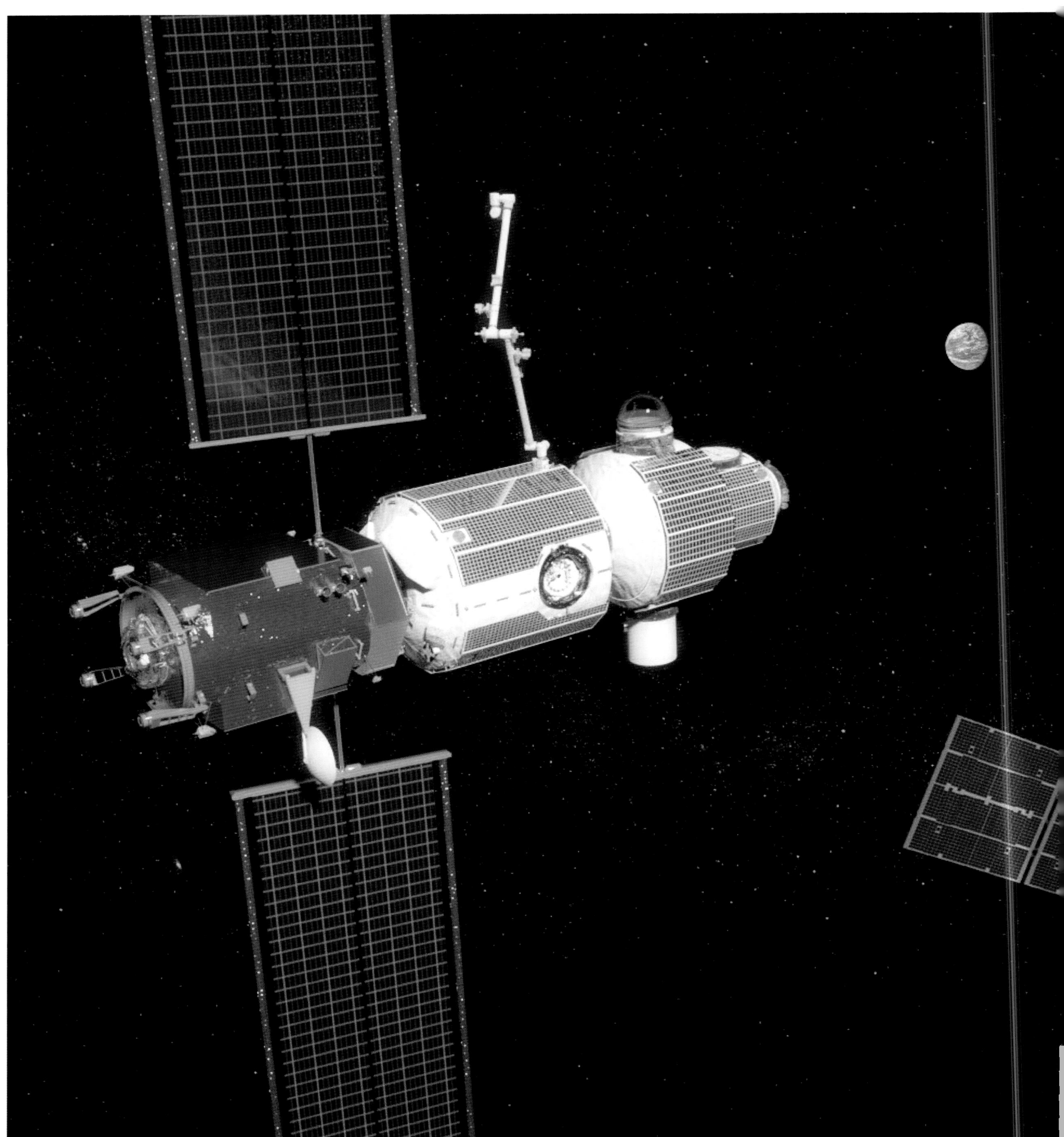

## CHINA GOES ALONE?

As China gains power and technological prowess at a record pace, so Chinese aspirations to explore the cosmos have risen as well. The Chinese timetable for lunar exploration roughly parallels that of the United States and its partners. In 2013, China landed the rover Yutu at Mare Imbrium on the moon. They are aggressively pursuing lunar missions. In 2019, they were the first to land on the dark side of the moon and are eying 2036 for their first manned mission.

**Above** On December 23, 2013, the Chinese Yutu rover embarks on its mission to explore the moon's Mare Imbrium. Portions of the lander are seen in the foreground. The Yutu included instruments to study lunar geology. The lander houses the first moon-based telescope.

**Above** The final image of "Starman" shared on social media by Space X CEO Elon Musk. The image was shared widely and shows the power of social media to drive interest in space exploration.

**Left** A rendering of the Lunar Orbital Platform-Gateway (LOP-G) that will be a staging point for exploration of the moon's surface and beyond.

# TRANSLATION

**PAGES 42–43 *PRAVDA* NEWSPAPER**

THE MOTHERLAND HONOURS ITS HEROES

[photo]
The cosmonauts at the Cosmodrome: Colonel V. A. SHATALOV, Colonel B. V. VOLYNOV, A. S. ELISEEV and Colonel E. V. KHRUNOV. Telephoto TASS

A COSMIC PERSPECTIVE IN THE WORKPLACE

The voyage of the spaceships Soyuz-4 and Soyuz-5 demonstrates to the whole world the might of our country and its constant endeavour to use the achievements of science and technology for peaceful purposes, to benefit the Soviet people and all mankind. This is how the remarkable event was assessed by A. Sapozhnikov, lathe operator at the Lepse factory. A crowded meeting, devoted to the completion of this voyage by the four Soviet cosmonauts, took place at the factory yesterday.

'We live in an age when the boundaries between fantasy and reality are steadily disappearing. But what our people have done is beyond all fantasy,' said design engineer E. Shtangei.

Komsomol member Nikolai Dmitriev, a drill operator, emphasised that this new victory in the conquest of space has created a powerful wave of enthusiasm among factory workers around the country. He called on young people and all factory workers to spread the spirit of emulation, in order to increase the productivity of labour and exceed the targets for the fulfilment of socialist obligations.

'The Soviet people have marked the beginning of the New Year 1969 with a brilliant cosmic firework, launching the spacecraft manned by four brave cosmonauts, following the Venus-5 and Venus-6 launches,' said I. V. Akhutin, Candidate of Technical Sciences, Deputy Head of Department, speaking yesterday at a meeting of employees of the S. N. Vavilov State Optical Institute. 'We have lived to see the first Soviet space station assembled in orbit around the Earth. I believe entire integrated laboratories will soon be orbiting the Earth.'

The head of the scientific department of the B. K. Baranov Institute called the achievement of the space crews a wonder of our times. He said the employees of the institute, inspired by the remarkable triumph in space, are doing their utmost to create perfect optical instruments and equipment to serve the national economy.

N. G. Yaroslavsky, Doctor of Physico-Mathematical Sciences, emphasised the exceptional accuracy with which the space experiment was conducted, the consummate skill of the cosmonauts, and the excellent quality of the entire battery of instruments and equipment used in the latest space flights around the Earth.

In the decision they adopted, those attending the meeting underlined the determination of the members of the institute to respond to the heroic feat of the "space quartet" with new achievements, and to meet the 100th anniversary of Lenin's birth in a fitting manner.

A meeting devoted to the latest achievements of Soviet science and technology in space was held yesterday at the "Vozrozhdenie" thread-spinning factory.

'The docking of such huge spaceships as Soyuz-4 and Soyuz-5, and the transfer of cosmonauts from one ship to the other – this is a brilliant achievement of the Soviet people,' said M. N. Bolshukhin, a fitter from the engineering shop. 'Only through dogged hard work and fruitful effort was it possible to achieve such a remarkable experiment, opening up great potential for the further conquest of space.'

B. A. Korzin, sub-foreman, called on textile workers to work even better and more productively in response to the success in space.

On behalf of young people, Galina Salodar, secretary of the VLKSM [young communists' organisation] committee of the enterprise, addressed words of gratitude to the cosmonauts. She confirmed that young workers were successfully achieving the production tasks in this new year of the Five-Year Plan.

Meetings devoted to the heroic voyage of the Soviet cosmonauts were also held at the Leningrad Pipe Foundry (Lentrublit) and the Zhelyabov weaving and dyeing plant. (LenTASS).

TWO STRIDE OVER THE ABYSS
The technology of the space walk

A distinctive aspect of the Soyuz-4 and Soyuz-5 flight, setting it apart from all earlier space flights, was the fact that after the docking of the spacecraft in orbit, the world's first space walk was performed by two cosmonauts from the orbital section of one spacecraft to the orbital section of the other, through open space.

The significance of this achievement of Soviet space flight is hard to overestimate.

In addition to actions directly related to the space walk, the programme of this complex experiment was densely packed with scientific observations, filming and photography.

Let us try to retrace the steps making up this unprecedented operation, the 'walk over the abyss'. We should remember that before the walk, the two cosmonauts had to leave the orbital section of the spacecraft, which is also an airlock chamber, put on spacesuits, cross to the orbital section of the other spacecraft and, after taking off their spacesuits there, continue their scheduled tasks.

So, during the preparation and while carrying out the space walk, the space crew had to perform a whole range of actions and operations, such as putting on the spacesuits and testing them for airtightness, putting the autonomous life support systems into operation, controlling the airlock system, and working with scientific and photographic equipment.

Obviously, if the entire team had not undergone thorough, concentrated training in these tasks, it would not have been possible to carry out the programme successfully.

From the experience of A. A. Leonov's first space walk in March 1965, and also on the basis of the research carried out, it is known that when walking in space, cosmonauts experience not only weightlessness, but also other adverse factors. These include reduced atmospheric pressure, limited mobility in the spacesuit, unusual temperature conditions, and also the psychological barrier to be overcome when exiting into open space and when working in a vacuum.

During the team's training for this flight, in addition to basic professional skills, the correct reaction to each of these factors had to be developed in the cosmonauts who were to take part in the space walk.

Because of the complexity and novelty of the issues arising during preparation of the simulators needed for this purpose, specialists had to find creative solutions to a whole range of technical and methodological problems. A system of specialised simulators was needed, to enable the cosmonauts to practise and strengthen the skills necessary for performing the space walk. Such a system of simulators was created. One of them became known as the 'flying laboratory'. Here, in conditions of weightlessness, they gained experience in putting on their spacesuits and preparing them for work in a vacuum; performing experiments with various apparatus during the walk; the dynamics of exiting and entering the hatch of the orbital section; switching over the connections for communications and remote measurement.

This laboratory, with its life-sized model of the transfer zone between the docked spacecraft, and also its life support and control equipment, allowed the cosmonauts to practise all the necessary skills.

The ability to handle the airlock and life-support systems during the space walk were practised in pressure chambers by the cosmonauts in their spacesuits. In the pressure chambers, the atmosphere was rarefied to a point approaching the natural vacuum of space.

The interaction between crew members during the walk, and also the work with the scientific and photographic equipment, were practised as separate elements in the flying laboratory and in the pressure chambers, and then in a fully integrated manner in a special all-round simulator.

In tandem with the creation of this system of simulators, training methodology was developed to ensure that the cosmonauts were effectively trained and were able to practise and consolidate the necessary skills.

The cosmonauts' training for carrying out the space-walk programme was based on two main principles: the closest possible approximation of the cosmonauts' working conditions to the real conditions of the space walk, and a progressive increase in the complexity of the actions practised, until they could be performed in their totality.

The implementation of these principles, in combination with the necessary number of training sessions, ensured a high standard of training for the crews of the spacecraft Soyuz-4 and Soyuz-5.

This remarkable experiment, including the performance by the cosmonauts Evgeny Khrunov and Alexei Eliseev of the walk from one spacecraft to the other, is an important step in the mastery of space. The experience gained from this flight will form the basis for the training of other teams whose task it will be to build new scientific research stations in space orbit.

N. ANDREEV
Engineer (TASS)

A LENINGRAD SCIENTIST COMMENTS
A very valuable experiment

The flight of the spaceships Soyuz-4 and Soyuz-5 remains at the centre of public attention. Yesterday the correspondent of Leningradskaya Pravda, V. Zakharko, asked the Department of Aviation Medicine of the S. M. Kirov Military Medical Academy for some comments on the results of this orbital flight.

'The storming of the cosmos, initiated by the Soviet people, is steadily gaining pace,' said the director of the department, Prof. G. I. Gurvich, Doctor of Medical Sciences. 'Experience has shown that a fuller solution to the problem of research in outer space will not be possible until humans spend prolonged periods in space. This in turn will not be possible until habitable space stations are constructed in orbit, with capacity to carry shifts of crew members, various apparatus and other cargoes. This is why the docking of spacecraft is an outstanding achievement, opening up a new stage in the conquest of space and in the development of space medicine.'

The data from medical examinations of the cosmonauts, especially those who went into open space, A. Eliseevich and E. Khrunov, show the way to further improvements in spacecraft and autonomous spacesuits, and will help to create better conditions for human activity in space. Of huge value to doctors are the data on the nervous and emotional tension which the participants in the flight experienced.

The first cosmonaut doctor, B. Egorov, worked in the rather confined conditions of the spacecraft Voskhod-1. Orbiting laboratories offer immeasurably greater possibilities for scientific experiments by all members of the crew, including doctors. They will be able to carry out detailed research, using various apparatus, and directly and comprehensively study the reaction of the cosmonauts to weightlessness, varying barometric pressure, temperature, and many other parameters of the flight.

In such laboratories, doctors will obtain very important information on the adaptability of the human body to unusual, extraterrestrial conditions. All this material will not only serve progress in the conquest of space. There is no doubt that it can also facilitate and improve prophylactic and medical work among the population as a whole.

G. I. Gurvich concluded, 'This unique experiment by the courageous Soviet cosmonauts is of vital significance for many branches of science, and especially for medicine.'

AN EPISODE REMEMBERED...
Does the cosmonaut need much?

The name of Evgeny Khrunov – one of the four courageous spacemen – is now known throughout the world. This makes it all the more interesting today to recall a little episode which K. Petrov, the cosmonauts' mentor, once mentioned in one of his public speeches. He was simply talking about someone called Zhenya. Now we know this was Khrunov...

One of our cosmonauts was visited by a friend, a fighter pilot from a distant garrison. When the former regimental comrades got together, there was a lot of catching up to be done, and many tales to be told. The guest told him news of the regiment... Then, as if in passing, he asked, 'How are you doing these days, Zhenya?' 'Nothing new. The same rank. And I'm not chasing after promotion. The main thing is, I'm in my element. It has simply taken over my life.'

The major looked at the bookshelves in his friend's room. Quite a library! Resolutions of party congresses, history, metal alloys, art, electronics, medicine, rockets, meteorology, sport, poetry, astronomy, mathematics, psychology, construction of scientific instruments, geography, physics... The guest asked doubtfully, 'Do you really need all that?' 'Of course,' replied the host. The major was not convinced. 'Well, I understand Tsiolkovsky, Kibalchich, Efremov's "Andromeda", contemporary rocket-building – it's your bread and butter, so to speak. But Makarenko, Repin, Pavlov, Stanislavsky – do these books really have anything to do with outer space?'

In reply, the cosmonaut told his friend how once he happened to be at an institute with close links to the field of astronautical science. They were talking shop. Suddenly the conversation turned to art. One of the scientific workers asked the cosmonaut, 'What do you think of Picasso's painting, Evgeny Vasilyevich? The tones of his colours are just fantastic! He seems to have looked at our planet from outer space. Just wonderful!'

For politeness' sake, the cosmonaut agreed that Picasso really does achieve some 'wonderful' tones, though he didn't know the first thing about Picasso's paintings. He arrived home disheartened: they had talked to him as an equal among equals, and he had felt like an ignoramus. And perhaps that was when Evgeny understood for the first time, not just in theory, but in practice, how much he needed to know. The cosmonaut is regarded as a highly educated man: in the arsenal of human knowledge, there are so many sciences which are directly or indirectly related to his profession. He needs psychology and electronics and sport and medicine and physical metallurgy and much, much more.

'So, judge for yourself, is that a lot of different things that we cosmonauts need?' the host asked with a smile, and his guest replied, 'Yes, I certainly see your point!'

# INDEX

# CREDITS

The publishers would like to thank the following sources for their kind permission to reproduce the pictures in this book.

Pages 2-3: GRIN/NASA; 4: Universal/Getty Images; 6: NIX/NASA; 9: NASA; 10: NASA; 11: Wikimedia; 12 (top left): Bettmann/Getty Images, (bottom left): Bettmann/Getty Images, (bottom right): Bettmann/Getty Images; 13 (left): Bettmann/Getty Images, (top right): Bettmann/Getty Images, (bottom right): Public Domain; 14: NASA; 15: NASA; 16 (top): NASA, (bottom): NASA; 17 (left): NASA, (top right): NASA, (bottom right): NASA; 18-19: JSC History Collection, University of Houston/Clear Lake; 20: NASA; 21 (left): Author's collection, (right): Wikimedia; 22: NIX/NASA; 23 (left): NIX/NASA, (right): NIX/NASA; 24: NASA; 25 (left): Wikimedia, (right): NIX/NASA; 26: GRIN/NASA; 27: JSC History Collection, University of Houston/Clear Lake; 28 (top): NIX/NASA, (bottom): NIX/NASA; 29: GRIN/NASA; 30: NASA; 31 (left): NASA, (top right): GRIN/NASA, (bottom right): GRIN/NASA; 32 (top): JSC History Collection, University of Houston/Clear Lake, (bottom): NIX/NASA; 33: NIX/NASA; 34: NIX/NASA; 35: JSC History Collection, University of Houston/Clear Lake; 36-37: JSC History Collection, University of Houston/Clear Lake; 38: NASA; 39: NIX/NASA; 40 (left): Mark Wade, Encyclopedia Astronautica, (right): NIX/NASA; 41 (top): NIX/NASA, (bottom left): NIX/NASA, (centre): Author's collection, (bottom right): Wikimedia; 42-43: Kansas Cosmosphere Archives; 44: NASA; 45: NSSDC/NASA; 46: GRIN/NASA; 47: GRIN/NASA; 48: NSSDC/NASA; 49: NIX/NASA; 50-51: NIX/NASA; 52: NASA; 53 (left): NIX/NASA, (right): GRIN/NASA; 54-55: JSC History Collection, University of Houston/Clear Lake; 56 (left): GRIN/NASA, (right): NIX/NASA; 57 (top): GRIN/NASA, (bottom): GRIN/NASA; 58: NASA; 59 (left): NIX/NASA, (right): GRIN/NASA; 60: NIX/NASA; 60-61: GRIN/NASA; 61 (top): Kansas Cosmosphere Archives, (bottom): NIX/NASA; 62-63: JSC History Collection, University of Houston/Clear Lake; 64: NASA; 65: GRIN/NASA; 66 (top): NIX/NASA, (bottom): GRIN/NASA; 67 (top left): NSSDC/NASA, (bottom left): JSC History Collection, University of Houston/Clear Lake, (right): JSC History Collection, University of Houston/Clear Lake; 68: NASA; 69 (left): NIX/NASA, (right): GRIN/NASA; 70 (left): NIX/NASA, (right): NIX/NASA; 71 (top): GRIN/NASA, (bottom): Wikimedia; 72: NASA; 73 (left): NIX/NASA, (right): GRIN/NASA; 74 (top): NIX/NASA, (bottom): GRIN/NASA; 75: NSSDC/NASA; 76: NASA; 77 (top): GRIN/NASA, (bottom): JAXA/NHK, Japan; 78: NASA; 79: GRIN/NASA; 80: NIX/NASA; 81 (left): NIX/NASA, (right): GRIN/NASA; 82: NIX/NASA; 83: JSC History Collection, University of Houston/Clear Lake; 84-85: JSC History Collection, University of Houston/Clear Lake; 86: NASA; 87 (left): NIX/NASA, (right): GRIN/NASA; 88: GRIN/NASA; 89 (top): NIX/NASA, (bottom): NIX/NASA; 90: GRIN/NASA; 91: NIX/NASA; 92: NASA; 93 (top): GRIN/NASA, (bottom): NIX/NASA; 94: Eric Jones, the Apollo Lunar Surface Journal; 95: GRIN/NASA; 96-97: JSC History Collection, University of Houston/Clear Lake; 98: NASA; 99 (left): NIX/NASA, (right): GRIN/NASA; 100: NASA; 101: GRIN/NASA; 102 (top): NIX/NASA, (bottom): GRIN/NASA; 103: GRIN/NASA; 104 (left): NIX/NASA, (right): JSC History Collection, University of Houston/Clear Lake; 105: JSC History Collection, University of Houston/Clear Lake; 106-107: JSC History Collection, University of Houston/Clear Lake; 108: NASA; 109 (left): NIX/NASA, (right): GRIN/NASA; 110 (top left): NIX/NASA, (bottom left): NIX/NASA, (right): GRIN/NASA; 111: JSC History Collection, University of Houston/Clear Lake; 112: GRIN/NASA; 113: NIX/NASA; 114: NASA; 115 (left): GRIN/NASA, (right): NIX/NASA; 116 (top): NIX/NASA, (bottom): GRIN/NASA; 117 (top): NIX/NASA, (bottom): NASA; 118 (top): GRIN/NASA, (bottom): NIX/NASA; 119 (top): GRIN/NASA, (bottom): Universal/Getty Images; 120 (top): GRIN/NASA, (bottom): NIX/NASA; 121: JSC History Collection, University of Houston/Clear Lake; 122-123: JSC History Collection, University of Houston/Clear Lake; 124: NASA; 125 (top): NIX/NASA, (bottom): GRIN/NASA; 126 (top): NSSDC/NASA, (bottom): NASA; 127: GRIN/NASA; 128: GRIN/NASA; 129 (top): NIX/NASA, (bottom): Author's collection; 130: NASA; 131: NIX/NASA; 132 (top): GRIN/NASA, (bottom): NASA; 133 (top left): NIX/NASA, (top right): Wikimedia, (bottom left): NIX/NASA; 134: NASA; 135 (top): NIX/NASA, (bottom): GRIN/NASA; 136 (top): GRIN/NASA, (bottom left): NIX/NASA, (bottom right): NASA; 137 (top left): NIX/NASA, (top right): JSC History Collection, University of Houston/Clear Lake, (bottom right): NIX/NASA; 138: NASA; 139: GRIN/NASA; 140 (top): GRIN/NASA, (bottom): GRIN/NASA; 141 (top): GRIN/NASA, (bottom): NIX/NASA; 142-143: JSC History Collection, University of Houston/Clear Lake; 144: NASA; 145: NIX/NASA; 146: GRIN/NASA; 147 (top): NIX/NASA, (bottom): NASA; 148: GRIN/NASA; 149: NIX/NASA; 150: NASA; 151 (left): NSSDC/NASA, (right): NSSDC/NASA; 152: GRIN/NASA; 153 (top): USAF/BOEING, (bottom): NIX/NASA; 154 (top): NIX/NASA, (bottom): GRIN/NASA; 155: JSC History Collection, University of Houston/Clear Lake; 156: NASA; 157 (left): GRIN/NASA, (right): ESA; 158: ESA; 158-159: NIX/NASA; 160: NIX/NASA; 161: Emil Petrinic; 162: NASA; 163: Corbis/Getty Images; 164: NIX/NASA; 165: JAXA/NHK, Japan; 166 (top): NIX/NASA, (bottom): Xinhua/AP Photo; 167: JAXA/NHK, Japan; 168: NASA; 169: NASA; 170: MSFC/NASA; 171: NASA; 172-173: NASA; 173 (top): Chinese Academy of Sciences/NAOC/Science and Application Center for Moon and Deepspace Exploration, (bottom): SpaceX

Every effort has been made to acknowledge correctly and contact the source and/or copyright holder of each picture and Carlton Publishing Group apologises for any unintentional errors or omissions that will be corrected in future editions of this book.

Publishing credits
Editorial Manager: Anna Darke
Project Editor: Victoria Marshallsay
Design Manager: Russell Knowles
Design: Emma Wicks
Production Controller: Emily Noto